Saving America

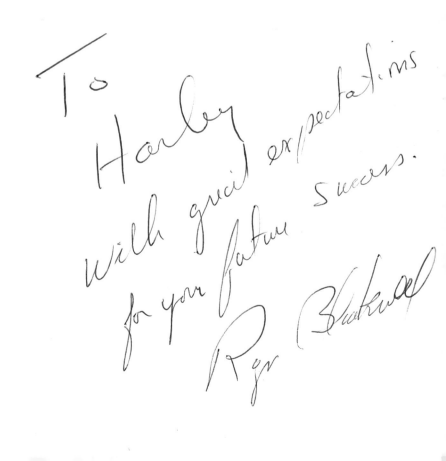

To
Harley
with great expectations
for your future success.

Roger Blackwell

Other Books by Roger Blackwell

Consumer Behavior, 10th Edition

Consumer Driven Health Care

*Brands That Rock – What Business Leaders
Can Learn from the World of Rock and Roll*

*Customers Rule! Why the E-commerce Honeymoon
is Over and Where Winning Businesses Go from Here*

From Mind to Market

From the Edge of the World

How to Grow Profits in Slow-Growth Times

Global Marketing: Perspectives and Cases

Contemporary Cases in Consumer Behavior

Cases in Marketing Management and Strategy

Consumer Attitudes Toward Physicians and Malpractice

A Christian Approach to Transcendental Meditation

Strategic Marketing

Laboratory Equipment for Marketing Research

Research in Consumer Behavior

Cases in Consumer Behavior

Saving America

How Garage Entrepreneurs Grow Small Firms Into Large Fortunes

by

Roger D. Blackwell, Ph.D.

ABOUT THE AUTHOR

Dr. Roger Blackwell is co-author of *Consumer Behavior*, published in seven languages and ten editions and used in universities around the world. His best-selling business books include *From the Edge of the World* (Ohio State Press, 1995), *From Mind to Market* (Harper Business, 1997), *Customers Rule!* (Random House, 2001), *Brands That Rock* (Wiley, 2004), and *Consumer Driven Health Care* (with Dr. Tom Williams and Alan Ayers, 2005). He published over 100 articles in *Journal of Marketing Research*, *Journal of Advertising Research* and other scholarly and trade journals and twenty-five books and research reports.

He retired as Professor of Marketing at The Ohio State University, where he received the Alumni Distinguished Teaching award and 26 other awards teaching more than 65,000 students. Lecturing on six continents, the *New York Times* described him as one of America's top business speakers. He was named Outstanding Marketing Professor in America by Sales and Marketing Executives and recognized for his leadership by Junior Achievement, The American Marketing Association and other groups.

Table of Contents

1

Conversation ONE

How to Bootstrap the Economy, Create Jobs and Enlarge the Middle Class

"If you don't know the cause, you won't know the cure." Most people realize that truth about health challenges, but it is also true about jobs and the economy. Politicians and economists gnash their teeth at each other debating fiscal and monetary fixes for the economy without understanding governments do not create jobs or determine the future of the economy. Consumers do, empowered by firms knowing what customers will buy.

Understanding what *causes* jobs is the first step in creating *more* jobs, and this book is about people who create jobs, bootstrap the economy, and enlarge the prosperous middle class. A nation cannot expect economic health unless its leaders understand what causes economic illness.

"Jobs" and "economy" are not the same. The "economy" generally means GDP, or Gross Domestic Product, the monetary value of goods and services produced in a nation. The economy can be good, but jobs bad, a truth often ignored or confused.

Jobs are created building small ideas into middle-sized or large firms. In this book, I will show you how to do that, rescuing the economy while creating prosperity for you and your family. Jobs are also created investing in successful entrepreneurs, but do not expect to build a fortune as an investor unless you understand what causes successful entrepreneurs. In this book, I will show you why some entrepreneurs fail and others succeed.

Starting and building firms is like building an airplane, computer or skyscraper. It is easier (and much safer) to build airplanes or fortunes when you know theories explaining why planes or firms fly. How to create high-flying fortunes is as knowable as how to build airplanes, but those theories remain secrets to people who do not put in hard work to learn them.

Before you say, "I'm not interested in theory, I just want to know what works," give me a chance to prove to you nothing works as well as good theory. Theory predicts success, avoiding the pain of trial and error. Relax and read on. The rest of the book is a manual how to create prosperity not just for the economy, but for you, your family and investors.

Bigger is Not Always Better

Large corporations, especially mature publicly owned ones, thrive by *reducing* jobs; entrepreneurs thrive by *creating* jobs. By the time we finish our conversations, I think you will see employment is not about the economy. It is about entrepreneurs.

Managers and employees of public corporations keep their jobs by increasing earnings per share (EPS), measured quarterly or annually. In mature corporations with many products, about the only way to increase profits fast enough to satisfy investors is to cut labor costs. When a company announces growing revenues and profits and fewer employees, share price typically increases and everyone is happy except workers who lost their jobs. Those who keep their jobs breathe a sigh of relief and perhaps smile if they own the company's stock.

Consumers *say* they want more workers employed, but consumers *behave* with their wallets, rewarding firms producing the most output with the least input, and labor is a costly input. Especially in the United States, with the highest health care costs in the world, large, public corporations prosper producing products with as few humans as possible. Motivation to reduce employment is highest during recessions, but by the time recessions end and sales increase, firms discover how to produce more products with fewer people. Managers and employees keep their jobs by learning how to do more with less people.

When the economy slows because of recession or because the nation's population stops growing—the reality in North America and Europe--EPS tends also to stop growing. Large corporations cope by introducing new products, but usually new products are such a small proportion of total sales, they produce minimal increases in EPS. Large firms increase EPS by expanding to nations with rapidly growing population or affluence, creating jobs in those nations and delighting shareholders in all nations, but that does not add many jobs domestically.

Large corporations may also increase EPS by acquiring other large companies. What does that do to employment? If Company A with 100,000 employees merges with Company B with 100,000 employees, will the result be a firm with 250,000 or 150,000 employees? Profits may increase, but the number of jobs usually decreases. Front-line employees in sales and manufacturing may remain, but the number of "overhead" employees--- usually people in offices— generally decreases. Where there were two accounting, R and D, HR, or marketing departments, only one survives the merger, with only slightly more employees than either of the pre-merger firms. If both companies operate similar factories and warehouses, you can count on closing the least efficient.

The Federal Reserve for years followed policies to ease credit, creating nearly negligible interest rates. Large corporations benefit from low interest rates because of their accumulated equity and good credit ratings, giving them access to big banks and public sources of low-cost capital. Fledgling firms receive little benefit because banks generally do not finance start-ups. Banks have a weird philosophy believing they should only make loans to firms (and people) that will pay them back, and most entrepreneurial firms in their formative years are too risky to qualify. Low interest rates also provide little incentive for individuals to deposit savings in small and medium-sized banks, the ones most likely to make loans to small and medium-sized firms. Low interest rates can decrease employment, an unintended result of well-intentioned policy.

Low interest rates stimulate loans to large corporations for capital equipment, but let me ask you, "When is the last time you saw banks loan money to add people?" Banks loan money to large firms to buy machines, especially when machines serve as collateral, but people are not collateral.

Who adds people to payrolls instead of capital-intensive automation and productivity programs? Small and mid-level firms, adding people instead of million-dollar robots. Yes, some giant corporations add people when sales increase, but not as many people as they lay off during declining years or mergers, and some small and mid-size firms invest in productivity improvements, as well as people. Overall, however, net new jobs originate in small and mid-sized employers, making them most likely to rescue a nation from economic malaise.

Lifting America

Entrepreneurs ride to the rescue of the economy as surely as the Cavalry did for settlers in old-time westerns. "Entrepreneurs can solve almost all the problems we have in this country, in this world. It's just that they have to be allowed and afforded the opportunity." Those are the words of Clayton Mathile, creator of thousands of jobs building a small business into a large one. He also created a fortune for his family when he sold his dog food firm, Iams, to P & G for $2.3 billion.

Mathile donated a chunk of the proceeds to help entrepreneurs, giving $130 million launching Aileron, a Dayton, Ohio, institute dedicated to small business owners. It is named Aileron, based on the wing part that helps lift an airplane during flight. The Institute's purpose is to "help uplift our clients," says Mathile. That is also the purpose of this book. Entrepreneurs in small and mid-sized firms are the ailerons lifting employment and the economy.

Who Wins? Who Loses?

High unemployment may be the result of a *good* economy, rather than a bad economy. I think you will want me to explain that statement, illustrated by a soaring sector of the economy.

Agriculture is doing well in the U.S. economy, exporting to nations around the world. China buys 18 billion metric tons of soybeans a year. Mexico buys huge amounts of corn and Japan buys huge amounts of almost everything the U.S. produces. American farms are so efficient producing everything from corn to beef that the nation's greatest health costs are associated with obesity. With all the growth in the agricultural economy, the number of jobs in agri-business must also be growing. Right?

Wrong, of course. The average number of hired farmworkers has declined steadily the last century, from roughly 3.4 million to 1 million. As a proportion of workers, agriculture declined from seventy percent to less than two percent. Why? The U.S., especially land-grant universities, invested heavily in education and technology, causing farms to be highly efficient. *The economy soared, but employment collapsed.*

Did consumers benefit from massive increases in agri-productivity? You bet! Since 1950, food costs for consumers dropped from 24 percent of their income to 10 percent. Entrepreneurial farmers, sometimes now on farms of 5,000 acres or more, evolved efficient demand chains with distribution partners ranging from Aldi to Whole Foods. The process created fortunes for agri-business giving consumers what they want, whether it is lowest prices or organic, locally grown products, with wide selection and convenience, but the thriving economy ended up with fewer workers "down on the farm." That is agriculture, you might say, wondering if it applies to the rest of the economy.

The same trends are now happening in many sectors of the economy---notably in manufacturing--but also in software programming, health care, legal and accounting services, architecture and just about all labor-intensive forms of output. I was in the accounting office recently of a firm whose sales grew rapidly the past twenty years, but the number of accounting employees dropped from 45 to 16. That is not good news if you want a job in accounting. Consumers benefit and so does the firm, but an improving economy reduces employment when the causes of unemployment are structural rather than fluctural.

Structural Unemployment:
The New Normal

"Manufacturing and construction are the keys to increasing employment," is the vociferous cry of naive individuals proposing government spending "to improve the economy." They propose such solutions, called fiscal stimulus, because monetary policies have been exhausted and government officials do not know or understand other solutions. They propose "cures" for unemployment without understanding its causes.

Manufacturing output is doing well in the United States and other industrialized nations, a fact that might surprise some readers – but not people operating factories or logistics firms. Products made in America are rolling along over rails and highways of America at record rates, operated by firms struggling to find qualified workers (who need both a CDL and a "clean UA") for unfilled trucking and logistics jobs.

The output of U.S. factories doubled the past twenty years, but just because factories produce more products does not mean they need more workers. It is the opposite.

During the last half of the century, factory jobs as a percentage of non-farm employment headed the same direction as farm jobs in the first half of the century, starkly revealed in data from the Bureau of Labor Statistics.

Percentage of Non-farm Labor Force Employed in Manufacturing

1950	-	31 %
1960	-	28.4
1970	-	25.1
1980	-	20.5
1990	-	16.2
2000	-	13.1
2010	-	9.0

Why? It's simple; what took 1,000 workers to produce in 1950 could be produced with 177 workers in 2010, according to BLS data. Just like agriculture, factories (and accounting offices, law offices, and many other sectors of the economy) need fewer workers to produce the same or greater output. Investments in education, technology, and research by universities, business, and government paid off.

Here is the grimy secret often ignored about the new economic environment. In the past, an improved economy meant adding workers. In the new environment, improving the economy stimulates technology investments to reduce workers. *In large firms with ready access to capital, a good economy produces fewer jobs.*

Structural unemployment is the "new normal," and cures from "old economics" may cause the disease of unemployment to get worse instead of better. Fiscal and monetary stimulants to the economy were useful prescriptions in the past, but applying those principles without understanding what causes jobs may *increase* structural unemployment, creating fewer jobs, not more. A troubling enigma confronting contemporary economists is that structural unemployment increases in both good times and bad. Rising unemployment is not even about "jobs going to other countries." Many people are surprised when they discover that just 2.7% of all goods bought by U.S. consumers are produced in China, mainly footwear, apparel and electronics.

Yes, jobs increase a little when the economy improves a lot, and yes, some jobs have gone to lower-cost countries, but rising unemployment is more closely tied to rising *productivity*, especially in large corporations. *The cause of high unemployment* is *structural rather than fluctual.*

Computer-guided tractors and high-yield hybrids reduced farm laborers from the majority of workers a hundred years ago to minuscule numbers today. Americans have to face the reality that the same trend is happening in factories and other large sources of employment ranging from architecture to pharmacies. Do not expect a "good economy" to eliminate unemployment.

If you find this troubling, you may be concluding the only answer to more jobs is more and more-effective entrepreneurs, starting and growing firms producing new products hiring additional workers, instead of robots. You would be right. The Bureau of Labor Statistics reports that 65% of all net new jobs in the last 17 years were created by small businesses, entrepreneurs like the ones you meet in this book. Failing to understand entrepreneurs causes futile economic policies to cure unemployment. Prescribing the wrong economic medicine to the disease of unemployment is as lethal as treating cancer with a heart medicine. A dismal economy is not likely to be fixed by people who do not understand what broke it. Fortunately, entrepreneurs have answers. In truth, entrepreneurs *are* the answers, as you will discover in the rest of the book.

As difficult as it is to accept, structural unemployment and declining income is the new normal, even if the economy were "fixed." With the exception of high-education professions, you should not expect high income as an employee of most firms. If you are unemployed with no one offering a good job to you and you desire to be in the *prosperous* middle class, it may be time to offer yourself a job by starting your own business.

I wrote this book to disseminate decades of research and practical experience with entrepreneurs, written for three types of readers:

1. People with the dream of starting a business. There are manuals about tactics of starting and operating an entrepreneurial business, but this book is about strategies to grow your firm into a fortune. You will discover practical theories determining which firms succeed and which fail, but don't give up your day job until you discover how to convert ideas into profits.

2. Owners of existing firms wanting to grow larger. If you have between five and five hundred employees, this book describes how to grow to a firm employing thousands or tens of thousands, creating a legacy for your family.

3. Investors wanting to grow their savings. You do not have to be an entrepreneur to make a fortune, but you do have to predict which entrepreneurs will succeed. In this book, I will show you how to do that and how anyone can be millionaire, even retiring baby-boomers fearing their IRA will expire before they do.

Why Nations Succeed

Why do economies of nations succeed or fail? Profound insights are found in Daron Acemoglu and James Robinson *Why Nations Fail: The Origins of Power, Prosperity, and Poverty.* (Crown Business, 2012). Their analysis of nations as diverse as Colonial America, Australia and Botswana demonstrates "inclusive" nations prosper, but "extractive" nations languish in poverty, even with similar resources, culture and geography. Nations dominated by government bureaucrats, such as North Korea and Zimbabwe create wealthy political leaders, but poverty for the masses. Nations dominated by entrepreneurs such as

South Korea and Botswana yield prosperity and democracy. The reason is "creative destruction," a concept pioneered by economist Joseph Schumpeter and popularized by Harvard Business Professor Clayton Christenson in *The Innovator's Dilemma*, (Harper Paperbacks, 2003).

The research of Acemoglu and Robinson reveals the importance of entrepreneurs in the history of prosperous "inclusive" nations, but stops short of describing how to achieve that in contemporary America. How does a nation include the formation and growth of small, entrepreneurial firms into firms employing thousands? How do those firms prosper, creating additional jobs and a revitalized economy? That is what you discover in the rest of this book.

Let's Have a Conversation

You probably wondered why I started this book with the title "Conversation 1." Here is why.

People like you often stopped me after a lecture or even a chance encounter with the question, "Can we talk?" My answer was usually, "yes." That is how I met and learned the secrets of entrepreneurs, some for whom I became a consultant or investor. In this book, you will learn what I learned about how they started and built firms into fortunes.

The conversations continued for decades. I heard about successes from people with whom I talked. Only rarely did failed entrepreneurs talk about their failures. I learned about them talking to their former customers and reading documents from bankruptcy court.

After years of listening, asking questions and offering suggestions, I discovered theories that determine which entrepreneurs succeed and which fail, how to predict what works and what does not. Increasingly, my partners in dialogue ended by saying, "I wish your experiences were available for my employees and investors to read. You should write a book."

So, I did. And, here it is, for you to read.

I could have written a textbook. I did that many times during my career.

"Textbooks are boring," students say, usually correctly. So, I decided *not* to write a textbook full of boring citations and footnotes. Some entrepreneurs who read an early manuscript said, "It feels like a conversation in which you are talking just to me."

One of the early readers was Bill Cloyd, a successful entrepreneur in both non-profit and for-profit organizations. He suggested I organize the book as "conversations" instead of chapters. I followed his advice. So let's start our second conversation, about people who build fortunes for their families and investors.

**Maybe the answer to the
next question is you.**

2

Conversation TWO

Who Wants to Be a Millionaire?

"Who Wants to Be a Millionaire?" That question resonates in dormitories, offices, kitchens and golf courses. Before answering, consider the secret revealed in *The Millionaire Next Door*, by Thomas Stanley and William Danko. If you do not have time to read the book, here is what they discovered. *The best chance of becoming a millionaire is starting and building your own business.*

Here's another secret that surprises some people--most wealthy people start poor. Millionaires are mostly self-made people, bootstrapping firms into fortunes. Time and hard work help, but are not enough. Many people work hard all their life and remain poor. The difference between success and failure is not hard work, it is *knowledge*. *The best hope for reducing poverty is teaching poor people knowledge needed to be prosperous.*

Most everyone knows Steve Jobs, Jeff Bezos, and Sam Walton created fortunes, but far fewer know why they succeeded in the face of failure by so many others. Lots of books and magazines describe *what* they did; my purpose is to reveal *how* they did it, *why* they succeeded and the *knowledge* needed to achieve similar success. Financial success is not a random walk down the economic path of life.

In the popular TV show *Who Wants to Be a Millionaire?* contestants stumped by a question could call a "life-line" for help. This book is your "life-line" on the entrepreneurial highway, smoothing the bumpy road to success.

The Most Useful Secret of All

You may hear people say, "that's just theory," usually a disparaging comment. College students sit in classes listening to professors drone on about "theory," dutifully pecking out notes on their laptops, hoping to memorize enough theory to pass the next exam. Only a few students have a light bulb go on, recognizing they just learned the secret of turning ideas into fortunes. Theory is available to all, but turning theory into profits is a secret hidden to many. By the time you finish this book, you will know the theories behind the most successful entrepreneurs of our era and how to turn your own firm into a fortune.

Nothing is as practical as good theory, tested in the laboratory of life. The laboratory for entrepreneurial theory is the market place, releasing discipline to turn theory into profit. It is easy to push "print" on a computer spreadsheet and project sales and profits in future years, but more important to understand the theory that helps entrepreneurs turn an ordinary start-up into a spectacular success. But, it takes grueling work to make those projections come true.

Taking ideas from possible to profitable is the focus of this book. Theories are validated by Apple, Google, Limited Brands' Victoria's Secret, Abercrombie & Fitch, Aldi, CheckFree (now Fiserve), Dell, Hewlett-Packard and Walmart, and a host of firms with less-familiar names. From Amazon to Worthington Industries, winning is about implementing down-to-earth theories empowering ordinary men and women to rise to extraordinary heights.

You can also achieve spectacular success investing in such firms, if you know why, when and which entrepreneurs will win. By the conclusion of our conversations, you will see that entrepreneurs vary greatly, coming in many shades of gray.

My own career as an entrepreneur started at age 8, selling greeting cards door-to-door under the watchful eyes of my mother waiting on the sidewalk. By age 12, that small business was earning as much as the fathers of some of my school friends. When I was in high school, my father returned to the University of Missouri to complete his education. My parents were poor, so at age 15, I loaned them money to buy a new car, the Buick in which I passed my driver's test at age 16. I drove it until I bought my own car with cash earned as an entrepreneur. I worked full-time the last two years of high school and all of college, eventually receiving a Ph.D. from Northwestern University with no debt and no financial assistance from my parents. Following my youthful years in business, I began researching and teaching business at The Ohio State University. I applied the theories I taught, helping students and friends start and grow firms, as well as investing in entrepreneurial companies. The theories worked well enough that by retirement, I was able to donate my lifetime salary and more back to the university I loved and the students I served. There is nothing as practical as good theory.

My research and experience taught me a secret – some theories are useful and some are not. Now, I am pleased to pass the useful theories to you to start your own successful business, or if you already have one, grow it as large as your vision. Do it well and you will create jobs for the masses, while enlarging the prosperous middle-class to include you and your family.

Neither ideas nor capital turn entrepreneurs into millionaires; fortunes are made by *transforming ideas into profits*. Winners pull themselves up by their own bootstraps, rather than relying on investors for capital. They know what Rocky Balboa knew, "It's not how many times you get knocked down. It's how many times you get up and go back into the fight."

Do You Want to Be a Billionaire?

Why stop with being a millionaire?

Have you studied the list of America's richest people, published by *Forbes* every year? You might believe that reading about billionaires is not relevant to ordinary people, especially the poor. Nothing could be less accurate because of the surprising revelation *most U.S. billionaires started with nearly nothing*. *Forbes* reports 70 percent of all people on its annual list are self-made billionaires, up from 55 percent two decades earlier. The firms they built employ tens of thousands of employees, who might otherwise be unemployed.

"The rich get richer, and the poor get poorer." You probably have heard that statement, but it is only half-true. The rich, measured as the top twenty-percent of household incomes, are getting richer over the years, but the rest of the statement needs some clarification. The poor are also getting richer, but less rapidly than the rich.

The *amount* of median income has *risen* among the poor (the bottom twenty percent of income), even though their *proportion* of total income *declined*. Income of the middle class rose 40 percent in inflation-adjusted dollars between 1979 and 2007, according to data from the Congressional Budget Office, while income of the poor increased only 18 percent, but income of the top 1 percent of Americans soared 275 percent. The poor are not keeping up with the rich, resulting in greater inequality each passing decade. And many (60 percent some studies indicate) in the bottom 20 percent are in the top 40 percent two decades lower. The poor don't always stay poor, and the rich don't always stay rich!

The quantity of consumer goods owned—things like smart phones, cable TV, cars, laptop computers and designer shoes—is also increasing even among the poor. The poor did not own most of those things in the past, and owning them in the future will be determined by the economy, but their ability to "bootstrap" themselves to prosperity, primarily by starting or growing a business. Only the educational elite can expect to prosper working for someone else.

Increasing inequality may (or may not) concern the rich, but it is distressing if you are poor. It is not fun remaining poor while reading about billionaires in *Forbes* or the rising proportion of income received by the rich, reported regularly in newspapers and TV. Learning how to be wealthy instead of poor is a vacuum filled in the following pages. The Gross Domestic Product (GDP) is going up, but Gross Domestic Happiness (GDH) is going down, because needs and desires are rising faster than income. Among the masses, there is usually more month than money when it is time to pay credit cards.

Whether rich or poor, everyone wants more. Economists call that "the insatiability of demand." A movie star described the problem succinctly when she said, "I've been poor, and I've been rich. Rich is better." This book is for those who prefer rich.

The way to join "the prosperous middle class" is success as an entrepreneur, whether you live in the United States, China, Russia, India, or other nations. Rather than lament rising inequality, you may decide not to be poor, using knowledge from this book. *A rising tide of affluence lifts all boats, but not equally.*

To become a billionaire, you do not have to be young like Mark Zuckerberg, who at age twenty founded Facebook in his college dormitory, dropped out of Harvard and became a multi-billionaire by age 24. At the other extreme of demographics, Sam Walton graduated from the University of Missouri, and at age 45 started an entrepreneurial firm making his family the richest in the world worth nearly $500 billion, according to *Bloomberg Business Week*. If you are a geek with a vision like Zuckerberg, you can make a fortune as a college dropout, but if you are 45, have a pick-up truck and understand retailing, there is still time for you to create the richest family in the world!

Investing in Entrepreneurs is Almost as Profitable as Being an Entrepreneur

You do not have to start your own firm to make a fortune. Another path to prosperity is *understanding which entrepreneurs will succeed and buying shares in their firms*. People who bought shares of Walmart in 1980—ten years after it went public—saw an investment of $5,000 become worth over $3 million.

Warren Buffet, second richest person in the United States, has done rather well buying shares of good companies when their prices are low and letting profits compound over decades. He earned money in high school delivering newspapers, saved his earnings to buy three shares of Cities Service, and continued the process of investing in other companies until his original investment became worth $40 billion.

Anyone with the good judgment to invest $10,000 in Buffett's partnership at its inception in 1956, transferring it into Buffett's Berkshire Hathaway corporation in 1972, would today be sitting on $432 million -- after all fees and expenses. Between now and the last pages of this book, you will discover Buffett-like principles for investing in successful entrepreneurs.

"I didn't have $10,000 to invest in 1972," might be your reaction. I didn't either, and hadn't heard of Warren Buffett. Those opportunities are rare, but they do happen. Based on the theories you read in this book, I discovered a firm in 2003 following Buffet's philosophy, headed by an entrepreneur who studied Buffet's theory. The shares I bought in his firm are now priced 24 times what I paid and pay an annual dividend twice what I paid for the stock. Similar firms start up and grow every day, but you must examine entrepreneurs closely to find both *knowledge and discipline* to follow Buffet's principles. This book provides the knowledge. For the discipline, you are on your own.

People often ask, "How can I get rich quickly?" I have no answer for that question because it rarely happens. I can answer questions about how to get rich slowly; answers embedded in theories why and how firms emerge from start-ups to giants. For the health of your IRA, this may be the best knowledge you acquire.

For Entrepreneurs who do NOT want to be a Millionaire

Entrepreneurs come in many shades with many motives, as you will soon see. An important discovery I made in researching this book is not all successful entrepreneurs want to be a millionaire, content with creating jobs for their family. Some put family ahead of fortune, like the following.

Francesco Scali is founder, proprietor, chef and greeter at what some consider the best Italian restaurant in Central Ohio. That was the opinion of a friend who told me about it and said he would take me there because it is a little difficult to find in a secluded mall in Reynoldsburg, Ohio. (1903 State Rt. 256.)

"I told him many times he should move to a better location,"
my friend said.

"Location, location, location," any entrepreneur guru will tell
you, is a principle for successful retailers and restaurants.

"Apparently this guy doesn't understand that," I thought to
myself the first time my friend took me to the restaurant, storing
that phrase in my memory bank in case the entrepreneur asked
for advice.

"We're lucky it is Friday," my friend informed me, "because the
restaurant is open for lunch only on Thursday and Friday. It
is closed all day on Sunday and Monday."

"I can help this guy grow his business a lot," I thought to myself.

When we arrived, Frank greeted and took the three of us to the favorite table of my friend, who eats there often. One wall was covered with racks of wine, all personally selected by the owner on his frequent trips to visit family in his native Italy.

"Not only can he pick the perfect wine and tell you the vineyard where it was produced, he will probably talk about the vineyard's winemaker by first name," my friend continued.

When he came to take our orders, my friend suggested we eat family style, a suggestion that delighted our host.

"What's your favorite food," he asked each of us, and proceeded to suggest we order one of each – plus a couple with which we might not be as familiar. That way, everyone was sure to have something they really liked, as well as the opportunity of trying something new, an experience some people avoid. I describe details such as these because it is not great ideas that determine success or failure of entrepreneurs; it is mastery of details.

When our server brought bread to the table, it was warm and delectable. I later learned why. The owner's mother—many years beyond normal retirement age—comes in each day and bakes bread as well as forms handmade pasta the family makes fresh in the kitchen. Mama speaks little English. She doesn't need to, because her food is universally expressive. Her granddaughter was our server.

As an immigrant from Italy, Frank knew food service was his calling, and he wanted his family to prosper. He began as a dishwasher, learning the restaurant business from the ground up. In 1993, he opened *Scali Ristorante* in a remote strip center, and has gradually grown it since then.

My favorite Italian dish is Fettuccini Alfredo, but I rarely order it. I know the calories it contains. But, I thought, if the food is this good, "What the heck!" I ate more than my share of the Fettuccini, cleaning out every crevice of the serving bowl. I have eaten in the some of the best restaurants in Italy, including the Cipriani Hotel in Venice. Never have I tasted fettuccini any better than what I had just eaten.

The service was a perfect blend of immediacy and relaxation, the noise level just right, the ambiance modest but spotless, and the prices reasonable. I could see why people made the effort to search out his location and, delighted with the experience, returned again and again, often bringing friends with them. *If you appreciate the importance of these details, you are on your way to understanding what it takes to succeed as an entrepreneur.*

Why not move to a better location? Why only one restaurant? Frank and his family could open several more, I thought. Maybe even start a whole chain of restaurants? There are ways to do that, as you see later in this book. Frank's reason is an important discovery to consider.

"I make a comfortable living, enough to support my family well. My wife runs the front of the house and she, my mother and my children surround me while working in the restaurant. I am able to pay college tuition for my children. We work evenings, but if I served lunch more than two days, I wouldn't get a good night's sleep each day. And we all go to church together on Sunday. What's more important? My family and time with them or making more money?"

He made a good point. Sometimes, the reason for being an entrepreneur is more about family than fortune. Not everyone wants to be a millionaire. And that is OK for entrepreneurs planning their future success, but remember *success is determined by details whether your motivation is fortune or family.*

Raise the Average Standard of the World

My mission as a professor, consultant and writer over the past decades has evolved into a simple vision: To improve the average standard of living throughout the world. It does not matter whether you create wealth as an entrepreneur or invest in entrepreneurs. After reading this book, if your standard of living increases, I accomplished my mission. I do not want anyone to be so poor they lack a reasonable standard of living.

Some people say, "I am willing to do the long, hard work to be successful, but I don't know how to start a successful business that will provide for my family and be prosperous." That is why I wrote this book.

The poor will always be with us. That is distressing, but also highly motivating in learning how not to be poor. History is brutally blunt in revealing that when most everyone is equal, most everyone is poor. There are theories, various forms of Communism and Socialism, that income equality benefits everyone. Those theories fall apart when analyzed with facts from empirical economic experiments. Some of the most notable experiments to "distribute to everyone according to their need, and take from everyone according to their ability" include Eastern Germany, the Soviet Union and China until recently. Cuba, North Korea and some African nations currently practice the economics of equality for everyone (except politicians who control the system, of course). History reveals *the inevitable consequence of equality is poverty, and the inevitable consequence of prosperity is inequality.*

When Russia and China changed to a market system based on "to everyone according to their ability," instead of the Communist approach "to everyone according to their need," the number of wealthy people increased dramatically. So did average income and standard of living for those who remained poor. And when people on the east side of the Berlin Wall (who started out with better land and more resources than western Germany) looked across the Wall to see what happened to average income of everyone when some become wealthy, they tore down that wall and traded in their Tavias for Volkswagens, Mercedes and BMWs.

It would be wonderful if someone discovers an economic system that produces wealth sufficient for everyone to have the same level of high income. So far, no one has. Affluence and inequality go hand-in-hand, and for those who choose affluence over poverty, starting and growing a business is the surest way to avoid poverty and gain affluence. Capitalism is successful as an economic system partly because of an internal discipline that allows for loss and even bankruptcy. *The possibility of failure creates the opportunity for success.*

So, if you want to be a millionaire or billionaire, be prepared to live with the knowledge there will also be many poor, some in poverty. Sometimes the poor are described as "those less fortunate." In reality, the poor are usually "those less knowledgeable" about how to prosper. One of the best sources of what works in reducing poverty and what does not is *Poor Economics: A Radical Rethinking of the Way to Fight Global Poverty* by Abhijit Banerjee and Esther Duflo (PublicAffairs, 2011).

As a successful entrepreneur, you will have to learn to live with criticism when you become wealthy. (When sports heroes earn ten million dollars a year and more, or Sofia Vergara and Kim Kardashian earn twenty million a year as actors, no one seems to object. When Oprah or the Rolling Stones become celebrity billionaires, there are no "Occupy" protests outside their corporate offices. But when you earn those amounts as an entrepreneur, creating thousands of jobs for others, you may be the subject of scorn and vilification.) Learn to live with it!

What Do Entrepreneurs
Do with Their Wealth?

Prosperous entrepreneurs create enough wealth they often share with people less knowledgeable. Sometimes sharing is achieved by force, through taxation. Sometimes sharing is voluntary through charitable giving.

Alexis de Tocqueville was so impressed with the tradition of charitable giving in America, he wrote about it as an admirable characteristic of people in the United States. It is a tradition carried on today by America's most successful entrepreneurs. Some follow the principle of tithing, or giving a certain percent of their income to religious and charitable organizations. Dan Ariely, author of the best-selling book *Predictably Irrational* (Harper Collins, 2008) reports that rules such as tithing are useful because they are strict and clear. I have observed that emerging entrepreneurs who understand the principle of tithing and practice it when they have little are often men and women who later have a lot. Some entrepreneurs tithe their time as well as their income.

If you observe organizations such as United Way, you usually find successful entrepreneurs as leaders. Entrepreneurs "tithe" their time in non-profit and educational organizations ranging from neighborhood schools and universities to the Salvation Army. Executives and staff of charitable organizations who emulate successful entrepreneurs increase their own effectiveness as a leader.

Whether the motivation is a desire to "pay forward," creating better communities, or following a religious commitment, most charitable organizations would accomplish little without involvement of entrepreneurs sharing time, money and leadership. People will always disagree about what is their "fair share" of rewards obtained from success as entrepreneurs, but *without affluence, there is little to share.*

It is easier to explain and understand theories that work when illustrated with organizations that are well known. That is why I write about firms you recognize, such as Amazon, Apple, and Victoria's Secret, but the same theories explain how lesser known firms succeed, as you see in the rest of this conversation.

Should I Go to Medical School or Start a Handyman Business?

"Do I want to go to medical school and become a doctor, or start a handyman business?" That unlikely question faced Chuck Nutter. If your answer, were "Handyman, because I don't want to do the long, hard work involved in completing medical school," you should probably choose medical school as an easier and shorter path to financial success. Chuck's story illustrates the path of many successful entrepreneurs.

How long does it take to get a college degree? Seven years in the case of Chuck Nutter. My father needed thirteen years, a story of perseverance told in the book *Farm Boy* (Outskirts, 2011) which Dad wrote in his last year of life. The reason for protracted college degrees for both Chuck and my dad was that they paid for their own education, a necessity if you are one of five children as my father was on a Missouri farm, or one of nine children for Chuck, growing up on an Ohio farm. Both persevered to receive their college degrees, a trait predicting success.

I am not saying college education is a necessity for financial success. Some entrepreneurs drop out of college to start their own business, and still do pretty well in life. Bill Gates, Steven Jobs and Michael Dell come to mind as examples. Some even drop out of high school, such as David Karp who sold Tumblr to Yahoo for $1.1 billion.

Nutter, however, completed his seven-year degree in the rigorous Chemical Engineering program at The Ohio State University and qualified for medical school. Instead, he accepted an offer from a large firm, embarking in a sales job taking him to Singapore and other global destinations. He was on his way to success climbing the corporate ladder, but Chuck was an entrepreneur at heart. What he really wanted to do was return to Columbus and start a business. He did, maintaining campus-area rental properties, using skills learned on a farm. On a farm, everyone has to be a "handyman," and everyone works.

Get the picture? Being an entrepreneur is not an easy task. Chuck could have chosen the "easy" path of being a physician, a certain path to prosperity or continued his corporate career. Perseverance is essential on any path to prosperity, including entrepreneurship.

How did it work out for Chuck? That is a story still unfolding, but here is a progress report. He has a rapidly expanding crew of workers with an increasing number of homes. The nation's construction industry collapsed because of overbuilding, but the less new homes built, the more the market increases for repair and remodeling. The readily available pool of skilled construction workers also increases, making it easier to start a business during a recession than during boom times.

Where do you go in the future after establishing a successful handy man business? Chuck's story illustrates how real-life entrepreneurs evolve. Chuck realized that someday he may not want to climb ladders all day, painting and repairing houses. He noticed the hardware store where he bought supplies was not adapting to changing times. He talked with the owner and suggested changes, but success had fossilized the firm.

Chuck started his own hardware store, choosing a good location and staffing it with some grandfatherly types. There are still a lot of customers who prefer knowledge and some gray hair to impersonal merchandise stacked high above the reach of customers. With the advantages of wholesaler-cooperative Ace for supply-chain and marketing support, Chuck's hardware added buying power, branding, and advertising support to localized, customer service.

Chuck has plenty of marketing savvy. In addition to product knowledge from sales people with decades of experience, Chuck's store features the charm of a neighborhood hardware store and service. For a fee, they will deliver to a customer's home for emergency repairs, even in the middle of the night. Kids may not know much more than the impersonal environment of big-box retailers, but Chuck is re-creating the ambiance of the hardware store with classes teaching how to build bird feeders and education about home repairs. Few kids resist his popcorn machine, popping away and sending out its aroma attracting a new, younger generation to the hometown hardware. Chuck understands competition from big box and internet stores, but adds, "We offer a different experience. Period."

If you are thinking about your own start-up business, what are the secrets you can learn from Chuck's story?

1. You can obtain a college education even if you are part of a large family and your parents cannot or do not want to pay for it.

2. A college education is not required to start a firm, but it may make you smarter in operating it.

3. It is useful to work for someone else for a while to develop your marketing and management skills. It is better to make your mistakes on someone else's payroll than your own.

4. The best business to start is one that serves needs of customers, not entrepreneurs. People who are paid well as entrepreneurs are those who do things others do not want (or do not know how) to do.

5. When existing firms stop improving, they create an opportunity for new firms to enter the market and capture their customers.

6. Hard work is the key to success, whether you want to be a physician, climb the corporate ladder or start your own business.

Walking the Dog

I have a friend with a dog. He works long hours at his job, earns high income and lives in an affluent, pleasant suburb of Dallas. At a community dog event sponsored by an veterinarian, he met an entrepreneur whose business is walking dogs. You do not want to trust the security code for your home to just anyone, but this man was a top sales person for H-P (formerly EDS). His new job is in his own firm, walking dogs for people who need dog care and can pay.

The basic charge is $17 for 30 minutes. A lot of people would be content with a job paying $34 an hour walking two dogs per hour, but my friend asked why he would leave his high-paying job at H-P to go into business for himself, walking dogs.

"I really don't want to have to go back to the office," was his reply.

His answer explains why some people choose the entrepreneurial path. His new career gives him flexibility in schedule, he likes to be outside instead of inside, and it does not require a lot of capital or education. It is not the type of entrepreneurial business likely to grow into a fortune, but it if you are trustworthy and like dogs, it provides a good income. If he were in New York, he might walk 4-6 dogs at a time, and as he grows his business, he might add lower-cost employees. Who knows, he might even find a way to franchise his concept to other cities and become a millionaire, but for now, he is happy, earning high income, and enjoys, as he explains it, "anything but the same old grind." He also demonstrates the power of one in decreasing the nation's unemployment rate.

I hope this conversation illustrates the range of possibilities as an entrepreneur, but also the consistency found in success. You can learn from the experiences of diverse types of entrepreneurs to grow your own business, achieving aspirations you have for yourself and your family, whatever those aspirations may be.

The job of a researcher is to look at what many people have observed, but see what few people have seen. The job of an author is to write what he or she learns, hoping the resulting words are helpful and inspirational to the reader. That is my aspiration for this book.

In our next conversation, we will discuss how to achieve prosperity as a "garage" entrepreneur.

{ 3 }

Conversation THREE

Garage Entrepreneurs

The term "garage entrepreneur" stems from a garage in Palo Alto, California where David Packard and William Hewlett started Hewlett-Packard (HP) in 1939, growing it into a global technology giant with revenues over $100 billion. Their original investment of $538 and a lifetime of hard work made both men multi-billionaires. Packard and Hewlett are not unique; they are typical of garage entrepreneurs who "bootstrap" small firms into large fortunes with little or no capital.

Shaping a Successful Strategy

"That was then, but can it still be done today?"

If you have doubts about that question, study Sara Blakely, who *Forbes* describes as America's newest self-made female billionaire.

Blakely started her first business in 1990, a kid's club, charging $8 a child for a few hours of babysitting. Later she worked for an office-supply company, learning the art of selling, an essential skill of successful entrepreneurs. She saved every dollar possible, gradually accumulating $5,000 and preparing a business plan solving the age-old problem of shaping the body, in a new way. While still working at her day job to pay rent and expenses, she stayed up much of the night filling orders for her invention. She did not have $3,000 a lawyer wanted to obtain a patent, so she spent hours in the library, learning how to prepare the application herself. She answered customer service calls on the telephone from her bathtub or bed. She could not afford a public relations firm, so she did it herself, tearing out journalist bylines from magazines and calling them with story ideas.

Today, her $30 Spanx Power Panties (along with about 200 other products) are in Nieman-Marcus, Target and many other stores. She employs a team of people (mostly female) selling in 11,500 stores and 40 countries online. With no outside investment and no debt, she owns Spanx, valued at a billion dollars. She was just one of over 200 new billionaires in the world on *Forbes* list of 1,226 of them, but the newest female to make that list without inheriting a chunk from a husband or father.

Garage Entrepreneurs Don't Always Have Garages

The study of billionaires reveals a pattern of starting with little or no capital, building dominant organizations like Hewlett and Packard, Bezos or Blakely. Many literally started in a garage, but when I use the term "garage" entrepreneurs, I do not mean they always start in garages. "Garage entrepreneurs" is a generic term describing a start-up with limited capital and inexpensive space. Successful entrepreneurs typically continue working at another firm, retaining health insurance and initially avoiding depending on the start-up for current income, beginning small and bootstrapping to survive.

Do not give up your day job until you know what works in your new job. Working on someone else's payroll allows you time and diligence to understand what customers like enough to pay a profitable price, perfect the product, develop the most efficient way to make or buy, develop trust-worthy supply-chain relationships, implement accurate accounting systems, and expand your people skills enough to manage well— attributes of success as an entrepreneur.

Patiently pursuing perfection in management functions gives you time to accumulate capital to strike out on your own instead of handing over a large portion of your business to outside investors. Start-ups focused on raising capital from outside sources generally do not learn what works until they burn through the capital. Then, it is usually too late. If you learn fast, follow your passion, and keep expenses lean, investors will flock to you when you need capital to grow. Ideas do not have financial value; results do. You can find help at Small Business Development Centers (SBDCs) providing an array of technical assistance to small businesses and aspiring entrepreneurs at no cost, often in cooperation with universities and community groups. As a taxpayer, you pay for SBDCs, so use them. They're free!

A Dorm Room is Even Cheaper than a Garage

Michael Dell started a fledgling firm in his dorm room at the University of Texas. He bought and sold computer parts on the Internet, making enough profit on each transaction to rent a nearby garage in Austin where he gradually hired a few employees and expanded operations.

I had the opportunity to work with Michael on a few occasions and heard him tell about having the only key to the garage. After a few years, he realized that if he did not show up for work, his employees would have no way to get into the garage. That is when he learned to delegate.

Some entrepreneurs think they can "hire someone to do things I don't want to do or don't know how." That is a mistake. In the beginning, Dell did it all. Successful entrepreneurs start out doing everything, and then learn how to hire others gradually assuming more responsibility, adding to the firm's knowledge and skills base as the business grows.

The reason Dell's story is valuable is because he didn't develop a new product. Dell developed a new method of marketing, transforming the existing supply chain into a demand chain, starting with the minds of consumers. Previously, firms such as IBM and Gateway decided which computers customers would buy, spent a lot of money to build and ship them, and then sold them to retailers hoping customers would buy what manufactures made. The process required a lot of financing up front and carried a huge risk of guessing wrong about customer preferences, a big problem in an industry with rapid product obsolescence.

> *Dell did the opposite. He let customers design computers to the precise configuration they needed, paying Dell before Dell paid suppliers. It was a model that transformed an industry and left competitors drowning in a sea of obsolete products and high carrying costs. You can study how he did it in his book Direct from Dell: Strategies That Revolutionized an Industry (HarperBusiness, 1999). It took years before competitors learned how to duplicate his strategy.*

Dorm rooms breed entrepreneurs such as Fred Smith, who wrote a term paper describing his business plan to lease airplanes and create an overnight package delivery in competition with the U.S. Postal Service. Can a "little David" by the name of Smith take on a giant such as the United States Government? His professor said it was impractical, reportedly giving Fred a "C" on the paper. Fred did the start-up anyway. The result was FedEx.

The most famous entrepreneur of the past decade, Steven Jobs, dropped out of college, but started a business that eventually became the most valuable corporation in the world. His story is so instructional for entrepreneurs and so complicated that it deserves a separate conversation later in the book, but his first "factory" was his father's garage.

Much the same scenario is true of Mark Zuckerberg. As a Harvard student in 2004, he created the online social website Facebook with fellow computer science majors and roommates Dustin Moskovitz and Chris Hughes. They decided to spread Facebook to other schools and within a few months released Facebook at almost forty-five schools, with hundreds of thousands of users.

Zuckerberg soon dropped out of Harvard, moving to Palo Alto, California, with Moskovitz and friends. They leased a small house during the summer of 2004 as their first office, where he met Peter Thiel who invested in the company. According to Zuckerberg, the group planned to return to Harvard in the fall but eventually decided to remain in California. I doubt he will ever return to complete his degree, but if Zuckerberg does go back to Harvard, I am confident he won't need to apply for financial aid.

From Geek to God

Yes, there was another famous Harvard student who dropped-out to start a successful entrepreneurial firm, named Bill Gates. He and his friend and fellow student, Paul Allen (who did graduate from college!), were computer geeks, both loving to program and work in computer labs, starting together in middle school. One time, Gates and Allen had their school computer privileges revoked for taking advantage of software glitches to obtain free computer time. They escaped punishment by offering to debug the computers, correcting the glitch they discovered and took advantage. Later, Gates and Allen formed a partnership called Micro-Soft, a blend of "micro-computer" and "software."

A voracious reader, a trait true of many successful entrepreneurs, Gates made his fortune by knowing how to use and improve ideas from others. He purchased an operating system (DOS) for $50,000 and licensed it to IBM for billions, his start to becoming one of the richest persons in the world.

Gates' success was based on perfection rather than invention. He observed inventions of others—word processing, spreadsheets, graphical interface and the Internet (whose value he was originally skeptical)--and made applications so practical customers chose his products instead of those of earlier entrepreneurs. *There is more money made from perfecting products and processes than inventing new ones.* That has been true since Edison realized his invention – DC electricity— was not profitable because it was not as efficient as Westinghouse's AC version. *Ideas are worthless; profits are priceless.*

Although Gates probably could have obtained capital from his influential family, Gates and Allen grew it internally from profits derived from their business acumen. If they had funded their firm primarily from Venture Capitalists (VCs), they might not have been as successful. If their success were built mostly with money from VCs, Gates would have sacrificed much of their firm to investors and be far less wealthy today.

What did Gates do with all his wealth? Mostly, gave it away, pledging ninety-percent of his fortune to the Bill and Melinda Gates Foundation, devoting money, time and involvement to solving the world's problems in health, education and literacy. Some people are skeptical of Gates playing "God" solving social problems. Some even call giving away your fortune "dumb," but never call Bill Gates dumb. For readers of this book still in high school, you may find it interesting – and motivating—to know that Bill Gates scored a 1590 (out of a possible 1600) on his SAT college-entrance exam.

Gates and Allen moved Microsoft to Seattle, their hometown, creating a computer culture that spawned hundreds of other entrepreneurial firms. Today, Seattle is the home not only of many computer-based corporations, but also the University of Washington's TMBA (Technology MBA), an innovative center to refine technological prowess into business supremacy.

The lesson learned from successful "dormitory entrepreneurs" is not to wait on someone investing capital in your idea. Follow the advice of Nike's famous slogan, "Just Do It!" Now, let me tell you about less-famous entrepreneurs.

A Smokin' Hot Success

How do you bootstrap a successful firm when you have no capital?

That was the dilemma facing Rick Malir who believed Columbus, Ohio needed barbeque and set out to create the perfect product. He looked for the best sauce in his home state of Kansas and for ribs, he went to St. Louis. He studied brisket and sausage in Texas and pulled pork from eastern North Carolina, developing a product he believed superior to anything on the market. Two friends shared his passion for barbeque, contributed their encouragement and recipes, and eventually became partners in his mission to market the best barbeque in the business.

Successful entrepreneurs live by the creed, "The devil is in the details." *Successful start-ups are built on passion, preparation, perfection and patience.*

After perfecting his product, all Malir needed was a good location, which he found on Henderson Road in Columbus, a market area with dense population and diverse incomes. He also needed money to lease and equip the building, which he did not have.

His solution was characteristic of successful entrepreneurs. He catered from his garage, booking profits from day one. He saved the profits, accumulating enough cash in a year to open the restaurant he passionately planned from the beginning. Instead of dreaming of opening a restaurant or seeking investors who would have owned the majority of the business, he found a way to start up his business with little capital. *The most successful entrepreneurs get capital from customers instead of investors.* The first restaurant opened in December 1999, under the name City Barbeque. It's pulled chicken sandwiches and beef brisket became known for miles around for their rich, smokin' good flavor. Within a year, he opened a second location.

"It was too soon to expand....we needed to focus on quality products, managing our cash and not getting stupid and thinking we are something we aren't," Rick Malir says. Managing multiple locations is a different skill than operating one well, and the second restaurant drained profits from the original success. Rick and his partners learned from their mistake, regrouped and analyzed what to do differently to succeed in a multiple-store format with more planned. Rick's on his way to creating financial success for himself and investors, all started perfecting a smokin' good product in his garage.

Creating Capital Creatively

Creating start-up capital may require creativity. An example isGeorge E. Johnson born in Richton, Mississippi. In 1954, he started Johnson Products, eventually becoming the first African-American company listed on a major stock exchange in 1971.

His father was a sharecropper and lived in a three-room house in Mississippi until his parents separated and his mother moved to Chicago, for a $16 a week job in a cafeteria. Johnson shined shoes and collected bottles for cash to help his mother. He attended high school when he could and began his first step toward becoming an entrepreneur by working at Fuller Products, founded by S.B. Fuller, another African-American entrepreneur. While working as a production chemist, he developed a hair straightener for men.

Johnson wanted to start his own business, but where could be obtain $250 start-up capital? He applied for a business loan at banks, but was told they didn't make loans for African-Americans to start a business. To find a solution to the discrimination he encountered, he applied for a $250 loan from a finance company as a "vacation loan," which was approved.

Johnson used the "vacation" money to establish a firm selling Ultra Wave, a hair straightener, sold from the back of his station wagon. He and his wife worked long hours for years, gradually expanding with products for hair care professionals targeting African-American women, giving black women versatility in hairstyling not previously known. As one of the largest black-owned firms in the nation, Johnson became the sole black advertiser to sponsor a nationally syndicated TV show, *Soul Train*.

Despite some rocky times personally and financially, the Harvard Club honored him with a public service award for the George E. Johnson Foundation, which he founded, funding educational and charitable programs for African-Americans. He was the recipient of the Horatio Alger Award, the Babson Medal from Babson College and many other honors and honorary degrees. When you question where you will get capital to start your business, consider how resourceful entrepreneurs can be. Perhaps you will also become creative and take a "vacation."

A Smart Cookie

Flexibility, determination, hard work, a solid background in retailing, and Grandma's cookie recipes were ingredients for the success of entrepreneurial super-star Cheryl Krueger, who made cookies everyone wanted. While working at retailing firms, Cheryl made cookies in her kitchen to share with friends, evoking compliments and thanks. They were so good, friends wanted to buy them as gifts. She could have quit her job, spent her savings or raised capital from investors and started a store. But, she didn't.

Cheryl maintained a high-energy career in retailing in order to finance a tiny store opened with her college roommate, Caryl Walker. Friends and family operated the business during the week while Cheryl commuted from New York City to Columbus, every weekend for three years. Cheryl comments, "I've made personal sacrifices, most of the time with a sense of guilt toward my family and friends, but sometimes it just becomes necessary. Excellence cannot come without sacrifice." *Success as an entrepreneur requires time, realism about finances and patience.*

Cheryl believes her key to success is giving the public what it wants. Eventually joining the company as CEO, she spent two or three days a week in the stores, often waiting on customers. *The best way to know what customers want is to listen to them yourself, modifying products to be what customers want instead of what you or investors want.*

At first the stores carried only cookies, in a store of about 250 square feet. Later, she added brownies and other innovations. A problem faced by the company, however, is large shopping malls usually want cookie stores located in the food court. In that environment, how can a little firm compete with what were then the cookie monsters—Mrs. Fields and David's?

The answer was evolution to gift stores, featuring special cheesecakes, breakfast rolls, gourmet coffees, chocolate sauces and other tasty delights. With gradual, concentric product expansion came larger stores—about 1,000 square feet—and a new name—Cheryl & Co., instead of Cheryl's Cookies.

Larger stores stimulated innovative new products, such as "cookie roses," a basic chocolate-chip cookie on a stick appearing to be a rose stem, wrapped in red cellophane and packaged in a rose box with appropriate greenery and florist paper. The result was improved margins by selling a cookie for $1.95 instead of the normal 50-60 cents per cookie. With a dozen "cookie roses," customers could say, "I love you" for $19.95, a good value (and much tastier!) than roses sold by floral stores.

The roses provided an innovative way to increase margins and average transactions. That grew revenue, but also helped negotiate better locations in malls. Centrifugal growth continued by evolving from "rose" gifts to baskets, containing all sorts of delectable, delicious treats. Soon customers began asking if the cookies could be shipped as gifts and Cheryl designed baskets, decorated tins holding a dozen cookies and towers as colorful, seasonable and fashionable as the retail stores where she worked.

The core of Cheryl's business was cookies, but over the years, she became a gift retailer, not only in stores, but also through catalogues. Cheryl moved with the times becoming a major presence on the Web, generating millions of dollars and corporate sales. This happened not just because the retail environment changed, but because Cheryl changed with it, often leading with creative merchandising, CRM (Customer Relationship Management software), web analytics and a strategy of delighting customers rather than simply satisfying them. She pioneered her field, becoming the first to move to catalogues, first on the Internet, first with individually wrapped cookies and first cookie company to add seasonal gifts. Customer retention rates hit 83 percent compared to competitors with twenty percentage points lower. She used her experience in merchandising and retail management to produce a shopping experience as innovative, attractive and exciting to consumers as the beautiful packages and retail ambiance that accompanied products, moving the average transaction from $1 to $8.15. She killed cookie-monster competitors with better-tasting products and a better customer experience than the giants she conquered. That is the pattern for success among garage entrepreneurs.

Cheryl's success may seem inevitable or easy. It wasn't. I served as an advisor and director from her early days with only two stores and a fledgling catalogue operation. You may not have heard of Cheryl, but I know her well enough to tell you I have never seen anyone work more diligently or persistently. After building her own factory, there were times when she worried about meeting the weekly payroll. Entrepreneurs learn that the last payroll check written is their own. In the end, it was a large check.

The exit strategy for Cheryl was sale of the company for many millions to 1-800-Flowers, a large, public company. Today, Cheryl uses the payoff from her decades of hard work to serve the community and family, in philanthropic activities and mother to a son who played football at Ohio State. She won many awards for work serving the James Cancer Hospital, Female Entrepreneur of the Year, Women's Business Board, Lung Association, and YWCA. Junior Achievement inducted her into its Hall of Fame. She is the consummate example of how to be an entrepreneur with great rewards to herself and others. For my money, Cheryl is a very smart "cookie."

The phrase "garage entrepreneur," as I use it, is defined by the pattern and life of Cheryl Krueger, even though her "garage" was a kitchen. You can read details of Cheryl's marketing strategy in *Contemporary Cases in Consumer Behavior*, 4th Edition (Dryden Press) which I co-wrote, but here are lessons I believe you can apply achieving your own success from Cheryl's success as an entrepreneur:

1. Start your career by working for the best firms you can. You become the best by learning from the best.

2. Work harder than other people--a lot harder!

3. Don't give up your day job until your new firm is on a firm foundation for survival and growth.

4. Make sure the *experience* with your firm meets or exceeds the quality of your product.

5. Constant change and innovation helps you break away from the pack of competitors congregating around the mediocrity of normalcy.

6. Give back to the community when you think you don't have the time to do anything except manage your business, and keep giving back even after you cash in your chips.

I hope our conversation about the meaning of "garage" entrepreneurs clarifies the term. Great fortunes do not always start in an actual garage. A kitchen or dorm room works just as well. For geeks, a university lab or incubator is even better with an abundance of technology and experts on any subject readily available, often at little or no cost. Expert advice is a key to success.

"Solopreneurs"

"Solopreneur" is another type of entrepreneur that flourishes when economic vagaries require greater occupational flexibility. The term refers to an independent professional; one who has started his or her own business, with little capital and often without additional employees, variations on the French word *entrepreneur*, originally referring to the director of a musical institution.

Lots of solopreneurs are stay-at-home moms looking to make an extra buck, eBay folks, storage wars folks, re-sale shops, and resellers of merchandise on Craigslist or other Web-based virtual places. To be complete, thousands of drug dealers should be included as entrepreneurs, making big bucks from homes and street corners. Most are "underground," estimated as much as $2 trillion a year in the U. S. economy.

There are thousands of solopreneurs such as Shawna Robinson, former female NASCAR driver, who operates a company called Happy Chair in Charlotte, NC, "recycling the old into the new." A recently divorced friend needing to start over furnishing her home told me Shawna found just the right chair online for $25, recovered it in glorious bright new fabrics, selling it to my friend for $400. You can find out more about her business at www.shawnarobinson.com. Instead of waiting for someone to offer them a job, solopreneurs create their own.

Millions of solopreneurs are found in direct-sales organizations such as Amway, Avon, Longaberger and ViSalus. A recent star is Thirty-One, taking its name from Chapter 31 in Proverbs. Growth has been blazing with revenues approaching a billion dollars of purses, totes, backpacks and similar items, creating jobs for nearly 2,000 corporate employees. Its founder, Cindy Monroe, encourages the firm's 115,00 entrepreneurial sales persons (mostly female) to find happiness not only in making money but from the relationships and good things that result. Monroe relates examples, "So often someone will be in tears and tell us, 'My marriage is saved', because the added cash lifted the family's income or allowed a husband to quit his job and get into a new career." Entrepreneurs come in many shades.

Non-Profits as Entrepreneurs

Non-profit organizations need to understand entrepreneurs; they also need to be entrepreneurs, using what they learn to start or grow non-profits meeting social needs. One such person is Susan Dell, wife of mega-billionaire Michael Dell.

"When I get a letter that tells me I changed this person's life, well, that resonates more than anything," Susan Dell told a *Forbes* reporter. Despite funding of medical, youth, Jewish and other projects by their foundation, "We really didn't have a focus," she says. Since then, she became convinced the focus of her home (and their four children) should become the mission of the Foundation, making sure kids have healthy options.

First, she started on projects close to home, ranging from classroom coaching initiatives to the Dell Children's Medical Center of Central Texas. As she gained experience in understanding effectiveness, the Foundation expanded to child obesity programs and "name brands" such as Teach for America, Livestrong, and the Dell Scholars Program, providing financial assistance and mentoring to help kids get through college. The evolution continued, much like concentric expansion in for-profit firms, funding microfinance and water-sanitation services in India and programs for orphans and vulnerable children in South Africa. Susan Dell is typical of entrepreneurial families who pay forward by solving community problems. "We surely don't need to have more money than necessary to take care of our family, so why wouldn't we give," she says.

In this conversation, I hope I convinced you that "garage" entrepreneurs live in many forms of "garages."

Where Do I Get Capital to Start My Firm?

"I want to start a firm and be an entrepreneur. Where do I get capital to start it?"

When people ask that question, I usually enquire what type of business they are planning.

"I don't know. I thought I would raise the capital first, and then figure out the best business to start."

My response in the next conversation may surprise you.

4

Conversation FOUR

TMC – Why Most Entrepreneurs Fail

"Where can I obtain capital to start a business?" I hear that question often, but when you understand why most entrepreneurs fail, I think you will conclude it is too early to talk about raising capital. We will save that topic for later.

"Why do most entrepreneurs fail?" I ask that question when teaching seminars on starting and growing firms. Answers vary depending on experience, but typically include lack of hard work, lack of focus, lack of people skills, lack of perseverance, not understanding needs of customers, poor cash control or insufficient time. Those are good answers. But when entrepreneurs say they failed because of lack of capital I roll my eyes and say, "Before we talk about raising capital, we need to talk about why so many entrepreneurs fail."

TMC and the *Best* Source of Capital

"Lack of capital," is the reason often given for failure. Call me a contrarian if you wish, but the cause is the opposite of lack of capital. Empirical analysis reveals dramatic cases of firms started with large quantities of capital invested in good ideas, ending in traumatic failures. Few reveal the causes of failure as clearly as the history of Webvan. Anyone who fails to learn the lessons of its history is likely to repeat them.

Webvan Hit a Wall Made of Bricks and Mortar

Webvan was born in Silicon Valley at the height of the technology boom. Investors salivated over the amount of money spent on groceries, eagerly investing nearly $1 billion to make Webvan successful selling groceries online. Anything can be sold on the Internet, right? Webvan opened for business with panache, selling groceries in ten U.S. markets, hoping to expand quickly to 26 cities.

A few years later, CNET named Webvan the largest dot-com flop in history, placing it above Pets.com and eight other techno-fallen stars. In 2001, the technology superstar declared bankruptcy (along with 330 other Internet companies), firing its employees and closing its doors. Webvan was technologically advanced, attracted highly motivated employees, well-funded and well-liked by a substantial base of loyal customers. What went wrong at a firm that was one of the best capitalized – nearly $1 billion --among technology firms?

A company representative attributed the problem to "being ahead of our time." The harsh truth is Webvan was about 40 years behind its time and entrepreneurs who earlier perfected bricks-and-mortar grocery stores. The reason it was 40 years behind the times is because, like many other failed technology firms, Webvan focused on the "e" of e-commerce. Failing to learn the lessons of history, Webvan was doomed to repeat them.

Webvan based its business model on home delivery, a model doomed to fail selling groceries as surely as it did forty years earlier among dairies, bakeries, department stores and other forms of retailing.

If you are mature enough, you might recall when regular delivery of milk to the home, as well as bread, groceries and department store merchandise was a normal retail practice.

Why did home delivery by retailers die decades earlier? There were two reasons.

First was cost. The last mile of logistics is the most expensive, even for simple products such as bread or milk. Home delivery of complex, heterogeneous grocery orders (fresh, frozen, and dry merchandise) costs about $30 to deliver, as any investor in this entrepreneurial firm could have known by examining similar business models of wholesale grocers delivering to small restaurants. Add expensive automated warehouses to "pick, pack and ship" and truck drivers travelling from delivery to delivery in expensive trucks, and there is no hope of getting the cost below the amount consumers are willing to add to their grocery bill.

There is a small segment of consumers packed closely together with limited existing retail alternatives in cities such as New York City, but they are few and far between. If Webvan had started small, like FreshDirect, (also the first New York grocer to accept food stamps over the internet) with minimal capital and a limited offering of high-quality products, the idea might have worked. A network of high-school students in cars (the "pizza delivery" model, requiring little capital) might also have worked, but that was not Webvan's strategy.

Another reason Webvan failed with home delivery is few people are home to accept delivery, at least those with families needing large quantities of food and the income to afford premium-priced groceries. Consumers at home in the daytime are mostly lower income, often with several children. They buy large quantities of groceries, but at stores with low prices such as Aldi and Sam's Club, retailing refuges for high-volume, price-sensitive shoppers.

Investors pouring capital into Webvan could have foreseen all these problems if they had understood that *the most important determinant of success is behavior of customers.* Webvan busied itself raising capital, with great success, and technological innovation instead of focusing on how consumers behave. With access to a billion dollars of capital, Webvan was not forced to learn what matters most to consumers and how to operate efficiently. The bottom line is *firms with their eyes on capital or technology instead of customers usually fail at turning ideas into profits.*

Investors seeking to maximize their IRAs could have predicted the downfall of Webvan. The only way to profit was selling its stock short after the Initial Public Offering (IPO). The reasons Webvan would fail are described in *From Mind to Market* (Harper, 1997) and a later book *Customers Rule! Why the E-Commerce Honeymoon is Over and Where Winning Businesses Go from Here* (Crown, 2001*).* These books show how to analyze what really matters to customers and how to deliver at prices they are willing to pay. *Entrepreneurs claim they are undercapitalized when actually they are over-expensed.*

Customers Rule!

Here are many lessons entrepreneurs can learn from the demise of Webvan, useful for anyone wondering "where to get capital." These lessons are especially important for entrepreneurs developing mobile apps, social media and other popular technologies, who will fail if they do not code the Webvan lessons.

The first lesson from Webvan demonstrates both sides of the e-commerce equation—the "e" and the "commerce." Whereas the glamorous "e" portion and raising capital is the focus of many entrepreneurs, the "commerce" portion determines ability to delight customers.

The Webvan business model was inferior to existing "bricks-and-mortar" retailers, who long ago mastered inventory management, sourcing, transportation and distribution, customer attraction and retention, personnel recruiting and training, warehousing, and logistics, the essential functions needed to move groceries from farms to homes. These functions are not eliminated by new technology, but had already shifted to the most efficient levels of the distribution channel. Retailers that didn't learn those lessons, didn't survive.

Consumers do more than just "shop" at a grocery store—they perform essential marketing functions, including picking and delivery, at no cost to the retailer. Some stores, such as Aldi and Sam's Club, ask customers to bag their own purchases. These retailers understand the cost efficiency of shifting functions to consumers, and many consumers willingly perform these functions in return for lower prices.

When consumers perform the picking function, their eyes scan over 900 items per minute in a retail store, selecting an average of 18 items. When a product is out of stock, consumers make instantaneous decisions about substitutions. Examined closely, the process and cost of the picking function at Webvan alone explains drains on precious revenues, burning up capital. Add the cost of home delivery for which retailers pay nothing when customers "deliver" groceries to themselves, and the model that attracted $1 billion capital quickly becomes too costly. Webvan was destined to die from the beginning, and IPO capital merely prolonged inevitable death. Webvan understood the "e" better than traditional retailers, but existing competitors understood "commerce" better than Webvan.

Despite what eager entrepreneurs may believe, technology determines only what can be *offered* to consumers; consumers determine which technologies are *accepted*. Consumers migrate to Internet buying when they are dissatisfied with present solutions, but studies show that 75-80% of consumers *like* today's grocery stores, especially those offering a superior *experience*. Investors in Webvan overlooked that reality, ultimately leading to Webvan's failure. Marketers propose, but consumers dispose.

The success of retailers such as Starbucks, Whole Foods, and Lululemon demonstrate that *experiences inside stores determine some consumer choices more than physical attributes or prices of products*. That fundamental retailing truth was missed by Webvan.

Webvan learned the painful (and eventually lethal) lesson that its business model appealed mostly to a small segment of the market, while the masses flocked to bricks-and-mortar masters. If Webvan had started with minimal capital in one or a few densely populated, high-income markets, its chance of developing a profitable model would have been better. Too Much Capital (TMC) allowed Webvan the luxury of surviving for a short time before learning that what it wanted to do, didn't match where, how and when consumers wanted to buy.

When firms have ample capital, they can—and often do—operate without learning how customers behave and how to supply products and services in ways delighting customers more than existing alternatives. Unfortunately, there is no reliable way to answer that question except testing your idea in the laboratory of the marketplace. A firm with ample capital can survive a long time without learning what is really important to customers, but when you don't have much capital except what you scrape together from savings, family and friends, you have little choice but to produce what customers will buy, learning how to make and distribute it at prices customers are willing to pay.

Entrepreneurs with TMC start big, but grow small or not at all. Entrepreneurs starting small with limited capital grow large by knowing what customers will buy at a profit, creating jobs for employees and fortunes for families.

How Barbers Become Billionaires

For investors, it is better to put your money in companies with little capital and lots of successful experience than entrepreneurs with lots of ideas and little experience at delighting customers. In contrast to highly capitalized Webvan, look at how a single grocery in Michigan started with capital saved from operating a barbershop. That store became, according to *Forbes* magazine, one of the 15 largest private companies in the United States, operating 117 supercenters in Michigan and surrounding states with sales of over $2 billion. It was started in 1934, at the depth of the Great Depression.

Hendrik Meijer (pronounced to rhyme with "buyer") emigrated

from The Netherlands to the United States in 1907, settling in Michigan. In 1914 he opened a barbershop, building an adjacent storefront hoping for rental income when he retired as a barber. When the Depression hit, Meijer could not find a tenant for the new space so he opened a grocery store, hoping to cover the building costs from store profits, knowing that even during an economic depression, people find a way to buy groceries.

With $338.76 of goods bought on credit, Meijer opened his food store, competing with a grocer across the street and 20 more competitors in town. Starting with essentially no capital except what he saved as a barber, Hendrik and his son Fred knew they had to work harder than more-established stores. They had to offer the lowest prices, because that is what mattered most to consumers in the Depression-dominated 1930s.

Meijer's goal was to help customers save money at their "Thrift Market." To speed shoppers through the store, Fred displayed baskets near the door with a handwritten sign inviting customers to take one and help themselves. This "self-service" innovation ("new technology") increased the number of customers Meijer could serve, becoming his foundation for growth. Technology that functions better than previous solutions is a better investment than technology that is "cool."

By 1937, Hendrik Meijer had doubled the size of his original store. With the help of his family, he opened a second store in 1942 with profits from the first store, perfecting operations to keep costs low and prices attractive. In the 1950s, the family built four new stores and opened a supermarket chain in western Michigan. After a fire leveled Meijer's first store, the company relocated to its present Grand Rapids headquarters.

Meijer had ten stores in operation by the late 1950s, when trading stamps became popular in supermarkets across the country. Meijer was offered a "stamp program" from major vendors, but declined. Then the company, with some trepidation, initiated its own Goodwill stamp campaign in 1956 at a cost of $10,000 a week. Although gross sales increased, costs increased more. That is the kind of lesson firms with little capital learn by necessity and in 1961, Meijer dropped the stamp program. Entrepreneurs learn from experience there is neither profit nor reputation to be gained from doing what nearly all other firms are doing.

With a thoroughly planned campaign, Meijer advertised, "Nobody, but nobody gets nothin' for nothin'," announcing its plan to drop stamps. In the following Sunday paper, Meijer announced it was closing stores the following Monday to lower hundreds of prices. Banners urged buyers to "Save U.S. Green Currency--Redeemable Anywhere for Almost Anything!" When shoppers arrived at Meijer on Tuesday, they found shelves lined with tags listing "Typical Stamp Store Price" compared with "Meijer No-Stamp Price." While competitors offered double- and triple-coupons, Meijer increased its market share with the image of a different kind of supermarket.

Meijer entered Ohio in the late 1960s, pioneering a "one-stop shopping theme," offering, in addition to food, garden and pet supplies, small appliances, jewelry, sporting goods, clothing, and home fashions. In the 1970s, Meijer had more than 20 stores open, some with gasoline pumps as well. By the 1980s the *hypermarket*, a concept from Europe, was adapted by Meijer to the U.S. market, adding in-store delis, bakeries, and fresh meat and fish departments.

A major change in Meijer's practices occurred when the company announced it would keep most stores open 24 hours a day. Unlike competitors who followed, Meijer operated the stores with policies and management providing services to its customers, many employed by multi-shift firms, as customer-friendly in the middle of the night as the middle of the day. Meijer evolved over the years to its multi-billion dollar size, but it didn't succeed with Webvan-style venture capital. It started with limited capital from the earnings of an immigrant barber.

I hope you are beginning to understand how entrepreneurs become billionaires.

Centrifugal Growth

Growth from small to large at firms such as Meijer provides a stark contrast with TMC start-ups such as Webvan who start big and grow small. Here's one of the most important secrets entrepreneurs can learn: Turning small beginnings into large fortunes is largely explained by the principle of *centrifugal growth*, a logical alternative to TMC.

Centrifugal growth is based on the principle in physics that effects occur in connection with concentric rotation as an outward force away from the center of rotation. Great fortunes are created from outward, concentric, incremental growth starting with the center or "core" product, evolving over years to a greatly expanded array of locations, products and services related to central attributes that provided the initial foundation for success.

Superficially, it might seem that Meijer's grocery store was unrelated to his barbershop. Closer analysis reveals that expansion extended the core attributes of the barber store. First, was an adjacent location, giving Meijer ability to operate a store next door without abandoning the barbershop. Second, the customers in the new store included many from the barber store. Customers of the new grocery store knew Meijer, his family, and his quality of service. *Knowing and serving similar customers is key to growing new and expanded product offerings.* If you own a small firm and understand the principle of centrifugal growth, you are on the way to building a large firm, as the next example reveals.

Geographic Centrifugal Growth

Here is one of the most important theories of growing small firms into large ones with limited capital, illustrated by Max & Erma's, a restaurant chain evolving from a single store in 1958 serving as a neighborhood gathering spot in the German Village area of Columbus, Ohio. After the original owners sold the store to Barry Zacks and Todd Barnum in

1972, they successfully added a few stores and went public, deciding to grow more by adding stores in Toledo, Cincinnati, and Kansas City.

Big mistake, because home office was too far away to manage well or achieve advertising and supply chain efficiencies. After closing the distant locations, the firm concentrated on the Columbus market, eventually developing over a dozen successful stores in its hometown city, planting similar "clusters" in Detroit, Pittsburgh, Dayton and other cities. From what was originally a neighborhood bar and gathering place, the firm grew *centrifugally* to a chain of over 100 stores creating millions of dollars of wealth for its entrepreneurial owners, before selling in 2008.

Centrifugal growth allows small firms to become giant killers. Walmart started with one store in rural Arkansas, gradually growing by concentric expansion into neighboring states, avoiding cities where they would have competed with giants such as Montgomery Ward, Sears and K-Mart. Who would you rather compete, Sears or Harry's Hardware?

Eventually, Walmart grew so large and efficient, it could invade major cities and crush giants avoided in earlier years, before those competitors knew they had been engaged by a superior force. You kill both giants and independents by delighting customers better than competitors, but entrepreneurs cannot kill giants until they learn how to stamp out gnats.

Non-Profit Growth

Centrifugal growth is the key to growing entrepreneurial non-profit organizations . Whether the organization is medical, social services, or spiritual, sound growth is achieved by expanding services to target audiences with similar attributes, whether those audiences are defined by demographics, location or social problems.

An example of centrifugal growth in the non-profit sector is

Directions for Youth (DFY), providing services to teenagers in a neighborhood where crime, drugs and other problems are omnipresent. DFY began its mission teaching arts to students after school. The visual arts and dance products were so attractive, people wanted to buy some of them. DFY added classes in business and marketing skills, teaching students how to sell their art as greeting cards for business organizations.

High school students served by DFY often came from homes with limited parental engagement and those students brought younger siblings with them to classes. Before long, DFY developed after-school and evening programs teaching younger kids and tutoring them to achieve success in school, adding computers to help with homework.

Attacking problems central to DFY's mission eventually required expansion to home services for single mothers, allowing DFY in 2002 to merge with an organization dedicated to family services and a long history that included the "Crittenton Home for Unwed Mothers" where young ladies avoided embarrassment by having their baby away from home. The Director of the "Home for Unwed Mothers" was a member of the church I attended. She sometimes invited me to give talks to women in various stages of pregnancy about family finances, where I observed the importance of the mission. Years later, the stigma of being an unwed mother decreased and abortions increased, dictating a change in mission for Crittenton. A merger of DFY and Crittenton Family services was a logical form of centrifugal expansion for both organizations. They combined, together solving urban problems with expanded services and funding. And, a new name---Directions for Youth and Families (DFYF) enabling the organization to serve over 6,000 troubled families and youth. www.dfyf.org.

Problems Caused by TMC

Too Much Capital—TMC—allows firms to fumble along until they die. When firms start with little or no capital, they have no choice but to be better than competitors, changing operations, perfecting them to meet customer expectations. Sometimes "better" means better products, but more often it is better marketing, better sourcing, better logistics, or better customer service. When entrepreneurs bootstrap their way to success, they learn how to operate well or they die. Firms with TMC die slowly, burning through capital, until it is too late to resuscitate. *TMC is not the cause of failure, but rather a blindfold over the causes of success.*

There are many failures caused by TMC in firms whose names would be unknown to most readers, such as a technology firm you wouldn't recognize. I met an entrepreneur in one who is a near-genius. He introduced a good product in the e-technology market. He had a business plan so good a major computer firm invested $20 million in seed capital to perfect the product and its marketing. The entrepreneur burned through the entire $20 million in nine months. The product never made it to market and the firm failed in less than a year. If he had started with "too little capital" and tested a few prototypes, he might have discovered the mismatch between what he wanted to make and what the market wanted to buy. The flaws in his plan were hidden by TMC.

I know of an investment by a major Silicon Valley venture capital firm whose name you would recognize, investing $150 million in a technology start-up having little more than an idea. The return was zero; the product never made it to market and every employee lost their job before the firm had a dollar of revenue. The entrepreneur started big—with TMC—and ended small. Actually, it ended not at all. *Patience thrills; impatience kills.*

Before you protest my controversial thesis too strongly, I should clarify that having ample capital in an entrepreneurial start-up is not inherently *wrong*; the problem is TMC keeps most people from discovering what is fundamentally *right* to achieve success. That is why firms are more likely to succeed when entrepreneurs bootstrap the process, taking time to determine what customers are willing to buy rather than using capital from investors trying to get customers to buy what the entrepreneur wants to sell. TMC feeds failure; limited capital fuels success by focusing a firm on what customers will buy at prices they are willing to pay.

TMC is a danger starkly revealed by firms such as Webvan and thousands of other entrepreneurial start-ups who drift into oblivion because they have capital allowing them to crumble and collapse. The secret many observers overlook is some of the most successful entrepreneurs start in a garage, but later populate lists of billionaires. I hope you see the principles of success and growth in the contrasting patterns of firms we discussed in this and the previous conversation.

Dangers from TMC are many, but here is a summary of some of the most blatant:

1. TMC permits entrepreneurs to produce what they want to make instead of understanding what customers will buy.

2. TMC funds entrepreneurs to operate without finding ways to lower costs.

3. TMC delays or prevents entrepreneurs from building efficient demand chains.

4. TMC encourages marketing programs based on attributes entrepreneurs value most instead of attributes customers value most.

5. TMC focuses attention on satisfying investors instead of satisfying customers.

6. TMC allows firms to muddle along without doing the right things right until eventually they fail or are owned by someone other than the founder.

7. TMC allows firms the luxury of burning cash until incinerated by failure

Entrepreneurs are often described as "risk takers," but successful entrepreneurs are better described as "risk minimizers," and TMC is an enabler of too much risk. If you invest in entrepreneurial firms, follow Warren Buffet's goal to, "Never lose money." *Successful entrepreneurs and investors focus on what could go wrong instead of what they hope will go right.*

If you are an entrepreneur whose first firm failed, do not despair. If you understand why it failed, your next attempt may be a winner. Second firms, like second marriages, can be better than the first.

I acknowledge some people create successful firms even though burdened by TMC. Sons and daughters of wealthy parents have greater ease in attracting investors because of their family name, and some do well even with that millstone. One who succeeded was the son of Sam Walton, who ably created an additional fortune in a new business. When he died in the tragic crash of an experimental plane he built himself, his widow became one of the wealthiest women in the world. Success is possible, even among the wealthy.

The opposite outcome is more common---sons and daughters of entrepreneurial parents turning their families' billions into millions. In private consulting and Executive MBA programs, I sometimes observe sons and daughters who do not understand why and how their parents created the family fortune. If young moguls understood the theories that create entrepreneurial success, they might avoid turning billions into millions. Some entrepreneurs succeed blessed with the lucky sperm of a wealthy parent, but they are the exception rather than the expectation.

So, as the song says, "if your daddy's rich, take a wrapper from him." But, if your daddy's poor, you don't need to remain on the floor because of limited capital. You can create capital at low cost in your garage— or kitchen, or a small rented space, a university facility or incubator. Entrepreneurs should not let investors define their lives and the life of their firm; entrepreneurs who bootstrap their own capital define life themselves.

Taking a Small Firm to the Next Level

Once you have a firm started and stable, how do you take it to the next level, perhaps to an organization worth millions or even billions?

There are three fundamental ideas explaining how profitable "breakthrough" success is built, the topic of our next conversation. But I warn you, these concepts are more intellectually challenging than examples we've discussed so far. So grab a cup of coffee (and maybe a Cheryl's cookie!), get rid of the kids or other distractions and prepare to have a dialogue about the three most important concepts in marketing.

5

Conversation FIVE

The Three Most Valuable Concepts in Marketing

Warning! The content of this conversation is theoretical, and theory can be toxic to mental alertness. If you have problems with insomnia, reading about marketing theory might be a prescription to help you fall asleep. By the time you finish this book, however, I believe you will understand there is nothing as practical and valuable as good theory.

Good teachers discover there are two ways to make theory understandable and interesting:

1. Provide examples, and

2. Use humor

Providing examples is easy. You already read case examples in previous conversations, and there are more to come. Using humor to teach theory is more challenging.

Years ago, I spoke to a group in Sheboygan, Wisconsin. After the presentation, a newspaper reporter told me he recorded the entire lecture. He thought it would be sufficiently interesting to print verbatim. I agreed, with one caveat.

"Jokes are useful in oral presentations, but usually don't translate well on the printed page," I told him. "It's OK to print the verbatim narrative, but please delete the jokes from your transcript. Humor just doesn't translate well onto the printed page." He agreed to my request and promised to send the newspaper to me.

A few days later, the paper arrived containing the full-transcript with a notation at the end, "In addition to the comments reported above, Dr. Blackwell told a few jokes that can't be printed."

I learned a lesson from that episode, so in the following conversation, I will stick to written words, without attempting humor.

Why Study Theory?

"Just tell me what I need to know. Don't waste my time with theory."

If that is how you feel, let me explain why theory is both practical and essential to building break-through firms, creating small, successful firms and growing them into a Dell, Google, Amazon, Limited or Walmart.

Theory makes it possible to predict what will happen before something not previously undertaken is attempted. It is like dropping an apple from the second story of a building. You know whether the apple will go up or down because of Newton's theory of Universal Gravitation.

Starting a business based on the hope it will succeed instead of sound theory is as dangerous as building an airplane, hoping it will fly without theories of aeronautics and structural engineering. It might, and some businesses are successful with little understanding of theory, but if you are investing time, energy and money in a firm, you should be like a test pilot on the plane's first flight. You really hope the plane was built with good theory. Not just any theory, but correct theories about lift, structural strength and aerodynamics. It is the same when creating a business or nonprofit organization. The probability your business will "fly" is much higher when built with good theory.

Author John Steinbeck once said, "Ideas are like rabbits. You get a couple and learn how to handle them, and pretty soon you have a dozen." The same process applies to theories. You get a couple of them, mix them around in the laboratory of the marketplace, and soon you have a billion-dollar business. When entrepreneurs do that, they rescue lethargic economies.

The Meaning of Marketing

Marketing may be the most misunderstood word in the vocabulary of business. Some people equate marketing with sales and advertising. Others associate marketing with manipulating people. Both views are sometimes true, but marketing means much more than either of these common misunderstandings about marketing.

Marketing means making and selling what customers want at prices they are willing to pay, in places, times and ways they choose to consume, with enough profit to sustain and grow the business. Marketing starts with customers and their motives for behavior. The marketing process ends with satisfaction so intense, customers keep coming back to buy more.

At Amazon.com, Jeff Bezos says, "We start with the mind of the customer and work backward." Marketing is a process built on models and methods, including a supply chain to accomplish that process profitably, starting by understanding consumer behavior. Simply stated, *marketing means making what people will buy instead of trying to get people to buy what an organization makes.*

"Does marketing manipulate people?" That's a question I've heard for decades.

"Yes, marketing, when practiced well, does manipulate people," I respond, "but it might not be the people about whom you are thinking." Marketing is about understanding customers so well they "manipulate" the firm to have what customers profitably buy.

When marketing is working well, who is "manipulated?" It is not customers; it is owners and employees of the firm. When marketing is skillfully practiced, the result is a lot of profit for firms that know how to please the boss. *The "boss" of entrepreneurs is customers.*

After studying entrepreneurs for decades, I recognized theories or marketing concepts explaining how organizations delight customers, evolving small firms into large fortunes. The three most valuable concepts are:

1. Market segmentation

2. Functional shiftability

3. Global thinking

Let's talk about each.

Market Segmentation

In an ideal marketing world, every product would be designed to individual preferences and behavior of each customer. If all human beings were identical, all products would be identical because every customer would prefer the same flavor, color, size and every product attribute. But if each customer is different from any other, each product would be custom-designed and produced with no two products alike.

Which of these descriptions of customers is accurate? Every person is different, of course, and in an ideal world, maximum customer satisfaction requires every product and marketing mix to be custom-designed. That is impractical, because custom-designed products cost more than standardized ones. This principle is evident in the price of a hand-tailored suit compared to one at Sears or JCPenney.

The dilemma for entrepreneurs arises because of the desire for *production homogeneity* (standardization, with all products the same), but faced with *demand heterogeneity* (desire by customers for customization). The solution to this dilemma is market segmentation, *finding groups of customers with behavior similar enough to be satisfied with similar products, but different enough from other groups to appeal to specific segments of the total market.* Competition is fought in a war between efficiency and low-costs of mass-produced products and the appeal of specific sizes, flavors, colors, functions, locations, or other attributes causing customers to be more loyal or pay higher prices than for standardized products.

Established organizations lower costs over time by making and marketing products all pretty much the same, based on average preferences of the market. Mass marketers end up with average products, average prices, average distribution channels and average communication messages. Usually the firm with the largest share of mass markets is the most profitable. Standardizing everything allowed Henry Ford to reduce car prices so much, he eliminated competitors and dominated an industry with the strategy, "Give customers any color they want, so long as it's black."

The way new entrepreneurs attack and destroy mass-market giants is by appealing to segments, discovering unmet needs or significant dissatisfaction with mass-market firms and their products. The ultimate form of market segmentation is customization for segments as small as one consumer or one firm. Usually that is too costly, although changing technology makes customization more feasible than in the past.

Extreme loyalty and high profitability occurs when entrepreneurial firms identify segments expressing strong behavioral preferences, and achieve passionate satisfaction (delight!) from customers in those segments, commanding a premium price. *The riches are in the niches.*

Appealing to a segment is how Apple Computers gained a strong hold among "creatives," specialized computer users in a mass market dominated by IBM, Gateway, and H-P. Along the path of segmented profitability and growth, Apple not only destroyed several of the undifferentiated "mass market" competitors, but created a group of loyal customers that followed Apple into new product categories including iPods, iPhones and iPads. With a different form of segmentation, Dell attacked dinosaurs not with specialized products, but a specialized and more efficient demand chain.

Market segmentation allowed Victoria's Secret to focus on consumers who value glamour and sexiness, taking market share from mass-market retailers Target, Walmart and department stores. Sexiness sells more profitably than lowest price. Customer loyalty and higher margins are reasons riches are in the niches, a theory allowing Sarah Blakely to become a billionaire with Spanx.

A strategy of "average" everything appeals to the maximum number of customers, and if you are one of a few firms in a market, average everything can be profitable. When you identify segments not satisfied with average offerings, you have an opening to attack existing competitors.

If you believe all customers are the same, check their fingerprints or DNA. When products appeal to "typical" or "average" customers, the only ones truly satisfied with existing firms are "typical" customers who fit the profile of "average." It is like saying the average house household has 2.3 children. No one does. When you define and divide the market into segments, you discover only "average" customers are satisfied with mass market firms, leaving the door wide open for higher profits by a new entrant. *Volume kills; profit thrills.*

The tricky part is to find segments unique enough for products with special appeal, but large enough to be profitable. How do emerging and growing entrepreneurs define and reach the right segments?

How to Segment a Market

Defining market segments is often with demographics, psychographics, size, volume, industry or other attributes. Be careful in doing that.

Profitable segmentation should be based on similar *behavior*, not necessarily similar characteristics. When using demographics or other variables, remember those characteristics are only correlates, or "proxies" for behavior, not determinants of behavior. Demographics and psychographics are useful mainly in defining channels to reach segments; delivering delight to those customers is determined by *behavior* of those niches.

How should a firm choose segments as market targets? Here are four criteria.

1. *Measurability* refers to ability to obtain information about size, nature and behavior of market segments. Behavior must be measurable (or have close correlates) to formulate and implement an effective marketing mix to reach the segment.
2. *Accessibility* (or reachability) is the degree to which segments can be reached, either through targeted communication and sales programs or through specialized marketing channels, increasingly involving digital communications.
3. *Substantiality* refers to size of the market. Small segments may not generate enough volume to support development, production and distribution costs to satisfy those segments.
4. *Congruity* refers to how customers within the segment exhibit similar behavior or characteristics correlating with usage behavior. The more congruous a segment, the more efficient are product offerings, promotion and distribution channels directed specifically to that segment.

Market segmentation is the "secret weapon" entrepreneurs use to take customers away from established, larger competitors. It is not the only way, but usually the most profitable way.

If you and I were having a one-on-one, personal conversation about market segmentation, you might be asking if a segmentation strategy limits you to remaining small.

No! As you will see in later conversations, especially firms such as Apple and Limited, segmentation allows your firm to capture a niche as a foothold to larger markets. Entrepreneurs can use that foothold to add incremental segments centrifugally, bootstrapping the firm from small to large. Niche by niche, firms grow from successful single-segment marketing strategies to behemoth multi-segmentation marketing masters such as Apple, Google, Meijer and Walmart. Large firms start small. Too bad Webvan did not understand that principle!

Multi-segment strategies are the foundation for future fortunes, but only if you dominate each segment. Multi-segment strategies are the bane of firms without focus. The danger arises from doing well in a segment without dominating it, without "putting it away," leaving money on the table for others. The temptation is to chase one good segment, then another and then another, resulting in second or third place, or less, in all of them. Firms eventually dominating a segment generally have twice the profitability of second place, and firms in third place or lower are usually only marginally profitable, a process described by Jagdish Sheth and Rajendra Sisodia in *Rule of Three* (Free Press, 2010.)

Market dominance is much like Olympic medals. Gold is a big win with lots of fame, endorsements and money. Silver is OK and bronze is not bad. The difference between third and fourth place may be inches or milliseconds; the difference in profits is the difference between fame and forgotten. For a firm, the difference between dominance and survival in multiple segments is the difference between millions and billions.

Functional Shiftability

Do you know why Michael Dell's net worth is over $15 billion, even though his firm is past its peak? Or why the Walton family's fortune is over $500 billion? Or how the smallest bank in a medium-sized city (City National of Columbus) became one of the largest banks in the

United States(Banc One/Chase)? Or why there are few independent bookstores left in America? Or why Webvan failed? The theory explaining each is *functional shiftability*.

If you plan to grow your firm into a future fortune, it is essential to understand functional shiftability. Yet, many entrepreneurs think very little, or perhaps not at all, about functional shiftability.

A number of essential economic activities—called "functions"-- are inherent in the creation of value, pervading the entire marketing process of getting goods from producers to users. *Marketing functions shift but cannot be eliminated.* Entrepreneurs win by shifting them to the most effective level in the supply chain or performing them more efficiently than competitors. Firms performing essential marketing functions better than competitors grow, transform industries and create billion dollar fortunes.

Traditionally, the relationships between firms producing and distributing goods and services to consumers were called "supply chains." In the book *From Mind to Market*, I show why firms with the most permanent, profitable and successful relationships are better described as "demand chains." In the past, manufacturers designed and drove supply chains. Today, especially in an Internet era, it is customers who design and drive relationships between firms, the reason I call them "demand chains." And remember, even if you are a business selling to other businesses (B2B), ultimately it is consumer demand that determines what is produced by industrial firms, allocating profitability among members of a demand chain.

Essential Marketing Functions

Because your ability to shift functions to their most efficient level determines much of your success as an entrepreneur, it is crucial to understand and consider carefully the three types of marketing functions:

1. *Transactional*—determining consumer needs, designing products to satisfy those needs, branding, pricing, stimulating demand, stocking and displaying products and selling.
2. *Logistical*—materials management, warehousing, transportation, distribution and delivery.
3. *Facilitating*—financing, taking risks of holding ownership, providing marketing research and customer data.

When working with entrepreneurs planning a new firm or improving an existing one, I have watched their questioning faces, asking, "Do you mean I have to analyze and coordinate *all* those functions in designing my business?"

"Yes," is the correct answer, if you want the enterprise to grow beyond an initial start-up. Few entrepreneurs performed these functions more successfully than Jeff Bezos at Amazon.com, as you will see in a later conversation.

Dominating one specialized function is how CheckFree, part of Fiserv since 2007, pioneered Electronic Funds Transfer (EFT), creating a fortune for Pete Kight, its entrepreneurial innovator. If you understood the theory of functional shiftability from its beginning, you saw the profit in shifting the very specialized function of payments by consumers and processing by banks to EFT. With that knowledge, you saw your investment of $10,000 in CheckFree become $2,000,000. If you purchased Fiserv (FISV) for your IRA twenty-five years ago, it's risen over 6,000% since you bought it. Does this help explain why functional shiftability is a very, very practical theory for investors and entrepreneurs?

Functions always shift to the most efficient levels of a channel of distribution. If other firms find better ways of performing essential marketing functions, they may put you out of business, just as Amazon.com displaced thousands of bricks-and-mortar bookstores and Walmart displaced thousands of hardware stores, investing in technology to perform logistics functions more efficiently than competitors.

Remember how Hendrik Meijer changed his grocery store to provide self-service? Prior to his innovative approach, consumers gave lists to sales clerks who picked the items from shelves behind counters. By shifting the function of "picking inventory" from retailers to consumers, Meijer lowered costs enough to offer lower prices to Depression-dominated, price-driven consumers. Membership discounter Costco does the same thing today, achieving high profits with low margins of fifteen percent or less compared to grocery chains with margins of 25 percent or more, by performing functions more effectively than competitors. Investors who understood functional shiftability predicted failure for Webvan from the beginning, and avoided investing in it.

Global Thinking

Over the decades, my own understanding of business success evolved to the point I now consider global thinking one of the three most valuable concepts in growing small firms into large ones. I was fortunate to study the theory of cross-cultural research as a doctoral student at Northwestern University, learning how to analyze markets across cultures, both domestically and internationally. I was fortunate to teach and consult with firms on six continents, providing a real-life laboratory in understanding how business differs from country to country. Both theory and experience taught me this truth: *factors causing entrepreneurial success are more similar than different in nations throughout the world.* From those experiences arose the concept of "global thinking."

Global thinking is the ability to understand markets beyond one's own country of origin. It includes the ability:

1. To understand demand in diverse nations.
2. To source materials and services around the world.
3. To understand management and marketing processes across national boundaries.

Market growth today is faster in Brazil, Russia, India, China and South Africa (BRICS) and other emerging markets than in North America and Europe. Corporate giants such as Coca-Cola, IBM, P&G, and YUM derive the majority of their sales and have more employees in nations other than the United States, growing profits in fast-growing emerging markets. Because of the success of massive firms, you might be tempted to believe "global thinking" is primarily for corporate giants rather than entrepreneurs just starting on the road to success. Resist that temptation!

Years ago a small tool and die maker in Milwaukee worried it might die along with the U.S. auto industry. But this firm knew that in a post-Soviet Union environment, laissez-faire states such as Poland, Estonia, and the Czech Republic were expanding exports rapidly, supplying manufacturers in Europe and Russia. Many of those firms lacked technology and skills the Milwaukee firm acquired supplying U.S. manufacturers. The firm found it had another asset in selling to this small, but emerging market—a number of employees had cousins in Poland, and some still spoke Polish. They were dispatched to Eastern Europe and the small entrepreneurial firm soon had a new avenue for growth.

"Global Thinking" is not just for large firms. Small firms grow by identifying specific markets in other nations that, while perhaps small, loom large for growth-oriented entrepreneurs. Global thinking does not mean entrepreneurs market throughout the world; it means seeking markets similar enough in specific segments of the world to provide profitable growth.

How to Analyze Global Markets

Whether targeting Euro-customers or rapid-growth emerging markets, entrepreneurs benefit from understanding *intermarket segmentation*. This involves identifying groups of customers who transcend traditional market or geographic boundaries, customers with similar behavior regardless of where they live. The objective is to build marketing strategy on universals of behavior and distribution rather than differences caused by geography. That is "global thinking."

A critical decision for any entrepreneurial firm is its name, and today a firm's name should be considered from a global perspective. Global access to the worldwide web dictates thinking about names and logos as part of global brands. Questions to be answered before settling on an English brand name include the following:

1. Does the English name have another meaning, perhaps unfavorable in nations where it might be marketed?
2. Can the English name be pronounced everywhere?
3. Is the name close to that of a foreign brand, or does it duplicate another product sold in English-speaking nations?
4. If the product is distinctly American, will national pride and prejudice work against acceptance of the product, or for it?

I hope you see the importance of "global thinking" as a key ingredient in entrepreneurial success, even for those who currently are just puttering around a garage.

One of BRICS nations with great potential for U.S. entrepreneurs is Brazil. It is huge, prosperous, growing fast, relatively near the U.S. and politically stable. I taught in Brazil, observing similarities between U.S. and Brazilian marketing and the warmth and attractiveness of Brazilians. Be sure, however, you learn a lot about the people and culture before you consider going to other countries. I heard about a professor invited to lecture in Brazil. He wanted to fit into the Latin culture, so he spent a year preparing by learning Spanish.

The Female Entrepreneur Who Created a Dynasty

Have you survived our discussion of marketing theory without a snooze? I hope so, but maybe you thought, "Can entrepreneurs survive if they don't know these theories?"

"Yes," is the candid answer, but life is easier and fortunes faster when you understand *theories* causing growth and profits. Proof you can grow a business without reading books is evident, however, by studying successful entrepreneurs long before marketing professors ever entered a classroom. One of those was Bridgett Murphy, who lived a century before contemporary entrepreneurs such as Sarah Blakely or Cheryl Krueger. Her story may be a secret you have not heard before.

Bridget Murphy became a single mom in 1858, when her husband, Patrick, died of tuberculosis. At age 37, Bridget was faced with supporting four children, ages one through seven. She endured prejudice against Irish immigrants, with no relatives in America to provide assistance. There were no food stamps or WIC programs back then!

Bridget found work as a servant girl, depending on neighbors for childcare. Later, she became a sales woman in a "notions" store, eventually purchasing and running it with help from her three daughters and son. She increased the store's offerings (centrifugal expansion!) to include groceries (including liquor) and variety goods. By living in the building where she worked, she saved enough to buy the building (functional shiftability!), using profits to educate her son. She also provided capital to help him open a tavern nearby, including a wholesale liquor business (demand chain!). Her son, Patrick Joseph, worked hard, entered politics and built his mother's modest capital into a family fortune, allowing his son to become America's ambassador to Great Britain (global thinking!) and grandsons to attend nearby Harvard University.

By this time, you probably guessed the name of the husband who left Bridget a widow and single mother with children to support. His name was Patrick Joseph Kennedy. The grandsons were John Fitzgerald, Robert and Ted Kennedy. The Kennedy dynasty and fortune was established by the female entrepreneur Bridget Murphy Kennedy.

You might be concluding Bridget Murphy Kennedy was exceptional, but not so, according to a fascinating book by Susan Lewis, *Unexceptional Women: Female Entrepreneurs in Mid Nineteenth Century Albany, New York 1830-1885* (Ohio State Press, 2009), from which I learned the Kennedy saga. Lewis documents many, many more; that's why she chose the term "unexceptional" to describe female entrepreneurs a century ago.

The Hand that Rocks the Cradle Sometimes Creates a Fortune

Do you know the name of America's first millionaire? History books generally ascribe that honor to John Jacob Astor, calling him a "self-made" man in the Horatio Alger tradition of John D. Rockefeller, Henry Ford, J.P. Morgan and Dave Thomas. Do you know how Astor started the firm that created a family fortune? That story is also told in Susan Lewis' inspiring book (and I bet you didn't think a history book could be so absorbing it is difficult to stop reading).

Sarah Todd and her mother were running a boarding house in Buffalo, New York, a typical occupation of early female entrepreneurs. A young German immigrant, John Astor, arrived nearly penniless as a boarder from New York City. They married in 1785, investing her dowry in a small shop selling musical instruments and furs. He traveled, purchasing furs, and Sarah ran the shop. She also gave birth to eight children and raised them in rooms above the shop. Sarah assisted in the difficult work of processing the furs, becoming an expert on fur quality, encouraging John to go to Canada to find a better supply chain (functional shiftability) and eventually to Asia (global thinking).

Sarah also advised her husband to invest profits from the fur business in New York City real estate (centrifugal expansion!), which eventually became the basis of the family's fortune. Some people might call her a "stay-at-home" mom, but I call her the brains of an entrepreneurial endeavor. As the family fortune grew, the company paid her $500 an hour as a consultant. I don't know how much that would be as a modern-day equivalent, but if you contribute as much to a business as Sarah Todd did, you might want to calculate that amount.

Marketing is Everything and Everything is Marketing

From our conversations, you may be concluding marketing is everything in the success of entrepreneurs. No, manufacturing, finance, human resources and other skills are also important, but they have no value until someone sells something. You can develop the most brilliantly engineered product ever invented, a product Thomas Edison or Henry Ford would envy, but if you can't market it effectively, about all you can hope to do is to give the idea to someone else. *Ideas have little value in themselves; fortunes are built by creating and building organizations that market ideas well.*

Our conversation about the three most valuable marketing concepts is just a beginning. If you haven't studied marketing, obtain a marketing textbook and read it from start to finish, something Bridget Kennedy or Sarah Todd couldn't do because marketing textbooks were not written until well into the Twentieth Century. Today, there are many good ones, but a good place to begin is Philip Kotler's *Marketing Management* (Prentice Hall, 2002), the most widely read marketing text in the world.

There you have it, the "skeleton" of marketing. We will put "flesh" on the skeleton throughout the rest of the book. I realize I threw a lot of theory at you, but the following conversations show how theories produce fortunes. These three theories helped one entrepreneur build a multi-billion dollar empire with the sexiest brand in the world, as you will see by flipping the page or screen.

6

Conversation SIX

The World's Sexiest Brand

How can a teenager turn a few dollars into thousands of dollars? Let me give an example how one student turned her earnings from a paper route into substantial savings by investing in the world's sexiest brand.

Josie was a newspaper delivery person, rising early to deliver papers before going to school. On Sundays when the paper was too heavy for her to carry or on snowy days, the father also arose early to help. Occasionally the mother had to get up early to awaken both of them. Josie spent some of her money on clothes; teenagers do that, but she saved most of it. She deposited her savings in a bank and started an IRA, as entrepreneurs teach their children to do. Her father suggested she pick her own stocks, and Josie wisely chose shares in a popular apparel retailer, investing about $300.

Fast forward to now. Josie is nearing forty, still single, and beginning to think about retirement. The retailer did well, and so did Josie. After seven share splits and three decades of growth, her original investment with dividend reinvestment is worth nearly $100,000. Not a bad return from delivering newspapers.

If you are a teenager reading this book, the lesson should be clear. Get a job and invest at least part of your earnings. If you are reading this book as a successful entrepreneur or plan to be, here is some advice you may also want to consider:

1. Teach your children how to work as a teenager, even if that requires you and your child getting up early on cold, snowy mornings. If they learn the rewards of hard work early in life, they may be as successful as you.

2. If you own your own business, let your children work in it as soon as possible, while still in school. Make sure they learn basic skills of your business as well as respect for and names of employees in every part of the business. That is your best chance of having children to succeed you and keep the business growing in the future.

In what entrepreneurial firm did Josie buy stock to produce this kind of return? The answer, if you have not already guessed, is the subject of our current conversation, a firm producing billions for its founder and investors and tens of thousands of jobs for employees. The way it grew illustrates the three valuable theories in our last conversation.

How to Start a Billion Dollar Business When You Have No Money

How much capital do you need to start a business and bootstrap it to a firm generating billions in revenues and thousands of employees?

The answer is $5,000, a loan from a family member.

That is what Leslie Wexner borrowed from an aunt to start his first store on August 10, 1963 in a shopping center. The loan provided collateral for inventory, which he turned fast enough to grow with profits from sales. The store's design of used brick, dark wood, stained glass, and cork in rustic old-world motif displayed Wexner's characteristic attention to detail in creating ambiance and a store experience, attracting and delighting customers. Sales on the first day of business were $473. By the end of the first year, the store sold $160,000 worth of clothing. He used profits from the first store to open two more, expanding to six stores in 1969, when he took his firm public, using proceeds from the stock sale to finance expansion into malls.

There is a lesson here for entrepreneurs. If you open your first store with little capital and demonstrate ability to make money, do not worry about getting more capital. Banks, equity funds and public offerings will provide capital to ramp up expansion at much more attractive rates than when all you have is an idea and a business plan. People with capital seek entrepreneurs with a track record growing sales and profits.

Does theory help achieve entrepreneurial success? Wexner was exposed to marketing theory in classes at The Ohio State University, some taught by Dr. Arthur Cullman, an entrepreneur himself before becoming a professor and mentor to many. Topics such as market segmentation and marketing functions (and their shiftability) were an important part of the theory to which Wexner was exposed, for which he gives credit to Professor Cullman.

Years later, after Wexner's success became known, Professor Cullman admitted that Wexner didn't make a big impression as a student. That's understandable because Wexner is reserved; some describe him as shy. In my own classes, I observed successful entrepreneurs often are not extroverts as the media sometimes describes an "entrepreneurial personality." Students who turn out to be the most effective entrepreneurs often sit in class quietly absorbing knowledge they implement later with great success. Perhaps you are doing that now as you read this book.

Do you need experience and training in the industry in which you hope to succeed? Wexner had both growing up and working in a women's apparel store in downtown Columbus, operated by his parents. The budget-clothing store barely provided a living for the family, but Leslie used his modest earnings in the store to pay for his education, entering the industry he revolutionized with hands-on, practical experience. Wexner had both theory and experience--basic ingredients in the recipe for entrepreneurial success. He also displayed another trait explaining why some entrepreneurs are successful and others are not—attention to details.

Market Segmentation

Wexner observed closely the buying preferences of American women. He noted that sportswear sold fastest and suggested his parents specialize in that line of apparel. Harry Wexner, his father, refused, telling his son he would never be a merchant. Wexner's father apparently made the mistake of many entrepreneurs, believing success stems from selling to "everyone." With that strategy, entrepreneurs end up selling to no one well enough to compete with other firms, all doing the same thing with an "average" offering for the "average" customer. Using the loan from his aunt as collateral, Wexner struck out on his own, limited inventory to sportswear only and called the store, The Limited.

Wexner and The Limited illustrate the principle of market segmentation, discovering niches leading to riches. His segment was sportswear for women, who buy more clothes than men. Not just women, but fashion-aware women buying clothes as an important component of their lifestyle. His segment was also young (typically 17-25), a segment growing faster then than other ages. His positioning was to the moderately affluent; there were not enough affluent consumers to provide mass markets, and poor people do not have much money to spend on clothes. Success is based on Marketing 101, not rocket science!

In either consumer markets or industrial markets, define your market segments for primary appeal with as much precision as The Limited. If you are a non-profit leader, the market segmentation is just as important in defining segments you serve and donors who help accomplish your mission.

Wexner did well, expanding The Limited into enclosed malls, which were rapidly replacing downtown centers of business. In malls, he offered visual excitement, convenient parking, and a safe shopping environment, believing success was dependent more on location and right products than advertising. The Limited thrived by shifting the branding function from manufacturers to a retailer, dominating specialty retailing.

Wexner also pioneered *multi-segment marketing*. After a decade in business, The Limited's primary market target was a decade older with more sophisticated lifestyles, ability to purchase at higher prices, and sometimes, the need for a larger size. As its target market matured, so did the Limited. That provided opportunity for a second concept store, Express, catering to younger, trendier tastes, providing centrifugal growth for the entrepreneurial parent. Later, Express discovered a segment of men who liked the colors, fabrics and styles of the Express, developing a spin-off for men called Structure.

There is also a segment with lots of price-sensitive consumers, so Wexner acquired Lerner Stores, an established brand appealing to that segment, and revitalized it, sending even more revenue to the corporate office. Continuing the pattern of centrifugal growth, he added Lane Bryant, appealing to fashion-conscious women wearing size 14 and up.

"The key is our ability to change," Les Wexner is quoted in an annual report. "We are constantly in the stores looking for ideas and listening to our customers. If we listen carefully enough, she'll tell us all we need to know."

By 1993, the multi-segment strategy of the company had expanded from its initial focus to more than thirteen businesses including Abercrombie & Fitch, Galyan's (sporting goods), Limited Too (children), Bath & Body Works (home décor), White Barn Candle (home décor), Aura Science (skin care), Henri Bendel (high-income, thirty-something New York women), and of course, Victoria's Secret. In a move to demonstrate its fervent belief in the importance of brands, the company changed its name to Limited Brands and later to "L". Don't worry, we'll return in this conversation to Victoria's Secret, the ultimate brand icon for targeted marketing to lifestyle segments.

Functional Shiftability and Logistics

Once upon a time, there were tens of thousands of independent apparel stores scattered across the land. Each one had to accomplish the functions we discussed earlier. Manufacturers designed products, stores bought what they thought customers might buy, and transportation was cobbled together by manufacturers, retailers and transportation firms as best they could. It was slow, inefficient, costly and often resulted in having wrong products at wrong times, in wrong quantities and sometimes at wrong places and prices. The Limited changed all that and the apparel industry.

The Limited shifted each of those functions to their most efficient location in the demand chain, starting with what consumers want to buy instead of what manufacturers want to sell. Instead of manufacturer-designed clothes and brands, Limited shifted the function of design and branding to itself. The result was less cost and a consistent brand ---The Limited—instead of the hodge-podge of brands found in most apparel and department stores. Instead of manufacturers losing sleep over the finance function with receivables from tens of thousands of questionably financed merchants, manufacturers had only one firm to deal with, and that firm had access to efficient capital markets. Instead of thousands of separate manufacturers typically tied to antiquated factories and labor force, The Limited could search the world securing the latest, lowest cost and most responsive factories, contracting with them for specific, large quantities of merchandise linked directly to sales data from cash registers.

The Limited and competitors who adopted similar innovations revolutionized American retailing with responsive fashions, better inventory control and lower costs. It was a win-win strategy for everyone from consumers to shareholders of the Limited. The results were delighted, loyal customers in the stores and riches from the niches for Limited's investors--$100,000 for the former paper carrier and over $5 billion for Les Wexner and his family. Everyone benefitted except, of course, competitors who did not understand functional shiftability.

One of The Limited's greatest achievements in shifting functions was logistics, the flow of materials and products through a demand chain. Logistics includes procuring, maintaining, transporting and delivering materials and products through every stage of production from the source of supply to the final point of consumption, deriving its name from the combination of logic and statistics. Logistics streamlines the flow of products to the right places, at the right times, in the right condition, in the right quantities, and at the right prices.

Logistics leadership allowed the Limited to bring products from the minds of a consumer to her body in 1,000 hours, or about six weeks time. Accomplishing this goal gave the Limited huge time and cost savings over department stores and other competitors, traditionally taking five months or longer to complete the same functions in a mish-mash of competing objectives between retailers, manufacturers and transportation providers.

For the Limited, getting products to stores before competitors allowed it to reorder only the most popular colors and styles based on sales while competitors were still stocking their first runs. This allowed Wexner's stores to operate with fewer markdowns and stock-outs and more likely to have what consumers wanted at the peak of the season. While the logistics gap between The Limited and some competitors has tightened over the years, logistics efficiency continues to be a crucial competitive advantage. If you fail to plan logistics as efficiently in your business , expect the plan for your business to fail.

Logistics was just one of the functions shifted to their most efficient level at the Limited. Others include branding, marketing research, financing, selling, advertising. *Functional shiftability explains how entrepreneurs become billionaires.*

Global Thinking

The Limited was a leader in *global sourcing*, one component of "global thinking." While other firms were beginning to buy from manufacturers in countries such as China, the Limited established close relationships through its secret weapon, Mast Industries. Designs for new fashions may be conceived in Italy, manufactured in Asia, and shipped by specialized air cargo planes daily from Hong Kong. Mast made sure this happened seamlessly, with high quality standards, and usually at costs substantially below department stores.

Victoria's Secret became a global brand with the advent of electronic commerce, enabling products to be distributed from Tokyo to Riyadh. Initially reluctant to open stores in other nations because more profitable expansion was available domestically, "L" now has 1,000 stores in other countries, including La Sensa, its chain of lingerie stores based in Canada. The centrifugal growth that created a fortune for Wexner and Limited investors started with manufacturing efficiency in Asia, but now includes concentric expansion in other nations. Entrepreneurs survive and thrive in today's global economic environment with ability to "think globally." You can find more examples in my earlier books *From the Edge of the World*, (Ohio State Press, 1995) and the textbook (with Salah Hassan) *Global Marketing* (Harcourt Brace, 1994).

The Sexiest Brand in the World

Another paramount principle building a small firm into a worldwide fortune is *branding*, and Victoria's Secret ranks high on lists of the world's most valuable brands. Whether judged by recognition, allure or sales, Victoria's Secret is the sexiest brand in the world. Remarkably, and characteristic of Wexner's ability to see potential where others fail, the brand was rescued from bankruptcy and probable obscurity when it was acquired in 1987 for $1 million and added to the Limited portfolio of brands.

Famed for its tastefully risqué catalogues and web site, Victoria's Secret challenged and redefined conventional definitions of acceptability, sexuality, and creative freedom. Although some critics snipe at what they perceive as attempts to exploit women, the brand's fans see it as empowering women, giving them the choice to feel sexy, look great, and express sexuality, not just to please others, but to please their selves.

The brand and the stores remind women that their bodies are beautiful and they have the freedom to express beauty, similar to rock stars such as Lady Gaga and Madonna do with fans of their music, lyrics and actions. I once wrote why Victoria's Secret is like both sexual icons Madonna and Neil Diamond, an analogy more fully described in *Brands That Rock* (Wiley, 2004).

Entering a Victoria's Secret store or website evokes the sexiness of a Madonna performance, but Wexner, the entrepreneur, is more like Neil Diamond, who exudes a different form of sexiness to mature audiences. When observing Wexner's performance as an entrepreneur, as he leads a multi-billion dollar empire, one senses the direction is clear, the execution precise, the performance consistent, the business strategies sound and proven, and the values lasting and highly-profitable for everyone involved—much like a Neil Diamond concert. Like both Madonna and Diamond, becoming a Victoria's Secret fan is an experience that makes people feel good about themselves.

Converting Customers to Fans

As an entrepreneur, you face intense competition, regardless which industry you enter. Higher margins leading to higher profits derived by converting customers into not just repeat customers, but fans, in much the same fashion as legendary rock stars do in converting casual listeners into people who would not miss a concert by their favorite artist.

What are the differences between customers, repeat customers and *fans*?

All businesses have customers, but only the most successful have *fans*. In today's market there are three kinds of consumers: customers, friends, and fans.

1. *Customers* buy from a variety of sources, often influenced by price.
2. *Friends* are loyal customers who buy specific brands because of favorable past experiences.
3. *Fans* take loyalty to the next level. Fans close their minds to other alternatives. They add an app to their phone just to keep close tabs on that firm (also allowing that firm to keep close tabs on them!) Fans invest time, attention, energy, emotion, and money into building and maintaining a relationship with the brand. Fans don't drink coffee; they crave Starbucks. Fans don't drive a motorcycle; they pilot a Harley-Davidson. Fans do not buy "devices;" life would end without their iPhone. That is a strong emotional attachment difficult for competitors to break.

Taking your firm from an initial start-up to a multi-segment colossus requires rigorous attention to the details of building brands. Accomplishing that objective requires finding ways to develop emotional attachment with you, your firm and ultimately your brand. You want *fans!* If you want to create a fortune instead of just a small business, develop fans for your product by borrowing from methods of Victoria's Secret, Apple, Coca-Cola, IBM, Costco and a host of other firms that are masters at having more than customers; they have *fans*.

A Role Model for Entrepreneurs

If you are an entrepreneur at heart, and looking for a role model on many dimensions, you might examine closely Leslie Wexner as a master entrepreneur. In addition to starting, acquiring and building new ventures centrifugally, he demonstrates the rare quality of willingness to divest companies at the appropriate time, usually when they reach their peak of growth or when it is apparent they never will achieve higher return on investment. He did that with several brands including Lane Bryant, Lerner, Limited Too, and Abercrombie & Fitch. I watched with fascination at the fate of his original store when the mall in which it was located was on the skids. Would he close his first-born store? He did, a decision requiring more strength of character and objectivity than opening it.

Wexner reveals ability to change things before they stop working. In an interview with the *New York Times*, he explained, "I've always lived in my own world, and that world is very much in the future." Guiding his continual evolution, Wexner personifies the philosophy of his former marketing professor who said change should be a habit. He has the uncanny ability to re-invent both himself and his firm every decade or so, a trait worthy of emulation by successful entrepreneurs.

Another key to Wexner's success is his ability to surround himself with highly competent people. To a group of entrepreneurs, he cautioned, "Hire people different than you. If you only hire people like yourself, you end up with an organization full of misfits."

Like most entrepreneurs I observe, Wexner enjoys toys, but his toys include several with potential for appreciation and high yields. His largest and most innovative project was the 1,200-acre Easton Town Center located near the airport in Columbus, Ohio. Starting in 1987 he used personal funds to buy thousands of acres of countryside for a combined residential, entertainment, and commercial development. Opened in 1999, the complex pioneered the trend to open-air, lifestyle malls anchored with some of the nostalgia of old-fashioned downtowns.

Wexner is also described by Don Thompson in *The $12 Million Stuffed Shark,* (Palgrave Macmillan, 2008) as one of the world's most important collectors of contemporary art for his assembly of outstanding works by Picasso, de Kooning and others.

Wexner is not solely focused on his work, even though he is still CEO of the mega-firm he founded in 1963. After marrying for the first time at age 55 and devoting time to his children, he also extended his art collection, compiled a library of great books, and perfected a stunning yacht, the Limitless.

But it is in the area of philanthropy that Wexner sets the standard for successful entrepreneurs. He generously supports literacy programs, social services and Jewish charities and donated $25 million to establish the Wexner Center for the Arts at The Ohio State University, helping it become one of the most innovative centers of visual and performing arts in the world. In 2011, The Ohio State University announced a gift of $100,000,000 by Wexner to his alma mater advancing research and services in programs ranging from arts to athletics, but mostly to support cutting-edge cancer research and health care.

In announcing the award, Wexner stated, "But for Ohio State, I would have never been able to go to college.... I hope this gift stimulates those who have received an education here, or been touched by this remarkable institution, to think about how they, too, can give back." His gifts to Ohio State now total $200,000,000 and in recognition of his generosity, Ohio State's renowned medical center is known as the Wexner Medical Center. He also generously gives of his time, serving as an Ohio State trustee multiple years. In talks to entrepreneurs and others, Wexner tells a story about how his banker, John G. McCoy, once described the Biblical principle of tithing to him. Wexner goes further, tithing his time, as well as money.

The Practical Effects of Theory

In our first conversation in this book, I described starting new firms as a solution to reducing poverty. If you want to see what some entrepreneurs accomplish arising from a modest or even impoverished background, study the patterns you see expressed in the development of a single store started with almost no capital bootstrapped into a mega-billion empire, empowered by the entrepreneurial talents of Leslie Wexner. *Forbes* lists his assets as over $5 billion, empirical evidence, I submit, that there is nothing as practical as good theory. Now that you know the secrets of success, hopefully, you will do the same.

Perhaps more important, his entrepreneurial success created tens of thousands of good jobs for people in Ohio, much of the United States, and other countries. And millions more for investors, including paper carriers and workers in their 401k accounts, all benefitting from applying good theory.

Wexner's success happened on one end of the spectrum of a marketing concept called the Polarity of Retailing. In our next conversation, I will show you how another person created the world's wealthiest family prospering from the other end of the Polarity of Retailing.

7

Conversation SEVEN

Secrets of the World's Richest Family

The road to riches is a journey, not a destination. The path can take many directions, sometimes with dangerous forks in the road.

There is an old, but apt axiom. Entrepreneurs who sell to the class, live in the mass, while those who sell to the mass, live in the class. As you discovered in our previous conversation, you can harvest riches from niches and still sell to the masses with multiple-segment strategies, crushing firms trying to be all things to all people. Wexner worked his magic in one end of the spectrum, specialty stores. The subject of this conversation worked the other end, specializing in a high-volume, high-efficiency, price-based mass-market strategy, often called "discount stores."

Firms at polar extremes of retailing obliterate firms in the middle offering average costs, average prices, average merchandise and average levels of service to customers. Lacking neither special appeal nor special cost-efficiency, firms in the middle (which is where most businesses find themselves) are vulnerable to firms at polar ends of the normal distribution of demand.

The Polarity of Retailing

The *polarity of retailing* describes how entrepreneurs typically evolve.

Once up a time, long before automobiles changed the face of America, retailers were everything to everyone, and most consumers shopped only occasionally. In rural areas, they shopped on Saturday. In large cities, it was usually during the week (and mostly women), often taking a street car, going to one or a few stores spending hours comparing products and prices, buying many items in one store, often delivered by the store a few days later.

In every city and most small towns, department stores catered to all the needs of most all consumers, a magnet displacing less-entrepreneurial retailers. In Chicago, Marshall Field dominated, but Carson-Pirie-Scott, Wieboldt's and Goldblatt's also did well. In Seattle, it was Nordstrom's. In New York City, it was Gimbel's and Macy's. In southern cities, it was Rich's, Belk's or Dillard's; in Columbus, it was Lazarus, but every city had at least one department store giant. Most fell to entrepreneurs starting specialty stores.

After World War II, consumers moved to the suburbs and took their retail preferences with them. Downtown stores were no longer convenient, but proliferated in a new format---shopping centers. The most aggressive department stores migrated with their customers, serving as "magnets" to malls, negotiating lower rents than small stores occupying the center of the mall.

There was only one way for small stores to compete against department store giants, and that was to be special in selection, service, sales or satisfaction. They were called specialty stores, and to thrive they had to be *special*.

Some became so special their entrepreneurial owners opened additional stores in other malls. Wexner was one of the best, but he had plenty of competitors including Gap, and later Lululemon, Buckle, Forever 21, H&M, Zara and many others. Those stores lose allure when they cease being *special* in their products, service and ambiance, but when specialty stores learn how to multiply a single store into thousands, they create fortunes. I am always amused when small business owners say they can't compete with corporate giants. Many billionaires started as single-store shopkeepers.

The Price Choppers

The opposite end of the spectrum attracts customers primarily with low prices. But here's an important caveat. Never base your appeal on *lowest price,* unless you also operate at *lowest cost.* You can't lose money on every sale and hope to make it up on volume.

In the 1950s and 60s, "discount department stores" such as E.J. Korvette, Polk Brothers, Shopper's World and G.E.M developed radically new methods of operating, permitting both low prices and low costs, attaining such high volumes of sales they threatened both department stores and specialty stores. The "discounters" had lower rents than malls, lower labor costs, lower transaction costs, and higher inventory turnover, attracting masses of consumers seeking a better lifestyle at lower cost.

Mass-market discounters took a page from grocers such as Meijer, learning they could shift expensive functions to a more efficient level--consumers. Their innovation was self-selection made possible by centralized checkout and consumers performing the last mile of logistics. The master of mass discounting used all three marketing theories described in Conversation 5 to become the world's richest family.

If there is a watershed year in retailing, my vote is for 1962. That's the year three new discounters were established --- Kmart, Target, and Walmart. It was the beginning of the end for department store dinosaurs and "unspecial" firms squeezed in the middle of the polarity of retailing.

The Man from Missouri

Sam Walton grew up in Missouri, an Eagle Scout by age 13. His leadership was observed early as basketball star and quarterback on a state championship football team at Hickman High School in Columbia, Mo. He graduated from the University of Missouri in 1940 with a B.A. in economics.

His autobiography indicates Sam taught Sunday school in his church, prayed with his children, and had a strong sense of calling to improve people's lives. Accounts of his early life and reports I heard first-hand from people who knew him well indicate he had little interest in being wealthy. His *passion* was to *improve customers' living standards through low prices.* That's the secret of his success.

Walton's values included respect for individuals, thrift, and hard work. The firm he founded attracted workers at entry level starting as low-paid cashiers and warehouse workers, progressing to managers because of Walton's strong predisposition for promotion from within. Drive around Bentonville, Arkansas today, and you'll see acres of high-end homes owned by store and warehouse workers who bought stock in Walmart early and saw their fortunes grow with Sam's.

If you don't want to start at low wages, work hard, be promoted on results and live frugally, you probably should seek a job some place other than Walmart. I realize those values may not always be implemented by everyone at the firm, but they guided Mr. Sam. His early study of scriptures also helps explain polices making stores family-friendly places not selling music with lyrics glorifying drugs and violence, and placing protective covers over some magazines.

Walmart became the largest retailer of Christian-themed merchandise, with over $1 billion sales of such items, including books such as Rich Warren's *Purpose Filled Life*. When Target Corp., a major competitor, refused to allow Salvation Army bell-ringers in front of its stores at Christmas, Walmart not only welcomed them, but pledged to match what Salvation Army bell-ringers collected at its stores.

As an entrepreneur, take time to know and reflect on your values before starting a business. It is *values* that provide the *vision* to build ordinary firms into extraordinary ones. That was the conclusion of the best-selling business book of the 1990s, *Built to Last* by Collins and Porous, and also John Kotter and James Heskett, *Corporate Culture and Performance* (Free Press, 1992). Both of these research-based books supply evidence that founders' values mold firms' profitability, growth and sustainability.

Learn from Master Teachers

Extraordinarily successful entrepreneurs are students of life for life. They learn from books, experiences and master teachers. For Walton, his "Master of Retailing" degree was with J. C. Penney, founder of the firm where Walton began his retailing career as a young Mizzou grad.

The JCPenney Company was founded in 1902 by James C. ("Cash") Penney, regarded by many as the father of chain apparel retailing. J.C. Penney was an innovator, offering quality merchandise on a cash-only basis at one price for all. During the Great Depression, the JCPenney Company flourished while competitors floundered, in part because of its no-credit policy. Lights went out in stores all over America accepting checks from banks that folded and extending credit to customers who couldn't pay. Penney's cash-only organization meshed perfectly with consumer behavior in the price-obsessed, durability-driven market of the pre-war economy. Nearly fanatical attention to expense control and operational efficiency made J. C. Penney one of the most successful entrepreneurs of the century.

But times change, and Penney didn't, at least initially. In the post-World War II era, consumers indulged in binge buying, financed by credit. Archrival Sears, whose stronghold had long been the catalog business, beat JCPenney to the punch offering credit to its customers in 1953. Along with credit cards---which later became its most profitable product—Sears attracted legions of catalog customers to visit its giant new stores in malls.

It took years for Penney's to recover, and I can't help believing Walton in his early years at Penney's heard stories about the danger of assuming that what pleased customers in the past will serve them well in the future. I thought about this when Walton faced his "Buy American" dilemma years later.

Walton was one of the most pro-American citizens you could meet. He sourced mostly, if not exclusively, from American firms and advertised "Made in America" with signs proclaiming that philosophy throughout stores. He drove only American cars (usually a pickup truck) and reputedly didn't think highly of employees who drove "foreign cars." Even his suppliers knew if they were meeting Mr. Sam, they should park their Mercedes, Toyota or Beemer at the airport and rent a Ford or Chevy before meeting Walton.

So, what should Walton do when consumers expressed by their purchasing they preferred lower prices for products made in Bangladesh, India and China? Walton listened to the *behavior* of customers instead of voices of critics, and Walton gave customers what he knew they wanted --- quality products at lowest-possible prices.

It's a good lesson for all entrepreneurs: *Listen to how customers behave, not what critics say,* even when policies must be updated to fit a changing environment. Sam Walton fixated on customers with the same precision he kept his eyes focused on quail with shotgun in hand, wearing a flannel shirt, driving a Ford pick-up and Ol' Roy, his favorite hunting dog, by his side.

Market Segmentation

After his "higher education" with JCPenney, Walton made a foray on his own into retailing, first as a manager of Ben Franklin variety stores, and in 1962, opened his first store in Rogers, Ark., offering a wide selection of discount merchandise. How can selling such a wide variety of merchandise to normal, middle-Americans be an illustration of market segmentation?

Walmart's strategy, stated simply, was *geographic segmentation*, entering neglected markets with a store that gave customers a better retail experience than existed in rural America. Those who understand the military concept of flanking strategy recognize it's usually fatal to launch a frontal attack on a superior force. That's what would have happened if Walmart attacked Sears, Penney's, or Macy's on their home terrain in large cities. As you plan or evaluate your own firm, do you have a plan as strategic as Walmart?

Entrepreneurs often make the mistake of trying to attract customers from entrenched competitors. By avoiding large cities and suburbs, Walmart built its brand with devoted fans in rural America, segment by geographic segment mostly in the Midwest and South. By choosing "Harry's Hardware" as its competitor, "Little David" slung his slingshot at mice, avoiding competition with the "Goliaths" of Sears, Montgomery Ward and other giants in metropolitan areas.

Gradually, Walmart grew in concentric circles, moving from Arkansas to Missouri, markets he understood well, and gradually to other states. He avoided large cities, circling them with more and more stores in small towns, building highly efficient distribution and logistics centers, until Walmart had the volume and efficiency to mount a frontal attack on retail giants. The process took decades, perfecting operational details, preparing to attack giant retailers in cities. Starting out as a whale in a pond is less risky than starting out as a minnow in an ocean.

Walton's strategy sounds simple enough, but the key to success over time was *execution*—giving customers quality products at lower prices. Critics complain Walmart eliminates small firms, but its more striking accomplishment is showing how small firms kill giant firms before giants realize who is behind the sling shot with a rock headed for their head.

Although Walmart was not a sleek, sophisticated retailer like those in large cities, it was the hottest, biggest retail deal in small towns. In my book *Brands That Rock*, I compare Walmart's strategy to the rock group KISS. Its leader, Gene Simmons, admits he was not the best musician, but his brand of fireworks was the most exciting act to light up mid-western county fairs. Simmons built his fan base in small-town venues before entering big-city arenas head-to-head with Aerosmith, Rolling Stones and Madonna. Like KISS, Walmart was the rock star of small-town retailing.

Customers Rule!

The key to the Walmart shopping experience is its ability to offer customers what they want to buy, when and where they want to buy it at a price they are willing to pay. Consumers can buy everything from steak to tires under one roof, knowing they are getting quality products at low prices. As some consumers migrate to a preference for "green" products, Walmart is also on the forefront of that movement, renovating stores to be energy efficient and pushing suppliers toward green products, packaging and logistics.

Quality levels, shelf quantities, and sales methods are determined by customers, not by an entrepreneur named Walton. One of Walmart's executives explained to me, "At Walmart, we don't consider ourselves selling products to customers; we consider ourselves buying agents for our customers."

Walton was famous for listening to both customers and employees talk about what they liked and disliked about Walmart compared to competitors. One of his secrets of success was how he challenged employees to ask two questions:

1. *What are our competitors doing better than we are?* Walton knew that even the worst competitor probably did something better than he did. He knew if he examined all of his competitors' strengths, adopted and

improved on them, eventually Walmart could become the best of breed on nearly every attribute of its brand.

2. *What books have you read lately that would help our firm be better managed than our competitors?* Walton knew the need to get the best ideas in the world from the best thinkers in the world. Those ideas are usually found in books, not magazines, and not even on the Internet. Magazines and newspapers offer intellectual "snack food," useful, but not as nourishing as the "solid food" found in well-conceptualized books. If I ever have the privilege of visiting you in your office, don't be surprised if you find me loitering near your bookshelves, because when you see what people have on their bookshelves, you know what's in their head. And, some people have an empty bookshelf.

Invest Before Wall Street Gets It

Wall Street analysts didn't understand Walmart for decades, and perhaps still don't. That's fine with me, because it allowed ordinary people, often the same people who shopped or worked in its stores, to make fortunes buying Walmart shares. Today, Walmart is the most successful retailer in the world, with nearly a half trillion dollars of sales, more than its major competitors combined.

Sam Walton's mission was not to be wealthy, but by starting with very little capital (95% from Sam and Helen themselves) and putting customers first, at the time of his death Walton bootstrapped himself to the wealthiest person in the world. An analyst calculated the net worth of his family to be over $400 billion, making the Waltons the world's richest family, and the share price has risen twenty percent since that calculation. Until the last few years, the family still owned over 50 percent of all Walmart stock, causing Walmart to be accurately described a "family-owned corporation." If you are age 45 or less, learning from Mr. Sam, you still have time to become the richest family in the world.

I've heard people complain, "I don't shop at Walmart because the lines are too long." That's like the famous quote of Yogi Berra, who reportedly said, "No one goes to that restaurant no more, because it's too busy."

Functional Shiftability

Walmart's strategy is simple—conquer mass markets, segment by segment. Accomplishing that strategy is built upon *execution*, achieving consistency, or "sameness," in every store (although inventories are tailored to each store). Delivering what customers want at a low price was helped by weaknesses of existing firms in warehousing, transportation, and inventory control. At Walmart and surviving competitors, operational excellence today is built on sophisticated, complex logistics systems shifting marketing functions to the most efficient level in the demand chain. The result is an expense ratio several percentage points below competitors.

Some people assume a firm as large as Walmart offers low prices to consumers because it obtains lower prices from suppliers. That's not reality, for two reasons. First, offering lower prices to large competitors beyond actual differences in cost of sales, manufacturing and delivery is prohibited by law, specifically the Robinson-Patman Amendment to the Sherman Anti-Trust Act. More importantly, Walmart achieved its greatest growth when it *was* the small firm, competing against corporate behemoths.

Walmart offered lower prices than giants by shifting marketing functions such as buying, branding, market information, inventory control, transportation, and other essential activities to their most efficient level in the demand chain. Walmart exemplifies the axiom: *Don't rest your competitive strength on lowest prices unless you achieve lowest costs.* "Sameness" in every store requires operating *differently* than competitors.

Where did Sam Walton learn logistics so well? In our last conversation, I described the leading-edge logistics of the Limited. Sam Walton personally travelled to Columbus, Ohio and asked Les Wexner for help with logistics, and Wexner generously loaned logistics experts to Walmart. The result was logistics leadership by both the leading specialty chain and the leading discounter. Retailers performing marketing functions inefficiently perished in the middle of the polarity of retailing.

Today, execution of marketing functions is complex, requiring the most advanced logistics, technology, and supply-chain systems. Retail Link, Walmart's electronic data interchange (EDI), and Walmart's satellite communications network (probably the largest private network in the United States) have revolutionized logistics and supply chain strategies. Not only are stores connected to Bentonville via voice, data, or video, but over 30,000 suppliers are linked to dozens of warehouses monitoring daily sales figures. Walmart's systems help vendors improve inventory positions and reduce costs, thereby making some competitors' systems hopelessly out-of-date and inefficient. The firm's investment in technology to analyze inventory, assortment, costs, transportation, and delivery fuels Walmart's gains in productivity, profits, and customer satisfaction. The result is less out-of-stock items, sales and expenses several percentage points below competitors, and increasingly a greener retail environment than most competitors. If this sounds complex, remember, I never said building a small firm into a fortune is easy.

As you contemplate our conversation and how to apply it in your own firm, are you committed to understanding technology, investing in it, and *passing along the savings to customers instead of investors?* If so, you understand how to become the wealthiest family in the world.

The road to riches can be rocky. Jack Shewmaker, former COO of Walmart, once told me how he was fired several times when Walton was CEO. Shewmaker, an engineer by training, understood technology better than most retail executives, and authorized a massive, costly satellite system to link buyers and merchandisers in Bentonville with manufacturers in China and other countries. "It was many millions beyond my spending authority," Shewmaker told me, "and when Mr. Sam found out, he fired me and cancelled the order. But I didn't leave, and the next day, reauthorized the order to implement the system." The next day, Mr. Sam fired Shewmaker again. This happened several times, until Walton finally realized Shewmaker wasn't leaving and was serious about the need for this investment in technology.

Retailers in the past, and some still today, incur enormous travel expenses and interminable delays sending buyers around the world buying products they *hope* consumers will buy when finally on the shelves of stores. Walmart and similarly efficient retailers negotiate shipments for arrival in stores on time and in the right condition and quantities, driven by cash-register transactions in stores. The process yields lower sourcing cost, fewer out-of-stocks, lower transportation costs and fewer disappointed customers. That's the type of strategic advantage you need to achieve in your firm, if you hope to compete on price and become the largest firm in the world, creating enduring wealth for you and your family, and over two million jobs for employees. And remember, Walmart initiated that technology while it was the "Little David" of business, not Goliath.

Global Thinking

Today, Walmart has nearly 10,000 stores and club locations in 28 countries, employing well over two million associates, serving more than 176 million customers a year. The challenge is how to manage growth without losing sight of Sam Walton's values. His most basic value was customer service, the ability to give customers what they want at the lowest possible price.

Sam said, "… if you think about it from the point of view of the customer, you want everything: a wide assortment of quality merchandise; the lowest possible prices; guaranteed satisfaction; friendly, knowledgeable service; convenient hours; and a pleasant shopping experience. You love it when a store exceeds your expectations, and you hate it when a store inconveniences you, gives you a hard time, or pretends you're invisible."

I hope you remember from our earlier conversation, *global thinking* involves three components: Global demand, global sourcing, and global management. No one disputes that technology-enabled logistics helped Walmart dominate the U.S.A. Now, the challenge for managers in Bentonville is to understand demand and management in areas of the world with cultures, infrastructure, and lifestyles different than the U.S.

In nations such as Mexico and Brazil, Walmart stumbled by assuming what worked in the U.S. would work in other nations. It didn't, but the impressive attribute is how quickly the company learned from its mistakes, changed itself to conform to local preferences and management styles, and developed intermarket strategies based on core values of customer service and low price, tailored to local consumers and products. Walmart has been accused of going too far in tailoring its policies to local practices, facing allegations that conforming to local practices violates the U.S. Foreign Corrupt Practices Law (FCPA) forbidding U.S.-based companies compensating local officials for help. It's not difficult to understand why U.S. firms might adopt local practices when most future growth occurs in faster-growing, emerging economies.

Frugality

Why did Walton believe low price was such an important reason for patronage to masses of consumers around the world? Probably because Walton lived a frugal life himself.

As an entrepreneur, Sam Walton kept his personal expenses low and ran his company the same way. When Walmart executives travel, they travel economically, staying at inexpensive hotels two in a room, unless of different genders. Food allowances are strictly limited; fancy restaurants are not included, nor are suppliers permitted to buy meals and gifts for Walmart buyers. When he flew (in economy class, of course) to other cities to meet with corporate executives, Walton usually arrived at the meeting in a rented economy car he drove himself while watching luxury vehicles and limos unload executives from giant corporations he crushed. Walton knew the fine line between making a profit and losing money was being very "tight with the dollar." He expected that attribute in every person working at Walmart.

Ron Loveless is an example of a typical career at Walmart, starting as a stock person with a high school degree for $50 a week in 1964, and promoted through the ranks to become General Manager of Sam's Club. He wrote a book (which I highly recommend if you want the rest of the story about Walton and the company he founded) called *Walmart Inside Out* (Stephens Press, 2011). Loveless explains "Call it 'tight-fisted, miserly, chintzy,' or whatever you like, but the fact was we could sell merchandise at lower prices than our competitors because we spent less, and passed the savings on to the customers."

I have listened for hours to Ron Loveless telling about frugality and what it was like to work for "Mr. Sam." Everyone who has read much about Walton knows he drove a well-used pickup truck, but Mr. Sam's wife, Helen, wanted to buy a new Lincoln car. She made a deal with the local dealer to bring it over to the Home Office and have Sam write a check for it. When Walton examined the invoice, he raised an eyebrow and said, "How many cars is Helen buying? " He refused to pay and told the dealer to take the car with him. (I think Helen bought it anyway!)

My favorite example is Walton's "frugality speech" to managers when managers meet every Saturday morning to discuss strategy and operations. Ron tells the story, also in his book, about the time he bought a new Porsche, but was careful to park it where he didn't think Walton would see it. But Sam did.

"Busted," Ron thought. "I'm in big trouble now."

At that Saturday morning's "frugality speech," Walton said, "You know how I feel about buying big new cars and how it might look to the public. Now I saw Ronnie getting out of a new car this morning. I don't know if it was his, but it was one of the small economy cars. That's setting a good example."

Walton obviously didn't care enough about cars or their status value to know the Porsche cost about twice a Lincoln, but to him big was expensive and small was economy. Ron's not sure whether Mr. Sam ever found out Porsche is not an economy car.

The frugality of Walton is a trait I've observed in many successful entrepreneurs.

"Why are wealthy people so stingy with their money?" That's a question asked by many.

"How do you think they got their money?" is my answer.

An Instruction Manual for Success

These are a few of the secrets you can learn from the world's wealthiest entrepreneur. There's a lot more of them in Sam's autobiography, *Made in America* (Bantam, 1993). It's a book I've recommended to thousands of students over the years, many who've told me it's the most valuable book on entrepreneurship they ever read. It's an instruction manual for turning small firms into large fortunes.

What are the secrets you can learn from the master at building wealth? Here is a summary of some insights that may help you understand how entrepreneurs succeed:

1. Values and vision determine success as much or more than strategy and tactics. Be sure you know yourself and your values before embarking on an entrepreneurial journey.

2. Entrepreneurs who pursue a passion for customers and servant leadership to their team are more likely to succeed than entrepreneurs whose passion is to be wealthy.

3. Learn an industry well before you decide to compete in it. Years of knowledge at JCPenney served Sam Walton well. Gain experience learning from a master if you hope to become better than your competitors. (If you can't work personally for them, read books by or about them.)

4. Choose your competitors carefully; the path to killing giants starts by slaying mice.

5. Don't build your business on *lowest prices* unless you have a strategy achieving *lowest costs*. That usually involves shifting essential marketing functions to different institutions than competitors.

6. Focus on customers as relentlessly as Sam Walton did on quail with his shotgun. Listen to what customers express in their buying behavior, not what critics say with their voices.

7. When the environment of consumer behavior changes, change with it, even when that requires fundamental change from previous practices.

8. Practice extreme frugality and pass the savings on to customers instead of yourself. You'll attract customers away from competitors and, in the long run, create wealth for yourself and your investors.

There should be no doubt that Sam Walton and the firm he created knew how to pinch pennies. You can observe from our discussion that Walmart used this competitive advantage to cut expenses to the minimum, lower prices and create loyal fans. But there is another firm, just as entrepreneurial, with even lower prices and more frugal expense control than Walmart, as you'll see in our next conversation. But I will end this conversation with words of wisdom from "Mr. Sam."

> *"Somewhere out there, right now, there's somebody, probably hundreds of thousands of somebodies, really, with plenty good enough ideas to take it all the way. The only question, really, is does that somebody, do those many somebodies, want it badly enough to do what it takes to get there? The answer lies in attitude, and the capacity to constantly study and question."*
> **– Sam Walton**

8

Conversation EIGHT

Aldi Velocity and Expense Control

This conversation will be brief because I want to focus on just two secrets of growing small firms into large fortunes – *velocity* and *expenses*. Little things add up to large advantages over rivals.

"The devil is in the details," German entrepreneurs proclaim, and no firm illustrates that better than one you might not know a lot about. If you are affluent, you may not have heard of Aldi, probably the largest grocery chain in the world. If you are poor, you may depend on it to feed your family. If you shop there often, you may be an Aldi fan, helping you become wealthier than struggling neighbors. One thing is certain; you've never seen its share price on a stock exchange, and it's not in the Dow Jones Index, even though large enough to be listed among those corporate stalwarts.

If you want an advanced degree in controlling expenses, enroll in Aldi University. Your majors will be inventory velocity and functional shiftability with minors in global thinking and market segmentation. If you do as well as professors Theo and Karl Albrecht at Aldi U, your diploma will be worth twenty billion dollars.

Mother Knows Best

"We should not suffer like others. When the rest of the society takes to an easy life of merry-making whiling away their time, you two must work harder to come up in life." That was Mother talking to sons Theo and Karl. They heeded her advice, starting from a single store in Essen, Germany, building it into a nearly 10,000-store global demand chain with prices lower and profitability higher than Walmart.

The official name of their firm is ALDI Einkauf GmbH & Co. oHG. You can see why they do business under the banner of Aldi, short for "**Al**brecht **Di**scount." Based in Germany, it operates in about forty nations including an increasing presence in the United States. Karl retired, but is Germany's richest man with an estimated net worth of $20 billion. Theo was Germany's second richest man until his death in 2010. Mother's advice worked well.

The father of Karl and Theo Albrecht was a miner and later a baker's assistant, with Karl born in 1920 and Theo in 1922. Theo completed an apprenticeship in his mother's store, while Karl worked in a delicatessen. Karl worked at a food shop formerly advertised as the "cheapest food source," and in 1946, the brothers acquired their mother's business and opened another store nearby. By 1950, the Albrecht brothers owned 13 stores, cutting prices, slashing merchandise from shelves that did not turnover rapidly, cutting costs by not advertising, not selling fresh produce, and keeping the size of stores as small as possible.

The brothers split the company in 1960 over a dispute whether they should sell cigarettes, but used the *Aldi* brand name globally for both firms, dividing the globe for expansion by two entities, Aldi Nord (North) and Aldi Sud (South). Aldi Nord owns the U.S. stores. Both groups are financially and legally separate since 1966, describing their relationship as "friendly relation," appearing as a single enterprise. They use their combined purchasing and branding power to negotiate with suppliers for captive brands in stores. When the brothers retired as CEOs in 1993, they gave much of their wealth to charitable foundations.

Mother and father Albrecht instilled a work ethic that proved to be an effective tactic to rise above hard times. They couldn't give their sons capital to grow a business, but gave them something far superior—*a desire to work hard achieving their passion.*

As a writer and teacher, I know how to transmit *knowledge* permitting people to rise from rags to riches. I don't know how to teach *desire to do the extremely hard work required for upward mobility.* If you work eight hours a day on someone else's payroll for enough years, you may learn enough to start your own firm, become your own boss, and work twelve hours a day. Aspiring entrepreneurs with parents inculcating the value of hard work are blessed people.

The "Hard Discounter" Market Segment

Aldi is a "hard discounter," meaning it attracts customers willing to sacrifice selection and ambiance for really low prices. If you live on food stamps, unemployment checks, and WIC programs, you already know the value of buying top-quality food at rock-bottom prices. When a tank of gasoline (or "petrol" in many of the nations in which Aldi operates) doubles in price, the segment increases rapidly of people willing to do a little to save a lot.

Families with small incomes and large families are not the only ones attracted to buying the same cereal for $1.89 that sells for $3.89 in traditional supermarkets. When milk and tomatoes are days fresher because of inventory velocity and dollars less because of lower expenses, the segment of fans delighted by hard discounters increases markedly.

Aldi was once disparaged as being "cheap stores selling poor-quality goods," but first in Germany and now in the United States and other places, a kind of cult of upscale consumers has emerged as "fans" of Aldi because of high-quality products ranging from cereal and soda to wines and computers (based on special "buys") at exceptionally low prices. In the United States, Aldi initially targeted tight food budgets of lower-income segments in urban areas, different than Walmart's rural strategy, but both eventually invaded suburbs in addition to their core markets.

When I mention the Albrecht's sister organization, Trader Joe's, named favorite American supermarket in recent consumer surveys, I observe more nods of recognition among affluent market segments. Walk through either Aldi or Trader Joe's, and you see the same principles of velocity and expense control. Some consumers are also enthusiastic about one of America's best-selling wines, marketed by Trader Joe's under the label of Charles Shaw. College students call it by its less formal name, Two-Buck Chuck.

It's Science, But Not Rocket Science

The key to high value for consumers and high profits for Aldi is *velocity*, or "inventory turns", calculated by dividing annual sales by average (or ending) inventory, based on retail prices or cost of goods sold. The magic bullet for achieving velocity is *limited SKUs*, a key to profits for entrepreneurs in any industry. A SKU (Stock Keeping Unit) is the identification for each item sold by a firm, with a different SKU for every product, brand, size, and variation. The more "flavors" or sizes or brands a firm carries, the more SKUs, decreasing velocity.

The profit or gross margin of a firm is derived from a simple formula: Velocity x margin = profit of an item. If a SKU turns over (sells) two times a year, it needs a high margin to justify the cost of buying, stocking and selling that SKU. That's typical in jewelry, furniture and some apparel lines. If a SKU sells ten times a year instead of two, a firm can charge a lower margin and still make the same or more profit. It doesn't require rocket science to understand the higher the velocity, the lower the margin needed to be profitable.

High velocity allows Aldi to sell at margins half its competitors and still achieve higher profitability. Traditional grocery stores "turn" their inventory only a few times each year, selling at margins in the range of 22-40 percent or a little more for products with high carrying costs such as frozen foods. Aldi "turns" its inventory much faster, around twenty times, I've been told, although I can't verify that number because "numbers" are *very* private at Aldi. Aldi can sell its merchandise at 12-20 percent, and yield higher profits than most competitors except Costco, which has similar margins. A typical grocery store operates with a net profit of 1-2 percent, but many observers (including me) believe that Aldi is two to three times the profitability of competitors. The reason for higher profits at lower prices is *velocity*.

That's one of the "secrets" I hope you apply in your own business as a result of our conversations on growing small firms into large fortunes. I have observed entrepreneurs calculate the *margins* needed when pricing their product without fully considering the other half of the equation —*velocity*. As I say (very carefully) in seminars, "It's important to keep your assets moving."

The effect of velocity on sales volume is breathtaking. *High velocity permits an entrepreneur to sell the same products as competitors at lower prices,* attracting more customers than competitors. And more customers cause velocity to increase even higher. It's a circle than entraps your competitors and enriches you. The operating model developed by Aldi is so efficient that traditional firms may offer more selection, more unusual products, more ambiance, more service, "loyalty cards" and other neat things, but they can't compete on price.

Contrast the strategy of limited SKUs with a strategy of wide selection. Some entrepreneurs add more and more SKUs in their product line, hoping customers will find something they like as they wander through the store. Successful entrepreneurs *know* what patrons like based on their behavior, and offer only the fastest-moving items. The result is lower prices for customers and higher profits for entrepreneurs.

The problem of too many SKUs can be caused by TMC. Abundance of capital permits operating without truly knowing what customers will buy. Without much capital, entrepreneurs are forced to focus on the most desired products, resulting in greater velocity, lower costs and lower prices attracting more customers.

SKU simplification works so well at Aldi that it can meet 85-90 percent of customers' grocery needs with 750-1000 SKUs. That compares to 45,000 or more SKUs in a traditional supermarket and 150,000 in "supercenters." Customers may need to go to a traditional, larger store nearby to "fill-in" with some items they can't get at Aldi, but which customer would you rather have as a fan, one who buys 90 percent of their needs at your store, or one that shops at your stop mostly for items they can't get at Aldi? The effect is striking, yielding low prices and high profits. Costco, another productivity super star, recently reduced its SKU count to 3,750 from 4,100 items stocked a few years ago, with the company's top-selling 200 items representing about 35 to 40 percent of total sales. *Don't compete on lowest price unless you attain lowest cost.*

No Frills Cause Low Expenses

The difference between Aldi and most stores is evident the moment customers enter the parking lot. There are no carts sitting around the lot, waiting to bang into cars. The reason for no carts is customers "rent" carts at the door, usually for a quarter, returned to customers when they return carts after loading their cars. That cuts expenses in at least three ways. Labor costs corralling carts are drastically reduced, carts require less maintenance because they are not left outside in weather, and insurance is less for damage carts sometimes do to cars. Another plus—customers have dry, well-maintained carts to glide through the store instead of rusted ones with wheels wobbling in opposite directions.

Aldi's "strictly no frills" approach is evident everywhere. They don't decorate aisles or stock shelves. Instead, pallets of products are parked by forklift trucks in the aisles, and the "stocking" function is performed by customers picking products out of boxes. Customers even dispose of boxes instead of Aldi paying a refuse company because customers transport groceries home in empty boxes eagerly grabbed in stores.

Stocking shelves is a major labor cost at other grocery stores, but not at Aldi.

At checkout, customers place all items on the belt and push the cart to the other end of the belt, waiting to take groceries to their car and get their quarter back. The checkout process is nearly devoid of labor cost, because functions performed by cashiers are limited to scanning and transferring items to end of the belt. There's no bagging, no credit cards, and no checks, making the system fast and the finance function *very* inexpensive compared to competitors.

Aldi carries mostly its own brands, known as "captive brands." They are manufactured to Aldi's high-quality standards, usually the same formula as the best-selling national brand, sometimes with similar packages. Because packages are made to Aldi's specifications, they have barcodes on multiple sides, making scanning faster than supermarkets where a cashier may have to swipe an item several times before it registers. By shifting functions of stocking, picking, and transactions to customers, Aldi achieves a differential advantage in labor costs.

Don't bother searching for the phone number of your local Aldi store. They don't have them; answering phones is costly. Store employees concentrate on just one job—scanning products and getting customers through the line at break-neck speed, not distracted by phone requests about store hours and directions (available on website) or inquiries, "Do you have Star-Kist tuna?" Limited store hours concentrate high velocity through a highly-efficient checkout system with carts filled with a hundred or more items instead of small quantities at stores open all times of the day and night.

Premium Wages Cause Low Costs and Prices

Because of the huge reduction in labor costs operating stores with few employees, Aldi pays premium wages to attract the best people, yielding low turnover among personnel. The firm recruits at a handful of universities most likely to have graduates with good values, paying them $10,000 to $20,000 more starting salary than other firms to enter Aldi's retail training program. Paying more for the best people who remain their entire career reduces labor costs, a principle overlooked by some entrepreneurs, but not at firms such as Aldi and Costco.

Does velocity and expense reduction really allow much of a difference in prices? An analyst for Bear, Stearns & Co concluded that Aldi's prices are 36 percent lower than brand-name equivalents at Walmart and 6.6 percent lower than Walmart's comparable private labels. Some people believe Walmart has the lowest grocery prices, but not after they shop at Aldi.

Not every consumer cares about lowest price, but those who do are a segment big enough to make Karl and Leo Albrecht multi-billionaires. Aldi's operational efficiency should also remind the world's richest family that even they have to worry about competition!

As a result of our conversation, I hope you are motivated to study Aldi (and Costco) closely, adapting the principles of velocity based on limited SKUs and expense reduction to your own business. And if you are among those who believe cost control is sacred, you may want to visit an Aldi store and worship.

Traditional grocery retailers are caught in the shrinking middle of the market, a difficult location, at polar ends of consumer demand between hard discounters and extensive selection at firms such as Whole Foods, Kroger, Albertsons, and Safeway. They fight the price issue with advertised "loss leaders" concealed among shelves of higher margin items, and implement loyalty programs promising lower prices to frequent customers. Their most effective weapon is wider product selection and an enhanced shopping experience, but astute consumers ask, "Can nicer stores with high costs really have the lowest prices?"

Shifting Marketing Functions

Instead of a battle between multiple manufacturers and wholesalers, Aldi shifts functions to consumers. It controls the battlefield, delegating manufacturers to run factories, but controlling itself essential functions of product design, packaging, logistics and market information. Costs are lower and products fresher, thus lasting longer in consumers' homes.

Aldi is a favorite customer of vendors because of its policies of no "slotting" or advertising allowances, lower packaging and warehousing costs and an "open book" policy to vendor's financial records. Aldi expects low prices from its contract manufacturers, but also expects its supply chain partners to earn enough return on capital to deliver high-quality products and maintain ability to be the most efficient manufacturer in the supply chain. Aldi typically maintains a policy of two capable suppliers for each product, just in case one is hit by disaster or labor issue. The process works because of SKU simplification, carrying only high-velocity products.

Signage at Aldi features its "Double Quality Guarantee," which says, "Quality, taste and satisfaction are always *double* guaranteed at Aldi. If for any reason, you are not 100 percent satisfied with any product, we will gladly replace the product AND refund your money." It's a strategy difficult to defeat for competitors of Aldi, Captain of the Demand Chain among hard discounters.

ALDI interior

ALDI shelving

ALDI store in Germany

ALDI in Bethlehem, PA with an exterior

design common in U.S. Aldi stores

Lessons Learned at the University of Aldi

Entrepreneurs in any business can learn a lot of success secrets by studying principles the Albrecht family executed, turning a single store into a multi-billion dollar global empire. Here is how I summarize them:

1. Don't base your strategy on "lowest price" unless you have a strategy achieving lower costs.

2. High inventory velocity permits lower gross margins with higher net profits. *Keep your assets moving!*

3. The key to greater velocity is SKU simplification. Don't offer a wide selection hoping customers will find something they like; know what they like, becoming the most efficient supplier of what customers buy most.

4. Take command as Captain of the Demand Chain, shifting essential marketing functions to the most efficient level in the supply chain.

5. The most efficient, cost effective way of performing essential marketing functions is often by shifting them to customers.

6. Sometimes it costs less to pay people more, achieving employee efficiency, loyalty and longevity.

7. Retail is detail. (So is every business!)

Survival Strategies for Family Entrepreneurs

Entrepreneurs are often family enterprises. Some people start and grow firms to be near their families. Some leave for the opposite reason. The Albrechts provide a model for how family-owned entrepreneurs can work well together.

It is a little surprising how well. The two brothers played well with each other, even though both were titans in the same industry and, to some degree, competitors in global markets. They knew their strengths and weaknesses and didn't poke their noses unnecessarily in the other's life. Their strength was understanding the other's mind well. For instance, younger brother Theo was a quieter type who drafted business strategies, while the older Karl, a practical person, put them into practice. Karl liked to play golf, while Theo had a hobby of collecting vintage typewriters. Though there were minor likes and dislikes between them, they never let these block the successful running of ALDI supermarkets. It is easy to find out which supermarket was run by which of the two brothers, depending on the availability of cigarettes. The only real difference between them was their age; Karl is two years older than Theo was.

If you have siblings, parents or children in your business, I hope you manage family relationships as well as Karl and Theo Albrecht.

9

Conversation NINE

Why are Hamburgers Square?

In our previous conversations, I hope you recognized the relationship between theory and execution of essential marketing concepts in growing small firms into large fortunes, but here's another secret of success. It is the personality, determination and values of the entrepreneur applying theory.

In many years of observing entrepreneurs, I've never found a more intriguing personality than Dave Thomas, or anyone with more dogged determination and commitment to values. Some might describe him as a simple person because of his limited education and homespun language, but I am not one of those. I found him to be extraordinarily complex, keenly insightful and solidly value-based. Simply stated, Dave Thomas is one of the most captivating entrepreneurs I've ever encountered.

The values of Dave Thomas gave him the *vision* to sell "the best hamburgers in the business." His vision grew a single hamburger store into Wendy's International, a global enterprise of 6,500 stores in 28 nations, $3.5 billion of sales, tens of millions delighted customers, and jobs for more than 200,000 employees of the company and its franchisees. That first store literally started in a garage, part of an auto dealership owned by a friend who bought stock in Dave's fledgling company at its beginning, an investment that paid off better than renting the garage.

Roots

It is better to have parents who give you good values than parents who give you capital to start a business. Values last, but capital doesn't. Karl and Theo Albrecht embodied that truth, rising from modest circumstances as sons of a father who was a baker's assistant and a mother who was a shopkeeper, instilling values of hard work and upward mobility. The same was true for entrepreneurial superstars Les Wexner and Sam Walton.

Can you still be successful, however, if your parents had bad values? It's difficult, but not impossible. I've met people who overcame the burden of really bad parents, sometimes as victims of abandonment, abuse and poverty. As you'll see in Conversation 15, Bonnie St. John rose from poverty, abandonment and the amputation of her leg to become an Olympic skier, Presidential advisor and entrepreneur.

But if you are an orphan, not even knowing the identity of your parents, can you still become a successful entrepreneur and humanitarian? That's the life story of a Horatio Alger award winner, the person featured in this conversation. If everyone on the planet adopted his values, we might eliminate poverty and war throughout the world.

Dave Thomas was born in Atlantic City, New Jersey on July 2, 1932, adopted six weeks later by a Michigan couple who experienced many hardships. Dave lost his adoptive mother at age 5, leaving his father, who struggled for years to find work, with the responsibility of raising Dave. As Rex Thomas looked for work, the family moved from state to state, staying in run-down boarding houses and trailers. Dave attended 12 different schools in a 10-year period, and knew hunger many times living with his itinerant father. That's the reason he told people he wanted to work in a restaurant—so he wouldn't have to go hungry again.

The stability in Dave's life came from a grandmother, Minnie Sinclair, a strong and loving woman who worked hard to provide for her own four children after her husband died. It was from her Dave learned the value of hard work, which she always told Dave was good for the soul. She also taught him about quality of life. "She used to always tell us, 'don't cut corners'," says Thomas, "something I remembered when developing Wendy's hamburgers."

Living with a single, sometimes-working father meant Dave and his father ate most of their meals in restaurants, mostly ones specializing in hot dogs and Dave's favorite food—hamburgers. During their dinners together, conversation was sparse, "I spent a lot of time watching other families eat together, having a great time," he says. "I realized that eating out was about a lot more than food—it was about having a good time and sharing special events."

It was then Thomas decided he would one day own a restaurant. But, first, he needed experience, which he obtained working at the lunch counter of Regas Restaurant in Knoxville, starting at the ripe old age of 12. There he learned to "work as if your job depends on every single customer, every day." He later adopted principles learned at Regas Restaurant, passing them on to employees working at Wendy's restaurants.

His father moved the family (now fortified with a stepmother and three step sisters) to Ft. Wayne, Indiana. Phil Clauss, owner of the Hobby House, took Dave under his wing and eventually gave him the opportunity that changed his life in many ways. It was here Dave says he made his greatest mistake: he dropped out of school to work full-time. His father and stepfamily were preparing to move again and Dave decided to stay in Ft. Wayne, moving into the YMCA and working full-time. This decision to drop out haunted him until he went back to school 45 years later and received his GED from Coconut Creek High School in Ft. Lauderdale. He said getting his GED was one of his greatest accomplishments. The graduating class of 1993 also named him, "Most Likely to Succeed."

Dave met Lorraine Buskirk, an 18-year old waitress at the Hobby House, and married her one year later. They were still married when Dave died in 2002. They would go on to have five children—Pam, Kenny, Molly, Lori, and Wendy.

The Colonel

Mentor and employer Clauss introduced Dave to a 65-year-old gentleman who had concocted a secret blend of herbs and spices and a "better way of frying chicken." He sold his spices and special pressure cookers to restaurants, and they paid him a nickel for each chicken they sold.

What was the name of that gentleman? Colonel Sanders, of course. In his white suit and famous mustache and goatee, the Colonel was taking the restaurant business by storm, eventually relying on franchises to spread Kentucky Fried Chicken restaurants around the world, now known as KFC. *If you want to be the best entrepreneur, spend time working for the best firm you can.* And, learn a lot.

Among the KFC restaurants were four in Columbus, Ohio, owned by Phil Clauss. They were struggling, something I observed when I ate at those restaurants. Clauss offered Dave 40 percent ownership if he could turn around the operations. The likelihood of success was slim—the restaurants had few sales and no credit; even Col. Sanders required cash on delivery. Lorraine, Dave's wife, and Clauss, his mentor, were the only ones who thought he could make the restaurants a success. The Colonel himself told Thomas the stores were too far gone and that he should get out while he could. But Dave was determined.

Dave wanted to advertise, but with no cash, no credit, and no capital, how could he do that? The answer tells you a lot about how entrepreneurs without TMC survive and grow. He got his chicken supplier to sponsor a newspaper ad and traded chicken for air time at local TV and radio stations, which led to increased sales.

And then there was the "bucket." Thomas and Clauss had a marketing idea; put the chicken in a red-and-white striped bucket with Col. Sanders' picture on it. No other stores sold buckets of chicken. Dave hired an artist to create a sign with a wobbling chicken bucket for the outside of the restaurants. I wouldn't be surprised to learn Dave paid the artist with fried chicken. The bucket attracted so much attention that Sanders put one outside each of his restaurants. Thomas also suggested Sanders make commercials and appear in them himself.

From Rags to the Beginning of Riches

The Columbus restaurants flourished, and in 1968 Clauss sold his franchises back to Kentucky Fried Chicken. At age 35, Dave Thomas, the formerly-impoverished orphan, netted about a million dollars. What would you do with that money if you went from rags to riches by age 35?

Dave's boyhood dream became a reality in 1969, when he opened the first Wendy's, in downtown Columbus. Housed in a garage owned by car dealer Len Immke, who also had a passion for a good hamburger, Wendy's had an old-fashion look and feel. Patrons dined at tables covered with turn-of-the-century advertising, lit by hanging Tiffany lamps. Thomas offered a simple menu consisting of single, double and triple hamburgers, chili, French fries, and the now-famous Frosty© Dessert.

At McDonald's, customers got quick service, but it was accomplished by cooking hamburgers ahead of orders, letting them sit under heat lamps until customers ordered one, with managers hoping they didn't have to throw away too many because of wrong estimates of what customers would buy. When other restaurants were using frozen beef and mass-producing food, Dave developed an innovative method to prepare fresh, made-to-order hamburgers, allowing him quickly to serve high quality and variety to many customers each day. It was an example of functional shiftability—shifting the marketing research function of how many of each type should be produced to consumers. The result or benefit for consumers is captured in the phrase Dave coined, "Quality is our Recipe."

Dave figured out how to provide a grilled-to-order hamburger, served to the exact specifications of customers with no waste (cooked, but unsold hamburgers could be added to chili), and still provide quick service. Details determine differences between success and failure, and Dave not only got the details of hamburgers better, but with less waste and more quality at high efficiency. Like Aldi, the strategy of limited SKUs was essential in achieving both velocity and fresh-grilled hamburgers instantly, delighting the tastes of each individual customer.

Red Pig-Tails, Lots of Freckles and a Big Smile

To give the restaurant a wholesome image, he named it after his 8-year-old daughter, Wendy. The logo was created in her likeness—a little girl with red-pigtails, lots of freckles, and a big smile. It was the beginning of his strategy attaching a human personality to the Wendy's brand. The logo, still used today, allowed Wendy to live forever as an innocent 8-year-old in the minds of consumers, giving them a place to go when they longed for good, old-fashioned food and value.

The strategy worked. The church I attended was on the same street a couple of blocks from that original Wendy's store. The image appealed to me, and I stopped there the first week Wendy's opened. I marveled at the efficiency of the operation, the ambiance of carpet and Tiffany lamps instead of the stark atmosphere of competitors, the quality of the products, the value and quick service. I remember telling friends, "It's tough to open a new restaurant and succeed, but this could be a winner!"

Dave's plan was to open five restaurants in the Columbus area, but critics said there wasn't room in the market for another chain. He proved them wrong. He began franchising his chain in 1973 and by 1978 had opened 1000 restaurants. Wendy's later bought the Tim Horton's chain based in Canada, partly because Dave knew and liked its founder who shared similar values with Dave, but also because it led to decreased operating costs in shared locations and ability to serve customers in different day-parts offering foods that didn't compete with the traditional Wendy's menu.

Invest Early in Winners

When Dave decided to offer stock to finance geographic expansion, I bought shares as soon as they were publicly available. As a young teacher with little money to invest, I couldn't buy many shares, but my investment turned out well. Very well!

If you are reading this book as an investor seeking to grow your IRA, that's the way it works. *Look for firms just starting out that have clear advantages over existing competitors.* The best place to find those companies is from personal experience, often on the street where you live, or the stores where you shop. Look for growing firms before other investors, especially those in Wall Street offices, know much about the company. That's the way to buy stocks for a little and later sell them for a lot.

Components of a Brand

A brand has two essential components: Functional and Emotional.

In developing the functional components of the Wendy's brand, Dave appealed to a different segment than existing, larger competitors. Dave felt people wanted choices beyond the hamburger and fries of other quick service restaurants (QSR). He felt consumers were fed-up with poor quality and were ready for an upscale hamburger place.

"Plenty of adults grew up loving hamburgers, but they didn't like what they got at most fast-food places, where the food was designed for kids and teenagers who really didn't care what they were eating," says Dave. "We wanted to give customers a place to go for a hamburger the way they used to get them—with fresh, pure, American beef. We also wanted to create a warm, family-oriented, yet somewhat-upscale dining experience."

The physical attributes in the functional components of the brand, from its inception, represented Wendy's competitive advantage in the marketplace:

1. 100% pure hamburger—fresh (never frozen) and served hot

2. Condiments served cold

3. Meat not to touch the bun until it is sold

4. Customized, made-to-order items

5. Nice restaurant atmosphere—not a fast-food restaurant—but fast service.

In the branding strategy of your own firm, I encourage you to think through your brand proposition, just as Dave did, and be precise in defining physical or other characteristics in which your product or service offers a *differential advantage* compared to competitors. Differential advantage is the concept marketers use to express how the product really differs from competitors. "Me too" won't get you far as an entrepreneur. The other part of the concept is equally important. The differences should not be variations in colors, flavors, design, or attributes you consider important as the owner of the firm. They must be differences perceived to be an *advantage* by customers.

At Wendy's, attention to consumer changing wants and needs was the center of its vision and strategic direction. For example, Wendy's was the first national chain to add salad bars (1979), the first to offer baked potatoes (1983), and establish a specific Value Menu (1989). When consumers became more concerned about cholesterol and fat, Wendy's took a leadership role in formulating and offering chicken items, eventually adding a skinless, grilled chicken sandwich in 1990, and other items over the years in response to changing lifestyles and preferences.

These are the elements that make up a brand's functional components. In the book *Brands That Rock*, I describe in more detail than possible here the rest of the brand components, attributes often responsible for converting customers into fans. The other component of a brand is its *emotional* elements, established through communications programs, especially advertising.

Where's the Beef?

During the 1980s, QSRs entered what the media called "burger wars." The battle for consumer dollars began with a Burger King ad that featured what the company thought was its differential advantage—flame-broiled hamburgers. The ploy for consumer attention worked, and consumers flocked to Burger King to get a flame-broiled burger like the one they saw sizzling on their television screens.

Wendy's answer to flame-broiled hamburgers was Clara Peller. Short on stature, but big on attitude, Peller made advertising history when she first uttered the now famous words, "Where's the beef?" The seventy-something mighty-mouth touted Wendy's big, juicy hamburgers by complaining about the competitors' small hamburgers and large buns. The ad evoked a huge collective laugh from consumers and the ad industry alike. It also drove traffic to the stores and sales through the roof. The ads brought Wendy's numerous advertising awards, vividly and clearly positioning a quality image as Wendy's recipe and an emotional response to Wendy's brand in America's collective mind.

The attention-grabbing value of the Clara Peller ads had its downside, however. When Dave retired as CEO (he remained as Chairman), the quality of store operations declined and customers were often disappointed when they entered stores. The ads brought people into the stores to try Wendy's, but their experience in the store discouraged them from returning. The sales spike resulting from notable advertising was soon replaced by sales decline.

Effective advertising to drive sales of an ineffective product reveals an important lesson for all entrepreneurs. Don't use advertising to promote quality if customers are likely to be disappointed when they buy the product. *Good advertising accelerates the demise of a bad product!*

The Turn Around

Wendy's turned to its founder for inspiration and guidance in the process of resurrecting the brand. It hired James Near, a franchise owner known for operational excellence to orchestrate a turnaround. Wendy's implemented a "Sparkle" program to maintain managerial and operational excellence, realizing it needed to regain the trust of customers, reposition the Wendy's brand, and retain repeat traffic.

Basically, *a brand is a promise*. It tells customers what a marketer promises to do for them. It must establish a connection with core segments, promising to deliver attributes (or benefits derived from the attributes) customers want most—not just the first time, but every time.

The first step in that process was to reinforce the "Mop Bucket Attitude" Dave lived by when he managed the company. He was a legend as a CEO who visited stores unannounced. If he found them anything less than sparkling in both appearance and service, he immediately took the manager aside and privately instructed him how to do it right. Dave was so persistent about perfecting the customer experience, that the company designed a special certificate when an employee went above and beyond expectations, accomplishing something special for customers. The certificate looked similar to diplomas granted by universities to people receiving an M.B.A., the Master of Business Administration. At Wendy's, an M.B.A. stood for Mop Bucket Attitude.

Although not an employee, I received an M.B.A. certificate from Dave Thomas for advice as a consultant. Perhaps it surprised Dave to find a professor stressing theory willing to roll up his sleeves and get his hands dirty with the practical side of marketing, but it is a "degree" I cherish alongside my university diplomas. Observing how Wendy's restored a brand that lost its luster taught me the importance of entrepreneurs maintaining an active role insuring the quality upon which they founded the firm never become tarnished when leadership is handed over to others. I hope that is a caveat helpful to you in your own firm.

An Entrepreneur as the Brand

A marketing issue facing all entrepreneurs is whether or not to identify the entrepreneurial founder of a company as part of the brand of the firm. Dave answered that question well, perhaps better than any other since the days of Thomas Edison and Henry Ford.

To reinvigorate the Wendy's brand, the company partnered with its advertising agency partner, Bates USA. Together, they took a team-approach to branding, creating a unified, coordinated, integrated set of promotion and marketing activities to send messages to consumers about what makes Wendy's unique and why consumers should try and trust it. After, of course, operational problems in stores had been fixed.

Among the objectives for the brand and delivery of quality was the need to create a new and sustaining personality for the brand. Brands need a "story" to tell about a company and can have more emotional connection with customers when built around a human personality. It could be a fictional person such as "Victoria" for Victoria's Secret, "Ronald" at McDonald's, "Mickey" at Disney or real people such as Michael Jordan and Tiger Woods as spokespersons for Nike. There are some risks, however, in using real people. Even Colonel Sanders had a few spots on his white suit.

Regardless of what marketers intend the personality of a brand to be, what counts is what consumers perceive the personality to be. Perception is the reality. At this point in the history of the brand, the personality of Wendy's had been "old fashioned," exuding tradition, nostalgia, and a return to the basics of great food and service. The company's personality also resonated from the little girl pictured in the logo and a picture of Wendy that hung in every store.

The long-term nature of the goals required a strategic approach to the creation and implementation of a new advertising campaign. On what became an historic visit to the Bates agency, Dave sat down with the team and told them, in a way only Dave could, his vision for the company and consequently for the new campaign.

The proverbial light-bulb went on, the direction of the campaign was solidified, the goals were accepted by the entire team, and the rest is history. The creative team realized that no one could speak more passionately and from the heart about Wendy's than Dave could, and certainly, no one could express the values of the company quite the way he could. *Values are the foundation for a firm's vision.*

It was not Dave's idea to be in the ads; it was a team decision. I've been told by team members at Bates that Dave resisted the idea. Prior to launching a campaign, Bates conducted focus groups and recorded consumers' reactions in which consumers found Dave, above all, to be believable, honest, and sincere. They said Dave was natural, down to earth, and personified "a regular guy." They felt he would stand behind the company, was proud of his restaurants, and represented high quality standards. They also saw him as a true American success story.

The first ad of the Dave campaign featured Dave Thomas talking about Wendy's hamburgers and ended with him proclaiming, "Our hamburgers are the best in the business, or I wouldn't have named the place after my daughter." The only problem was that Dave pronounced business as "bidness."

The creative team debated whether to correct his pronunciation or leave it as "authentic Dave." His voice remained, along with some of his grammar mistakes, a decision which drew criticism by teachers, parents and advertising critics. A columnist for *Advertising Age* wrote that Dave had "the screen presence of a side of beef," and went on to predict doom and gloom for any sales the company hoped would result from the campaign.

Needless to say, the critics were wrong. The one group whose opinion counted most loved Dave—consumers. They believed him. Sure, Dave's commercials weren't polished, slick or fancy. But then, neither was Dave.

Over the years in Wendy's ads, Dave drove a Harley-Davidson, glided down slopes on a bobsled and pedaled a bike through the French countryside. He shared the screen with sports celebrities, and blues-great B.B. King. He donned a leather vest, wild ties, a French beret, punk-rock duds, hockey gear, and the ever-famous Wendy's apron. And, *he sold a lot of hamburgers!*

As the campaign evolved, Dave's popularity skyrocketed and he became a "star" in his own right. The more consumers saw Thomas, the stronger the personality of Wendy's became in their minds. He appeared in more than 800 commercial advertisements for the chain from 1989 to 2002, more than any other person in television history. In addition to watching what Dave Thomas did in front of the camera, his fans began watching what he did off-camera.

True Character

In 1991, he published his life story, *Dave's Way: A New Approach to Old-Fashioned Success*, in which he told the world about his childhood.

He described what it was like being an adopted child, his need to quit school in the tenth grade and how he entered and conquered the world of hamburgers. All of the proceeds of this book were donated to the cause of adoption. In 1992, he established the Dave Thomas Foundation for Adoption, championing the cause by speaking to groups around the world and visiting the White House and Congress.

Dave Thomas showed his true character in 1993 by graduating from high school, completing a GED (General Education Diploma), becoming a spokesperson on the importance of getting an education. He generously donated his time to working with students, including many at The Ohio State University and never failed to respond when I requested him to talk with my students.

On one occasion, while speaking to my class of over 700 marketing students, he dropped the note cards he (or his good friend Charlie Rath) had prepared to keep him on subject during the lecture. That didn't bother Dave; he just talked from his heart about his values and the vision he had for giving consumers what they want at Wendy's. It was a sensational, informative, inspiring time for my students, and for me. During questions, one of my students asked him why he bothered to make the effort, retired and in his sixties, to go back to school and spend the considerable time and work required to achieve a GED. His answer explains the values of the man and what motivated him.

"Because I was adopted, I work with a lot of young people," he explained. "I realized I was telling them to get an education, but I wasn't a good role model for them to do that. That's why I thought I needed to get a GED." Values tell you a lot about why some people are successful and others are not.

On January 8, 2002, Dave passed away and the world lost one of its greatest advocates for children. Dave Thomas was respected for being a talented businessman and a caring philanthropist, but his unceasing desire to improve the lives of North America's most vulnerable children was arguably his greatest contribution to society.

Humility was a characteristic Dave exhibited to everyone. When walking out of the Waldorf-Astoria hotel in New York, a woman stopped him and said,

"I've seen you somewhere. Are you someone important?" she asked.

"I'm nobody, really, I just make hamburgers for a living," Dave replied.

Values and Vision

When entrepreneurs form a new business, they usually give a lot of attention to perfecting the product. Usually they prepare a business plan, often with a computer-generated set of forecasts of future sales, expenses and profits. Sometimes they write a mission statement and perhaps a market analysis. Those are good things to do, but far too often I see entrepreneurs fail to write a description of the values underlying all those other business prerequisites to success.

If you are starting out or already have years of experience as an entrepreneur, I encourage you to write down a statement of your values. They should include *terminal values*—the words that capture how you hope to finish life—and the *instrumental values*—specific behavior associated with accomplishing your values. Terminal values are words, and they are important, but instrumental values allow an affirmative answer when someone asks, "Does your walk match your talk?"

At the time of Dave's death, I was asked to write an article about him for a news publication. Writing that opinion piece caused me to reflect on Dave's values. You can also find most of them on the Wendy's International website, and I encourage you to look at it. To end this conversation, I'll summarize succinctly what I observed to be the values of Dave Thomas.

1. Don't cut corners when it comes to satisfying customers.

   His words "We don't cut corners on quality," affected everything from hamburgers to customer service. His values lived in behavior by selecting premium ingredients and serving food that's made fresh with every order, a philosophy that helped build a multi-billion dollar global enterprise.

2. Keep the store sparkling.

Dave was known for inspecting bathrooms and dining rooms of every Wendy's he entered. If they didn't meet his standards, he was also known to grab a mop and bucket and clean them himself. Not only does a sparkling restaurant mean clean and healthy food, it means the owner respects his or her customers and employees.

3. Develop a personality consumers relate to.

The personality of Wendy's started with an image of his daughter Wendy and became synonymous with that of its founder. Dave was believable and sincere in both what he said and how he communicated it. His imperfect English and shy grin made him a down-to-earth, regular guy in the eyes of his customers in a unique and convincing way.

4. Do what's right.

Dave lived by the Golden Rule: Treat others the way you want to be treated. He simplified this by saying, "Just Be Nice." When he met you, he looked you in the eye and remembered your name. He thought that was the greatest sign of respect. When he asked questions, he wanted answers, and after you answered, he either knew what you knew or knew you didn't know what you were talking about. Dave lived his life with honesty and integrity. He was a man of his word, and he believed that you earn your reputation by the things you do every day. He considered integrity the most imporant value one can have.

5. Profit is not a dirty word.

There's nothing wrong with making a profit and taking pride in your success. Profit in business means growth and opportunity. It also means being able to share your success with your team and community.

6. Give Something back.

Dave believed everyone has a responsibility to give back—to help those who can't help themselves. Giving back doesn't simply mean giving money to charities. It also means giving your time or sharing your special skills. When I asked him to give his time back to young people by speaking in my class, he did so without hesitation, except his humility about being a high-school drop out. Dave lived his values and walked his talk.

Dave often said he was lucky to have been born in America. "Only in America," he said, "would a guy like me, from humble beginnings and without a high school diploma become successful. America gave me a chance to live the life I want and work to make my dreams come true. We should never take our freedoms for granted, and we should seize every opportunity presented to us."

When I first bought shares in Wendy's as a young teacher, I only knew about the quality of the product, the efficiency of operations and the responses of consumers. I didn't know Dave Thomas nor did I know the values that were the foundation of his firm. At that time, I didn't even know the importance of values in determining the success or failure of a firm or the value of its shares. That took a few decades for me to realize and research, but I hope the lesson will be helpful to you in much less time by reading this book and recognizing the importance of values among leaders of a company as a predictor of success of a firm and the value of its shares.

If you doubt that values and profits go hand-in-hand, read the best-selling books *Built to Last* by Collins and Porras I mentioned earlier or *Corporate Culture and Performance* by Kotter and Heskett. They document well that firms with good values achieve the most financial success.

$16 Hamburgers

"The past is prologue," Shakespeare wrote in *The Tempest*. That seems an apt description of Wendy's. It has become the second largest hamburger restaurant after McDonald's and larger than Burger King, but most (about 92 percent) of its revenues are from U.S. stores.

Wendy's today has a new CEO, Emil Brolick, whose past experience is firmly rooted in the value-laden culture of Wendy's. Brolick's experience also includes being Chief Operating Officer of YUM Brands, a firm with impressive results establishing strong global presence for 37,000 Taco Bell, Pizza Hut and KFC stores. So, what's next for Wendy's under new CEO Brolick?

Wendy's most recent foreign foray is in Japan where it hopes to win over Japan's trendy consumers with the *Foie Gras Rossini* burger, introduced at 1,280 yen (about $16 U.S.), topped with truffles and goose-liver pate. In its public announcements, Wendy's said the premium, trendy burger will be available in about 100 of Wendy's Japan-based restaurants.

What would Dave say about a $16 hamburger in Japan? Knowing Dave as well as I did, I think he would take a big bite out of it, smile into Japanese cameras with a twinkle in his eye, and say, "Best hamburger in the bidness!"

"We Don't Cut Corners on Quality"

Not cutting corners was more than a slogan for Dave Thomas; it was a way of life and ultimately, the secret of his success. Square hamburgers are simply the icon of his philosophy of doing things, the way he treated people and his management methods.

Here's one more thing to contemplate. If you have good parents with good values, you are a blessed individual. If you didn't have parents with good values, remember that even though you can't choose your parents, you can choose your values.

(photo courtesy of Wendy's International)

10

Conversation TEN

What's Your Game?

The starting point in success as an entrepreneur is a good answer to the question, "What do you sell?"

"Hamburgers," you might answer when describing the product Wendy's sells. I hope you discovered in our last conversation that Dave Thomas sold much more than hamburgers in his restaurants, and I'm not referring to chili, chicken or a Frosty©.

"What's your game?" is a street term referring to what you are really good at, your specialty, something you are known for doing better than others. Successful entrepreneurs, the kind with an unlimited future, need to answer the question, "What are you good at?" Not just competent, or better than most, but what are you *really* good at doing? What sets you apart from all the others?

Jerry Garcia, leader of the Grateful Dead said it well, "It's not that we're the best at what we do, we're just the only ones who do what we do." Echoing Garcia, the leader of Cirque du Soleil added, "Our goal is not to be the best of the best, but to be the only ones who do what we do."

If you discover a large and growing industry and decide to jump in, don't, unless your game is different, offering more than the best of the rest. It's OK to incorporate superior attributes of competitors into your firm's offering, as Sam Walton did, but go beyond that by adding something more, often a lot more. *Distinctively better* is the key to creating jobs, transforming industries and building fortunes.

When I mentioned TMC as the reason most entrepreneurs fail, a wise person replied, "No, it is TFS." When I asked the meaning of "TFS," he replied, "Too Few Sales." He made a good point. Consider the topic of this conversation to be "preventing TFS."

It's Not the Product; it's the Benefit

Products don't turn customers into fans; superior benefits do. The secret of success is focusing on the benefit instead of the product. It is the key to survival and growth. Success requires viewing a product or service from the eyes of customers instead of the entrepreneur. That is not easy to do by an entrepreneur enamored with his or her product.

Why do people buy your product? What do they expect from it? What attributes do they prefer so strongly they shift behavior from one supplier to another? Those are critical questions in the marketing of any product, whether sold by a business to consumers (B2C) or by a business to businesses (B2B). The head of a famous fragrance brand was quoted saying, "In the factory, we make perfume, but in stores we sell hope." This could also be said about the lingerie and bras sold at Victoria's Secret.

"We Sell Up Time"

What's more glamorous than fragrance and lingerie? How about ball bearings and power transmission belts? OK, maybe not, but don't tell the management of Applied Industrial Technologies (AIT), because they are pretty passionate about bearings, drive systems, industrial rubber, fluid power and two million other products sold to customers ranging from local machine shops to global enterprises in paper, mining and manufacturing industries. The company started by selling bearings. In fact, in its early days, Applied's name was Bearings, Inc.

AIT management views its product in more than physical items such as industrial parts and components; its business is selling "uptime." It's the difference between selling commodities or building a business on delivering profitability for customers. Applied delivers the benefit of "uptime" through sophisticated information systems, integrated logistics, responsive sales representatives and a brand known for service, putting products where and when customers need them. That keeps machines, warehouses, and mines running dependably and profitably, delivering the benefit of "uptime.

Survival Insurance

There is probably no industry faced with a greater imperative of focusing on benefits instead of methods than music. If you were an entrepreneur focused on producing and selling the best albums, cassettes, or movies in the past, you are in trouble today. Consumers might say they want to buy the best CDs, DVDs or downloads, but what they really want is *entertainment*. There are a lot of 8-tracks and videotapes stacked in attics and basements!

Focusing on benefits instead of physical products lets entrepreneurs adapt and develop new methods or products solving ageless problems. Entertainment, information, "uptime," social acceptance, saving time, and a host of other basic customer problems don't go away, but methods of satisfying those needs change constantly and often rapidly. Defining a firm's business in terms of benefits instead of products buys survival insurance -- solving ageless problems with new or different methods and products.

Just look at what happened to one of the world's most successful firms that failed to adapt. Kodak dominated the globe with analog cameras and film, but the world now obtains those benefits digitally, bankrupting the former film star. Research in Motion (RIM) introduced the Blackberry smart phone, succeeding well until competitors such as Apple launched smarter phones. Firms committed to a specific technology or product open the door for new entrepreneurs to seize their customers. *The future often arrives before formerly prosperous firms give up the past.*

Consumption Process Analysis

Understanding customer behavior is the foundation for delivering benefits better than competitors, key to overcoming TFS. The study of consumer behavior has evolved over the past fifty years or so to provide an organized way to understand why people buy. It is easier to persuade customers to buy when an entrepreneur knows the *reasons* people buy specific products, services and brands, focusing on *benefits* expected from their purchases.

Establishing a successful business is like a good marriage. If you don't understand *why* customers or spouses behave the way they do, neither a business nor a marriage is likely to succeed for long. Understanding customer behavior focuses on obtaining, consuming, and disposing of goods and services.

Obtaining refers to the activities leading up to and purchase or receipt of a product, including searching for information regarding product features and choices, evaluating alternative products or brands, and purchasing. As you start or grow your business, study these processes to examine *how* and *why* customers buy. Do they shop primarily at specialty stores such as Victoria's Secret, Buckle and Lululemon or discounters such as Walmart, Costco and Aldi? Do they shop mostly in stores or on the Internet? Focus on how customers pay for products, how they transport them, where they get information about product and store alternatives and how brands affect their choices.

Consuming means how, where, when and under what circumstances customers use products. Do they use them in their cars, homes, or offices? Do they use products by themselves or with family and friends? Do they use products according to instructions as intended or do they find their own unique way of using products? Is the experience of using the product entertaining and satisfying or purely functional? Do they use the entire product before disposing of it or is some of it never consumed?

Disposing focuses on how customers get rid of products and packaging. How important are ecological concerns? Are products biodegradable? Recycled? Do customers employ methods to extend the life of the product? Do they hand them down to children, donate them to thrift shops or sell them on Craig's List and eBay?

When I confront entrepreneurs with these questions, challenging them to analyze the *consumption process* for their own product offering, I've often been met by a quizzical frown and the statement, "I never thought of all those things before I started my business."

Customer satisfaction requires good answers to all those questions. Customer delight depends on superior delivery on *all* elements of the consumption process, not just basic attributes of product, place, promotion and price. Failure to deliver what customers desire on *all* elements of the consumption process opens the door for new entrepreneurs to walk in and grab your customers.

Sam Walton used to tour stores telling employees, "The customer is the only one who can fire us all." Walton freely admitted that Walmart was an idea borrowed from Kmart. Rather than inventing some radical new idea, Walton focused on executing proven principles in the market place, eventually overtaking and threatening the existence of Kmart by focusing on what customers buy instead of what an organization sells.

After speaking to one of the early morning meetings held on Saturdays in Bentonville, a Walmart executive told me how Walmart views consumers. He explained Walmart's business is not selling *to* customers; it is sourcing *for* customers. The goal is to be a "buying agent" for consumers, finding out what they want and offering it at prices they are willing to pay. "Our job is to buy stuff people want in their homes and lives," he explained, "and get it to them in stores." (Today, he would probably add, "or online.")

You can make a fortune serving customers well, but not if you don't know *why* customers buy.

Why Do Customers Buy?

Marketing is an *exchange process* in which people pay for goods and services valued more than the money required to obtain them. You've never seen someone walk into a store and say, "I have an extra $100; just give me something and you can have my $100." No one becomes a customer unless you offer something of greater value than their cash or credit.

In one sense, all customer behavior is "rational" because if customers don't believe your product or service offers greater value than their money, they won't leave their cash or plastic at your cash register. They may decide later the product did not provide the desired utility or they could have received a better deal some other place, but at the time you hear the ka-ching of the cash register, customers are acting rationally by exchanging money for products and services.

Customers may evaluate the behavior of others and call it "irrational," and sometimes evaluate their own purchases later, considering them irrational. That's called "buyer's remorse" or what psychologists call cognitive dissonance. But at the time people buy something, they believe their purchase is rational or they wouldn't buy it.

If you want to read an excellent book about this, I recommend Dan Ariely's best-selling *Predictably Irrational: The Hidden Forces That Shape Our Decisions* (HarperCollins, 2008) in which he describes experiments and asks readers to predict outcomes. What some people consider irrational is at least predictably irrational. You'll also find most of these conclusions in any good textbook on the subject, including one I co-wrote with Paul Miniard and James Engel, *Consumer Behavior*, 10th edition (Southwestern, 2005).

Every result has a cause. If you understand what causes customer behavior, you will be more effective than competitors at predicting what works in your marketing program. When you know why customers buy, you can persuade them to buy from you instead of competitors, or buy at higher prices, more frequently or more loyally.

A road map is useful in getting where you want to go, especially if you have never been there before. You could ask for directions. That's what a lot of entrepreneurs do—asking or watching what customers buy at successful firms. The problem with directions based on the past arises when you need to go where no one has ever gone before, and that's often the situation for start-up firms and new products. Then you need a road map.

Lots of people don't ask directions or use road maps. They just listen to their Garmin, Tom-Tom or the GPS app on their phone or car. I do that, and I go where "Lady Gaga" on my Garmin tells me. It usually works, even though I don't understand the sophisticated math and models that permits Lady Gaga to track, re-calculate and tell me where I am and when to turn.

The same is true in the study of consumer behavior. There is a lot of math, sophisticated models and analytics useful in predicting consumer behavior. You can be sure Procter & Gamble, Coca-Cola, IBM and other major marketers use those sophisticated methodologies to understand customer behavior, but in this conversation, I will keep things simple.

There's a lot of science involved in understanding why people buy. When we wrote the first edition of *Consumer Behavior* in 1968, we read all the research available in psychology, sociology, economics, anthropology and decision making, integrating it in a model to predict how those variables affect consumer behavior. Over the years, marketing and other disciplines have evolved to include analytics,

Bayesian statistics, stochastic modeling and techniques far beyond our current discussion. I've taken what we learned and summarized it into a simple model of the customer decision process (CDP), a road-map you can use in designing marketing strategies for your firm.

Consumer Decision Process Model

Problem Recognition

Search for Information

Pre-purchase Evaluation of Alternatives

Purchase

Consumption

Post-consumption Evaluation

Divestment

Figure 1: How Consumers Make Decisions

for Goods and Services

Stage One: Recognizing the Problem

A purchase begins with *problem recognition*, also called *need recognition*. Problem or need recognition occurs when there is a difference between what people want to be true and what they perceive to be true about their lives. There are no markets for new products unless consumers perceive *felt needs*, including emotional or social needs. "I feel your pain," is the first step for an entrepreneur seeking to solve problems for potential customers.

A customer's need is *not* to help you make a profit. And you won't make much profit unless there is a substantial segment of people who feel the problem or need you hope to satisfy. Think of your product as a total bundle of utilities designed to solve a problem. The more pressing a problem is felt by lots of potential customers, the greater the opportunity to make a fortune solving that problem. *Successful entrepreneurs scratch where people itch.*

Unless you truly solve their problem and do it repeatedly and consistently, people will not buy your product. *Most firms don't fail because their products don't function well; products fail because they deliver benefits for which customers don't have a strong felt-need.* Firms also fail when the segment feeling the need is too small to be profitable.

To grow your firm into a large fortune, it is not enough to *satisfy* customers; you must *delight* them. Profits are caused by customers, but fortunes are caused by converting customers into *fans* of you and your brand. Fans bring their friends to your concert.

Stage Two: Search

Once problem recognition occurs, the *search* process begins, identifying methods and products to satisfy unmet needs.

Search may be internal, retrieving knowledge from memory, or it may be external, collecting information from the marketplace. At times consumers passively search, simply becoming more receptive to information such as advertising or targeted email blasts. Sometimes they engage in active search behavior, starting with Google or other search engines. If consumers are pretty certain what they want, the Internet offers the potential of finding a solution to their needs potentially any place in the world. In business applications such as looking for a special size or color, or for B2B products such as a specific machine part, grade of oil, or type of paper, the Internet shines.

If consumers are delighted with the products they currently use, they search very little. That's why triumphant firms place a high priority on keeping customers delighted. But if consumers are unhappy with current products, brands or experiences, search expands to include alternatives. Don't expect to succeed if your product is not dramatically better than existing alternatives. When customers feel they don't have enough information to make a decision, they become more receptive to advertising messages, sales persons' efforts, and alternative forms of distribution. Variables such as personality, social class, income and the size of purchase also determine amount and extent of search.

Some consumers enjoy search. Walking and browsing through malls is fun for some consumers; for others it is a chore. Understanding when search is fun and when it is a chore guides marketing strategies. For example, the search for microwave oven information doesn't excite many consumers. The most effective marketing channel in this instance minimizes time and effort required to obtain information, such as digital signage or mobile apps, providing in-depth information quickly, sometimes linking to the Internet to check inventory or prices. The search for a dress might be different. Browsing, trying on different styles, and experiencing the store may be more important than speed.

The Internet fits the search stage, while stores, catalogues, or other forms of selling may best fit the purchase stage of consumer decision making. Studies show, for example, that when consumers perceive the need for a new car, a majority search computer sites such as Consumer Reports, Edmunds, and others. They then use that information to buy the car at a dealer, at a price they learned on a web site to be realistic. Searching where to buy a car also helps consumers find information about issues such as service, an opportunity to test drive or evaluate appearance, or ability to talk to a real person when problems arise with the car. The Web site may be critically important searching for information, but the dealer is usually more important in the transaction stage.

Even for such functional products as soup or shampoo, the search process often includes examination of the package to judge whether or not the soup has genetically modified grains or too much sodium, artificial flavors or an ingredient to which the consumer has an allergic reaction. The "search" for exactly the right shampoo from the hundreds available may include judgment about whether the container is easy to grip in the shower and whether the aroma and color matches the desires of the consumer.

Why spend time and effort analyzing how people process information during the search stage of the CDP? That's how you decide whether communication programs should be built on advertising, in-store information and experiences, salespeople, publicity and third party communications (such as *Consumer Reports*), using celebrity reference group role models or the firm's web page. Which is the best way to get information circulated about your product? The answer increasingly is "all of the above."

Search and targeting segments go hand in hand. If you know how people search and the relative advantages of each media, you know a lot about developing a winning strategy. In today's digital economy, it's a Face-book, Linked-in, Googly world.

Stage Three: Alternative evaluation

"What are my options? Which is best?" Consumers seek answers to such questions in the *alternative evaluation* stage, when they evaluate and select from various products or services.

Although this process is intertwined with both the search and choice processes, understanding it separately as pre-purchase alternative evaluation helps design marketing strategies. During alternative evaluation, consumers compare what they know about different products, brands and stores with what they believe are their preferences. Consumers may not think about it consciously, but the process occurs in their minds.

How do customers evaluate alternatives? They choose products, services, and retailers based on attributes most important to them. Some attributes are *salient*, or the most important – things like does it function well, does it fit, and is it durable? If many alternatives perform well on salient attributes, customers make their choices on *determinant* attributes – things, perhaps minor in nature, which differentiate one product or supplier from another. All cars within a category perform well providing reliable transportation, similar mileage and are about the same price for similar space. The determinant attributes causing consumers to buy one SUV instead of another may be appearance, the availability of exact color and interior design or perhaps the number and design of cup holders. Honda and Toyota have sliding side doors on vans, causing parents unloading kids at schools to choose those brands over Ford or GM.

You might think that the most important (salient) attributes would determine purchase, but not always. When salient attributes are similar, customers choose products on less important things, *determinant* attributes. That's why success of entrepreneurs is closely allied with details. Get one detail wrong—even details like cup holders or sliding side doors—and competitors get the customers instead of you. Which details must you get right to succeed? All of them. The genius of Steve Jobs was his ability to get more details right than competitors.

Stage Four: Purchase

The fourth stage is *purchase* – buying the product. *Nothing else entrepreneurs do has any value unless customers---usually lots of them—buy the product.*

Customers move through the purchase stage in two phases. First, customers choose one form of supplier over others. The initial choice is between online, catalog, direct mail, personal selling (including direct sales such as Amway and Thirty-One) or location-based suppliers.

Part of the purchase stage involves in-store choices, influenced by salespersons, product displays, kiosks, and point-of-purchase advertising (POP) for location-based retailers. For on-line retailers, the purchase process includes finding sites (search engine optimization, or SEO), Web navigation, the influence of banners and other ads, payment systems (i.e. credit cards, increasingly from mobile devices), security issues and check-out procedures. Consumer expectations and satisfaction with these issues greatly affect choices. You must "get it right" with each to succeed.

To buy or not to buy? A customer might move through the first three stages according to plan – perceiving a problem, searching for information, and evaluating alternatives. The consumer intends to purchase a particular product or brand but ends up buying something quite different, or perhaps does not buy at all because of what happens during the purchase or choice stage. A consumer may prefer one retailer but choose another because of a sale or a promotional event at a competitor, hours of operation, location, or traffic flow problems. Inside the store, the consumer may talk with a sales person who changes the decision, see an end-of-aisle or digital display that switches brand preference, use a coupon or price discount, fail to find the intended product or brand, or lack the money or right credit card to make the purchase. Successful entrepreneurs manage the overall attributes and image, in micro detail, to perfect all aspects of the shopping experience, including the ability to capture a lot of that information with a mobile app.

Once on a Web site of an on-line retailer, a consumer may easily find what he or she is seeking, or may not. How well the web site navigates and handles transactions is critically important in determining whether or not the purchase is made. Perhaps the graphics and text do not provide enough information to build confidence the product will meet expectations. Studies indicate that about a third of consumers move to the check-out portion, but terminate without buying. Maybe it was because the credit card information was not close by or the process evoked concerns about security or other issues. Perhaps the Web site could not change quantities, sizes and colors easily with multiple purchases. Maybe the total included delivery charges or sales tax the customer finds unacceptable. Perhaps the only thing the customer really wanted was a printout of the price and product details to use for reference and negotiation at the location-based retailer. Or maybe a spouse just said "dinners ready, get off the computer."

Stage Five: Consumption and Evaluation

After a purchase, *consumption* occurs, either immediately or delayed. For example, if a customer sees a sales promotion, he or she may "stock-up" on the item, buying more than used in the normal time frame of consumption. If delivery costs are significant for small orders, they become a smaller proportion when leveraged against a "stock up" order. That's why Amazon pioneered free shipping over a certain dollar amount or unlimited shipping for an annual fee as a "prime" customer. B-2-B firms offer better prices for "truck load" instead of smaller orders. How people *use* products is key to how they *buy* products.

Customers also evaluate their purchases on the basis of satisfaction or dissatisfaction(S/DS), stored in memory to be used in future decisions. If customers are highly satisfied, subsequent decisions are much shorter, usually buying the same brand from the same seller, and paying little attention to your competitors. If people are dissatisfied with products or suppliers, they are ripe for picking by new entrepreneurs.

One of the most important reasons for studying the consumption process is determining the reason for satisfaction or dissatisfaction with products. The product might be good, but if consumers don't use it properly, dissatisfaction occurs. Successful entrepreneurs provide care and use instructions and offer warranties, service and instruction programs, and measure how well they work. Marriott built a vast hotel chain aided by comment cards in every room and follow-up mail surveys, done now by email. Successful entrepreneurs do the same.

Stage Six: Divestment

Divestment is the last stage in the consumer decision process model.

Customers have many options, including outright disposal, recycling, or remarketing. When customers no longer want or need clothing, cars or computers, they must dispose of them somehow. They can choose to sell (remarket) it to other customers online, trade it in on another product (common for cars, of course), or dump it in the trash. With many products, customers find themselves having to dispose of packaging and product literature as well as the product itself. In these situations, recycling and environmental concerns play a role in consumers' divestment methods. These concerns caused restaurants to switch from Styrofoam to paper cups.

Understanding divestment sometimes leads to profit opportunities. Goodwill and Salvation Army (Red Shield stores) have been in the business of remarketing for decades, and a stagnant economy encourages consumers to explore thrift stores for recycled, renewed and sometimes nearly- new merchandise at bargain prices. Farm auctions, garage sales and flea markets are major outlets in the disposition of no-longer-needed items ranging from clothing and appliances to restaurant equipment and business machines.

Profiting from Divestment

Entrepreneurs find opportunities divesting old products, some growing to substantial national corporations. Once Upon a Child provides a fun and convenient way to buy and sell "gently-used" kids' stuff. Started by a mom recognizing the need for new sizes of clothing almost every year for growing children, it matured to a system of franchised stores in the U.S. and Canada, selling children's clothes, toys, furniture and equipment. It is now owned by Winmark (formerly Grow Biz), which also franchises Music Go Round, Plato's Closet, and Play It Again Sports.

Such firms provide a sort of contemporary garage sale or flea market rationalized as a public corporation, helping buyers find products serving needs just as well as new products, but at much lower prices. They also serve sellers in need of a little cash and a lot more closet or attic space.

Can understanding divestment create billionaires? The stellar performer is Pierre Omidyar. At age 28, over a long holiday weekend, he wrote the computer code for what eventually became an Internet super brand — eBay. The word 'eBay' was made up quickly by Omidyar, when he was told his first choice for a name, "echobay," had already been registered. Not wanting to make a second trip to Sacramento to register a new name, he came up with the name eBay. Forbes described him as the 145th richest person in the world and the third richest person of Iranian descent. Understanding divestment worked out well for Omidyar.

CDP – Foundation for Entrepreneurial Success

Which of all the details we've just discussed are important to success as an entrepreneur? All of them! When you understand how consumers make decisions with a roadmap such as the CDP model, you can develop real businesses with real profits. You can also understand why many early technology firms were doomed from the beginning, started by people who understood the "e" part of e-commerce well. Unfortunately, for investors who plunked down their money at the wrong time, many e-commerce pioneers didn't understand the key ingredient of success, customers.

"Whew!" That may be your reaction absorbing the concepts and theory you've just read. It may seem too much to consider in defining "your game," but the process helps you answer a question crucial to your success. What do you sell that is better, cheaper, more convenient, more time-saving, or more fun than competitors? If you don't have a good answer, choose a different game.

11

Conversation ELEVEN

The Passion of Jeff Bezos

If you were selecting from the technology era one person as an exemplar of garage entrepreneurs, who would you choose? Steven Jobs and Bill Gates are conspicuous contenders. Michael Dell and Mark Zuckerberg are also notable nominees, starting in spaces smaller than a garage.

My nomination for outstanding technology entrepreneur is Jeff Bezos. It's not only because he started in a garage, nor his considerable financial success, but because he demonstrates many secrets vital to growing small firms into large fortunes. The most valuable secret, especially if you are a technology entrepreneur, is Bezos "gets" the commerce part of e-commerce, as well as the "e" or technology component.

Firms fail by focusing on technology instead of consumer needs. Bezos' passion is customers, applying technology to their problems and delivering better benefits. You might have questioned the time describing the CDP model, but it offers a systematic method for analyzing customer needs, a "check list" analyzing why customers buy. Using the CDP model to analyze consumers, I hope you *delight* them as well as Bezos. *Passion for customers is more important than passion for technology.* Passion for solving customers' problems fuels growth, profitability and market dominance. At Amazon, Bezos says it impeccably and succinctly, "Determine what your customers need and work backwards."

In our conversations about entrepreneurs, I hope you observe how successful entrepreneurs apply theory to profitable business strategies. *Knowing how to apply theory conquers competitors before they realize they have been engaged.* Ability to apply theory is more valuable than attracting capital. Jeff Bezos is a living textbook of how to start small and grow large—very large!

America's Most Successful Latino?

Bezos was born in New Mexico, working summers on a ranch. He developed a mechanical aptitude early, reportedly dismantling his crib with a screwdriver as a toddler. A teenager when Bezos was born, his mother's marriage lasted little more than a year. When Jeff was five, she remarried, this time to Miguel Bezos, an immigrant to the U.S. from Cuba who legally adopted Jeff. I believe that qualifies Jeff Bezos as Latino by adoption and cultural environment, if not birth.

Jeff converted his parents' garage into a laboratory for science projects, displaying talent for anything scientific at an early age. The family moved to Miami where Bezos attended high school and began winning science awards that won him admission to Princeton University, planning to study physics. He developed a passion for computers and graduated *summa cum laude* and Phi Beta Kappa with a degree in Electrical Engineering and Computer Science. He turned down a job from IBM to work at Wall Street firms, in the computer science field. It was there, among other things, he learned how to build a computer network.

Do you see a pattern in successful entrepreneurs?

1. Learn from the best

2. Learn the "hard stuff," including technology

3. Learn how financial markets work and capital is raised

4. Make your mistakes on someone else's payroll. That's how you get experience in areas needed to grow a small firm large.

I don't know whether hard work on a ranch, a modest family background, growing up in a Latino culture, high intelligence, or graduating *summa cum laude* from Princeton is the most important attribute of Bezos, but they clarify success and the passion with which Bezos lives life.

The most successful entrepreneurs are intimately involved in details of their business. Bezos' background may explain his reputation as a micro-manager, one who pays attention to details. You can find more background on his early life and formation of the company in Richard Brandt, *One Click: Jeff Bezos and the Rise of Amazon.com* (Portfolio, 2011).

What is the Best Business?

Aspiring entrepreneurs sometimes ask, "What is the best business to start?" The biggest opportunities are usually in fast growth industries.

While surfing the Internet back in 1994, Jeff Bezos discovered World Wide Web usage was growing 2,300 percent a month. He recognized the potential for selling online and began exploring entrepreneurial possibilities for developing an Internet business, compiling a list of 20 potential products that might sell well via the Internet, including software, CDs and books. After reviewing the list, books were the obvious choice, primarily because of the sheer number of titles. Bezos realized the largest superstores could stock only about a hundred thousand books, a mere fraction of what is available, but a "virtual" bookstore could offer millions of titles, an important consumer and retail problem that could be solved by the Internet.

There was no turning back for Bezos. He resigned his high-paying, secure job at the Wall Street firm where he worked and accumulated savings, packed his wife, MacKenzie, and their dog, Kamala (named after a "Star Trek" character), and headed for Seattle. Although Bezos was earning a good salary, he didn't spend his precious cash on luxuries like airplane tickets or moving vans. He put a few possessions in a station wagon and heeded the age-old advice, "Go west, young man, go west." When he arrived in Seattle, he started Amazon.com in a nondescript garage.

Why Seattle?

One of my all-time favorite cases is Amazon. I've taught it dozens of times in universities and business groups. It is Case #1 in *Consumer Behavior*, 10th Edition, taught by professors in universities around the world. It is a favorite of students because it illustrates a wide range of business principles and marketing concepts. As a catalyst to lively discussion, I usually ask the question, "Why did Jeff Bezos start Amazon in Seattle?"

"Because he liked rain," is almost always the answer of at least one wise-cracking student. That's not the correct answer, of course.

"Because he liked coffee," other students sometimes quip. Writing computer code does sometimes take all night, but I don't think it's abundant coffee that makes people sleepless in Seattle.

"The abundance of excellent computer resources and personnel," is a frequent answer. That's a good answer, but not the primary reason Bezos started Amazon in Seattle. The best explanation is functional shiftability, the key to marketing better products at lower prices.

The logistics component of functional shiftability is critically important to delivering lower costs and better service to customers. Logistics was ignored by many e-commerce firms, but not Amazon, explaining why Seattle is Amazon's home and pivotal to its success. Shifting logistics to Seattle allowed Amazon to accomplish its mission quickly, efficiently and with a minimum of capital.

If Amazon had built a major warehouse, developed picking and shipping expertise, and acquired huge quantities of books in inventory, the capital required to start Amazon would have been dramatically higher. But Amazon didn't do that; it shifted those functions to a more efficient member of the demand chain.

Seattle was home to Ingram Book Group, America's largest book wholesaler, a supply chain partner highly experienced in shipping small quantities of books—often one or two at a time—to thousands of small book retailers. Ingram knew how to pick, pack and ship, performing that function better than any start-up dot com. It had relationships to major publishers, knew what books were selling and held many of them in inventory at its giant warehouse in Seattle.

Raising Capital

While MacKenzie Bezos drove the family vehicle, Jeff pecked out a business plan on a laptop computer and called prospective investors on a cell phone. With $1 million raised from family and friends, Bezos rented a house, choosing one with a garage, to set up his business. I've read his desk was a door spread across two saw horses, revealing the frugality with which Amazon still operates. A million dollars of capital is minuscule to start a billion dollar business, but frugality in expenses and minimal outside investment is why Bezos still owns twenty percent of the most successful dot com of the era. He didn't have TMC, so he had to do the right things right. Bezos and a crew of five employees worked out of the garage, learning how to source books and set up a computer system making Amazon.com easy to navigate.

As a marketing visionary, Bezos created a user-friendly interface streamlining the "needle in a haystack" process that bookstore shopping by consumers previously required. He also wanted a "virtual community" where visitors could "hang out," allowing customers to add their own book reviews and recommendations. He employed "crowdsourcing" and CRM (Customer Relationship Management) before these terms became part of every entrepreneur's vocabulary.

In July 1995, Amazon.com opened its virtual doors, calling itself "Earth's Biggest Book Store," with more than 1 million titles to choose from, solving the perpetual problem of consumers failing to find the book they want in the small inventory carried by bricks-and-mortar stores. Retailers could order unique books for consumers, but often required weeks to receive them. Some consumers ordered a book to fit their special interests, but never returned to buy it, leaving the retailer with a store full of un-bought and often un-saleable books.

Fueled by word of mouth, or more accurately, word of e-mail, Amazon.com rocketed from the warehouse like the space rockets that also pique the passion of Bezos. Delighted by the enormous selection of books, superior customer service and user-friendly design of the site, Internet users quickly became fans of the new way to find exactly the book they wanted and get it without two or more trips to a book store. They also eagerly brought friends as "fans" to the concert given by Amazon.com.

The orders poured in, and by September 1996, Amazon.com had grown into a company of 100 employees and racked up more than $15.7 million in sales. Three years later, those figures would rocket to 3,000 employees (including some in Britain and Germany) and $610 million in sales.

Amazon.com's success did not go unnoticed by bookstore giant Barnes & Noble, who quickly put up its own Web site. To combat Amazon's claim it was "Earth's Biggest Bookstore," Barnes & Noble embarked on an aggressive marketing campaign proclaiming it offered twice as many books as Amazon.com, a strategy doomed to failure. The forward-thinking Bezos had already expanded Amazon.com's product line to include CDs and replaced "Earth's Biggest Book Store" with the tagline "Books, Music and More," leaving Barnes & Noble, as one writer put it, "wrapping its fingers around the neck of a phantom."

After success with centrifugal expansion into music, Bezos set his sights on expanding Amazon.com to other markets. Shortly before the 1998 Christmas season, Bezos added a temporary gift section to Amazon.com, where customers could buy toys and games. He also began experimenting with "Shop the Web," a program giving Amazon.com a commission for directing its customers to other, noncompeting online retailers. In 1999, Amazon.com added Drugstore.com, selling everything from breath mints to Viagra.

You know the story from there. Today, you can buy almost anything on Amazon and check prices and availability with your smart phone while shopping in stores of competitors. In an article in PC *Week* back in 1999, Bezos explained, "We are building something that can't be pigeonholed. We defy easy analogy. It's not a vision that can be communicated in a sound bite. We want to be the most customer-centric company in the world. Come and discover and buy anything online."

Cadaver.com?

When Jeff Bezos first started his virtual venture, he wanted to call the company Cadabra, from the magical incantation *abracadabra*. He phoned his Seattle lawyer to try out the name, but the attorney misheard Bezos and replied, "Cadaver! Why would you want to call your company that?" Bezos quickly reconsidered and adopted the name Amazon.com, after one of the world's largest rivers. A remarkable fact about Amazon.com is sales were growing at a rate of 3,000 percent annually, but the company wasn't making a dime. Financed with debt (in Euros), rather than equity Bezos grew rapidly despite losses. That didn't bother Bezos. "To be profitable [now] would be would be a bad decision," he told *PC Week*. "This is a critical formative time if you believe in investing in the future." Bezos' plan was to forego profits (including high salaries for himself and other executives), in favor of establishing brand recognition. To this end, he poured much of Amazon.com's revenue into marketing and promotion. "There are always three or four brands that matter," Bezos says. "With the lead we have today, we should be the No. 1 player." The strategy worked.

Amazonian Lessons for Entrepreneurs

Lessons learned from Amazon go far beyond the principle of functional shiftability. They include *frugality* and *delayed gratification*.

After leaving the garage, company headquarters moved to a nondescript building near Ingram Books' warehouse. That allowed Amazon to keep the warehousing function at the wholesale level, instead of absorbing those costs internally, stocking only 400 or so of the most popular titles. Scores of intelligent, computer-literate workers lived in Seattle, with much lower costs than New York where Bezos previously lived.

As it grew, Amazon invested hundreds of millions of dollars in its own warehouses in states such as Nevada and Delaware, partly to handle the "reverse logistics" (returns) problems that plague catalogue and Internet retailers. Amazon gradually developed its own expertise, shifting the "pick, pack, ship" functions back to itself with an infrastructure of warehouses and skilled workers, achieving inventory turns over 16 compared to 3 at Barnes and Noble at that time, 11 at Costco and 7 at Wal-Mart. Turns are lower today, but Amazon usually receives cash from customers before invoices are due suppliers, shifting financing to its most efficient level in the channel.

Changing execution illustrates the *dynamic* nature of functional shiftability. Bezos shifted warehousing to a wholesaler as an early-stage entrepreneur, requiring little capital, instead of the failed strategy of Webvan with TMC. As sales increased, the experience curve and volume led to shifting wholesale functions again, integrating the warehousing function and bringing logistics knowledge and assets back to Amazon. *Functional shiftability is dynamic.*

Within warehouses, Amazon is extraordinarily frugal. In 2012, Amazon.com acquired Kiva Systems, Inc. for $775.0 million. Kiva develops robots that zip around warehouses, grabbing and moving crates full of products, helping Amazon (and Kiva customers) fulfill online orders quickly with fewer workers.

Amazon chose states for its physical presence with no sales tax, passing tax savings to consumers. That strategy is under attack decried as "unfair" from bricks-and-mortar retailers required to collect sales tax, a significant advantage for e-commerce, but those are details (very important, in this instance) successful entrepreneurs consider in a business plan.

Similar shifts occurred in the delivery function. Amazon relied on supply chain partners including the Postal Service for fulfillment because it was more efficient for Amazon to shift those functions to specialists in the last mile of logistics. Now, Amazon also uses its own service Fulfillment By Amazon (FBA) filling many of its own orders as well as other online marketers.

Frugality pays in many ways. It is observable studying Amazon, beginning with its start in a garage to its footprint today in downtown Seattle. Amazon occupies a significant part of the city, including newly-built corporate facilities. They are massive, functional, and efficient, but still nondescript in both interior and exterior, and *frugal*.

Successful entrepreneurs don't waste money on ostentatious corporate facilities. If you want an additional example of how frugality fosters success, visit Bentonville, Arkansas, and observe how Walmart corporate executives house themselves. You might mistake the corporate headquarters of the world's largest retailer for an old brick high school. Corporate frugality is a reason Walmart employees can afford very nice personal residences!

For investors joining in this conversation, here's a tip in managing your portfolio. *When a previously successful corporation builds a luxurious new headquarters building, consider selling the stock.* When a firm lives in better facilities than its customers, there's trouble ahead.

Delayed gratification is another lesson of Amazonian proportions, separating entrepreneurs building long-term fortunes from people choosing short-term salaries. Are you familiar with the marshmallow study at Stanford University, examining the effects of immediate gratification compared to delayed gratification?

The original marshmallow study was conducted in 1972 by psychologist Walter Mischel, who observed children in a laboratory setting. After learning their preferred treat, a marshmallow was offered, placed on the table by a chair. The children were told they could eat the marshmallow, but if they waited for fifteen minutes without giving in to temptation, they would be rewarded with a second marshmallow. Some covered their eyes with their hands or faced the opposite direction while others simply ate the marshmallow as soon as the researchers left the room. Of the 600 children who took part in the experiment, about a third deferred gratification long enough to get the second marshmallow.

The results forecast success as an entrepreneur. In a follow-up study of the same kids in 1988, the ones who delayed gratification were significantly more competent. A second follow-up study, in 1990, showed the ability to delay gratification also correlated with higher SAT scores. These results have been replicated many times by researchers with chocolate bars and other variations. The conclusion: *People who delay gratification are the winners in most areas of life.*

Delayed gratification explains why some entrepreneurs build long-term fortunes, in contrast to entrepreneurs spending TMC on corporate facilities, high salaries, and personal perks instead of patiently discovering what customers want and providing it better than competitors. Winning entrepreneurs move across the nation to Seattle and work in a garage on a desk made from a door and two saw horses instead of swank facilities!

If you examine firms such as Costco (Amazon's nearby neighbor), Berkshire Hathaway and annual lists of "America's Best CEOs," the best executives are usually in firms where top executives receive modest salaries, but a payoff in growth and value of the company's stock. That's true at Amazon. It didn't pay high salaries in its early days, and still doesn't. The highest-paid executive receives $175,000 and Bezos salary in 2010 as CEO of the world's largest e-tailer was $81,840. He has also foregone stock options for years. His net worth, however, was over $19 billion on a recent *Forbes'* list of world's richest people.

In the early days of Amazon, Bezos endured the pain of hard work and low profits. Sales rose rapidly, but profits were elusive. The company's investments in technology, physical plant and marketing were so extensive that in 2005, the company's balance sheet still reported negative net worth. For a decade, the firm reported a Profit and Loss statement with negative or minuscule profits in most years, choosing to invest in future value for the company.

Because Bezos avoided TMC and resisted criticism for its low profits, Bezos still owns about one out of every five Amazon shares. I read the report of a financial analyst who said Amazon's shares have "defied gravity" in recent years, jumping 55% in 2011, adding another $6.5 billion to Bezos' already considerable wealth. That's a pretty good argument that delayed gratification beats immediate. If Jeff Bezos had been one of the kids in the Stanford experiment, I'm pretty sure he would have chosen two marshmallows in the future instead of one immediately.

Customer-Centricity

The original mission of Amazon was to be "the earth's largest bookstore." Mission accomplished!

Now, Amazon has a new mission, to be the most customer-centric firm in the world. That's the passion, and for my money, it is. I gave an academic paper a few years ago trying to explain what customer-centricity means. Here's the definition I used there and in *Consumer Behavior*:

> *Customer-centricity is a strategic commitment to focus every resource of the firm on serving and delighting profitable customers. It means new or improved products and evolving marketing methods focused on core, and sometimes changing, market targets.*

Amazon seeks to be Earth's most customer-centric company for three primary customer sets: consumer customers, seller customers and developer customers. When you examine financial statements of Amazon, you observe Amazon sells a lot of technology services to other firms, with higher profit margins in B2B sectors than B2C.

What does it mean to be "customer-centric" organization? A summit of leading retailers, technology firms, and academic researchers, sponsored by Cisco Systems and Dartmouth's Tuck School of Business addressed that question. My summary of the characteristics identified at that conference include the following:

Shared vision and values. Customer-centricity is not CRM software; it is vision, a set of values, and a belief that the future of the firm is embedded in the minds of customers. If senior management is not *obsessive* about delighting customers, don't expect the phrase "customer-centricity" to do much for the organization.

Cross-functional integration. Customer-centricity breaks down "silos" in organizations, focusing everyone on core customers. Customer-centricity is achieved by marketing and sales, customer call centers, and CRM software linked closely to production, human resources, and finance. Providing all functional areas with easily understandable information on all other business functions is characteristic of customer-centricity, supported by information technology.

System-wide simultaneous training. Don't blame your employees for mistakes if you haven't trained them well. In small organizations, this concept involves face-to-face interaction of *all* members of the team from CEO to front-line sales people and truck drivers. In large organizations, it means total organizational meetings, on a global basis, probably delivered by satellite, social media, or other technologies.

Customer-based metrics. Customer-centricity requires changing from metrics of profitability, productivity and customer satisfaction based on product lines, geographic divisions, or business units to metrics based on core customers and segments. It means retailers changing from tracking "comp store" sales to "comp customer" sales.

From what I observe and read, Amazon measures up well on most of these key characteristics, guidelines for all entrepreneurs in customer-centric organizations. Customer-centric organizations provide customers with more value than competitors, including time, money and "hassle."

Jeff Bezos displays passion for Amazon to be the world's most customer-centric organization, highly-effective in delivering value to customers. He states simply, ""Our vision is to be the world's most consumer-centric company, where customers can come to find anything they want to buy online."

Bezos shocked people when he used personal funds to buy the *Washington Post.* When asked how to resurrect this dinosaur, Bezos stressed three things that worked well at Amazon, "Put the customer first. Invent. And be patient."

He has other ambitious goals, far beyond, but not unrelated to Amazon's core business. To further those goals, he and his wife (who also graduated from Princeton) donated $15 million to establish a center within the Princeton Neuroscience Institute, the Bezos Center for Neural Circuit Dynamics. Its mission is to study brain patterns to determine how people make decisions and recall memories.

"We can hope for advancements that lead to understanding deep behaviors, more effective learning methods for young children, and cures for neurological diseases," Bezos said in a statement.

I believe research in this field is important, but if someone could just invent an electronic device to download the content of Bezos' brain, he could have saved the $15 million. I haven't observed any other entrepreneur who understands how human brains work and consumers make decisions better than Bezos.

It's All About Passion

Amazon broadened the river of online buying more than any organization, literally selling everything from soup to nuts and bolts. Why is Amazon foremost among organizations competing online, even larger firms such as Walmart? You've seen my attempt to analyze reasons in the words you just read, but I believe one attribute dominates all others. I illustrate with an example told to me by Steven Tyler.

When writing the book *Brands That Rock*, the objective was to discover why some musical groups become rock and roll legends while other talented musicians never achieve much success. Even those who reach number one on *Billboard* are often one-hit wonders, never to record another hit song. The Rock and Roll Hall of Fame requires twenty-five years of success before considering musicians for induction and that was the criteria used in the book to identify artists such as the Rolling Stones, KISS, Elton John, Madonna and Aerosmith, analyzing principles applicable to business brands.

I was fortunate to interview Steven Tyler, leader of Aerosmith, after winning "Teen Album of the Year" award which I regarded quite an accomplishment for a bunch of sixty-something musicians. I asked Tyler how he appealed to such wide demographics as teenagers and aging baby-boomers. Tyler pointed to his wrist where I saw his bracelet with seven letters made of diamonds.

"P-A-S-S-I-O-N," was the word spelled on his bracelet.

"It's passion for what we do, and who we do it for," Tyler explained.

Passion is the premier reason for Bezos' success, I believe, and the characteristic that provides highly successful entrepreneurs direction driving them into new markets, new products, new technologies and decades of success. Passion explains how entrepreneurs build small firms into large fortunes.

"What should my passion be?" That's a question aspiring entrepreneurs occasionally ask, hoping I suppose, I will tell them a new trend, new product, or new marketing technique causing financial success. It doesn't work that way. The best answer is a quotation by Jeff Bezos,

"You don't choose your passion. Your passion chooses you."

12

Conversation TWELVE

Good Jobs (Steve, that is)

A world of young people owe much of their education to what has long been the symbol of great teaching—the Apple. Instead of school-age children giving favorite teachers an apple to bite, a master entrepreneur gave teachers, their students and the rest of the world an Apple with a byte missing--an icon for opening a new world of sensory experiences and infinite information on a real-time basis. Steve Jobs told the team creating the McIntosh computer to "make a dent in the universe." Most people conclude that's what the team did, and much more. Good Job, Steve!

Conducting a conversation about Steve Jobs is problematic. Should we talk about good Jobs or bad Jobs? There are lessons to be learned from both personas. Jobs was an enigma of good and bad, simple and complex, intuitive and intense, romantic and ruthless, rebel hippie and master capitalist. His character included all of those qualities, and many more.

Some have called Jobs the greatest inventor of the technology age, but calling him an inventor is a misnomer. Master marketer is a more appropriate accolade, because Jobs wrote the book on sales, branding and marketing for garage entrepreneurs aspiring to lofty levels.

While creating the world's most valuable company (for a while) and a fortune for his family, another number demonstrates the role of entrepreneurs in a nation's economy. A report funded by the company, concludes that Apple created or supported over 500,000 jobs in the U.S., including 13,000 jobs in engineering at its Cupertino headquarters, 27,350 retail workers and 275,000 employees at nine suppliers in cities around the U.S. Add in 65,000 lawyers, hairdressers, and yoga instructors owing much of their income to Apple's well-paid designers and engineers, and it should make the severest critic of capitalism pleased Jobs didn't stay in college and become an employee at IBM, Starbucks or the government.

You Don't Have to Have a College Degree to be a Successful Entrepreneur

Steve Jobs possessed one attribute in common with other contenders for title of technology entrepreneur of the century. He dropped out of college. So did several (but certainly not all) of his technology colleagues Michael Dell, Mark Zuckerberg and Bill Gates, as well as David Karp who tumbled out of high school to become a billionaire. They dropped out to start computer companies, but Jobs dropped out to find enlightenment on a spiritual journey with an Indian guru. That first step of the Jobs journey ended up in a computer company worth more than any of his collegial dropouts.

Jobs possessed another attribute held in common with entrepreneurs such as Dave Thomas and Jeff Bezos; like them, Jobs was adopted. He was the child of a Syrian graduate student and his girlfriend, but adopted and raised in California by a man who repossessed cars for a living.

What's the proper background to become a successful entrepreneur? Syrian? Latino? Princeton graduate (Bezos)? Eighth grade dropout earning a GED at sixty (Thomas)? African-American son of a sharecropper (Johnson)? Cookie-baking home economics major

(Cheryl Krueger)? Or son of influential professional parents (Gates)? I mention all of these backgrounds, simply to illustrate an important theme. In the United States and other nations, a person from any background can make it to the top as a garage entrepreneur. It's useful to recall that 70 percent on the Forbes list of billionaires started with nothing. Another study indicates 50 percent of all start-ups currently funded by Venture Capitalists are started by immigrant entrepreneurs.

It is fitting that Steve Job's conquest of classrooms, homes and offices began in the dormitory room while a student at Reed College in Portland, Oregon. After dropping out, he "dropped in" by auditing courses, surviving by sleeping on the floor in friends' rooms, returning Coke bottles for food money, and getting weekly free meals at the local Hare Krishna temple. Jobs later said, "If I had never dropped in on that single calligraphy course in college, the Mac would have never had multiple typefaces or proportionally spaced fonts."

Jobs met Steve Wozniak in 1971, and it was Wozniak, not Jobs, who in 1976 invented the Apple I computer. Jobs, Wozniak, and another friend, Ronald Wayne, founded Apple computer in the garage of Jobs' parents, and Jobs assumed leadership in sales. They received funding from semi-retired, Intel product-marketing manager and engineer Mike Markula.

A lesson to be learned from Jobs and friends is the person who invents stuff does not become as wealthy, famous, or instrumental to its success as the person who sells it. It also doesn't hurt to get acquainted with someone such as Markula with years of experience in an industry, providing a little capital and lots of knowledge in moving a product from creative idea to market-place success. Nothing valuable happens to a product until someone sells it. Jobs did that masterfully throughout his career, creating jobs and, transforming industries and sparking economies.

Grand Theft

Jobs was a master marketer, whether the products were invented by Apple or not. Xerox invented the "mouse," but failed to market it effectively until Jobs concluded customers were tired of word commands and built a better mouse-trap. But Jobs is not the only entrepreneur to borrow (steal?) ideas from others. "Legal theft" is what some have called Gates' purchase for $50,000 of the multi-billion dollar operating system called DOS; Gates built better word processing and spread sheet software than the inventor of VisiWord and VisiCalc, making a fortune and dominating the world's PCs for decades.

Jobs did the same with graphical user interface(GUI). He admitted, "We have always been shameless about stealing great ideas." There were plenty of lawsuits both against and by Apple in building Apple's "better mousetrap," and the firm employed good lawyers for both sides of patent protection. The job of a good lawyer is to keep you out of jail, not out of trouble, and sometimes that requires frequent trips to court.

Apple profited greatly by dominating smartphones, but didn't invent them. That honor goes to Canadian firm Research in Motion (RIM) whose pioneering Blackberry put the world in the hands of time-strapped business people. RIM made money initially, but nothing compared to Apple.

When Android introduced a product similar to Apple's iPhone in Jobs' view, Jobs threatened to "go to thermonuclear death" to defend Apple against what he considered infringement of iPod patents. When Android became a subsidiary of Google in 2005, Google became Jobs' personal nemesis in the world of patent protection. In the last days before his death, Jobs vowed, "I will spend my last dying breath... and every penny of Apple's $40 billion in the bank to right this wrong," pursuing a lawsuit against Google for allegedly stealing the iPhone's operating system.

One of the great ironies of technology history is the war Jobs, a kleptomaniac of great ideas, fought to protect Apple patents. But it is a war and a warning from which all entrepreneurs can learn valuable lessons.

Patents, copyrights and trademark registration are important, and it is essential to have good legal advice on each of these by lawyers who are experts in this special area. Small firms find it difficult if not impossible, however, to protect their patents, because corporate giants with bulging balance sheets outspend and outlast little firms. Large, established firms may also simply "design around" the patents of smaller firms, knowing small firms usually don't have the bags of money needed to fight infringement by giants.

Even when patents and trademarks are properly registered, the government doesn't protect them, despite laws such as the Lanham Act under which trademark protection can be pursued. Protecting infringers is not the duty of government; it's the responsibility of the owner against alleged offenders. Entrepreneurs must spend money, usually lots of it, if they expect to keep other firms from infringing trademarks and patents.

The important lesson for emerging entrepreneurs is this: Don't expect patents and trademarks to protect your product or brand name. Continual product improvement and delighting customers is your only real protection, and that's also expensive, requiring innovation and continual change. Bill Gates reportedly said, "Intellectual property has the shelf life of a banana."

Should Investors Own Reins or Ride Horses?

Riding the thoroughbred and work horses of technology stocks such as Apple, Amazon, Microsoft and Google may not offer as high yields for investors as owning the reins and bits of those massive mounts. If you identify winning "horses" before leaving the starting gate, you might capture big winnings, but once Wall Street "discovers" Apple, Amazon, Walmart, and similar stocks, they become major holdings in the portfolios of mega mutual funds. Then it becomes difficult to get thrilling payoffs even when favored horses continue to win races. Everybody knows the chosen horses in the Kentucky Derby and Belmont, and odds on the best horses don't provide spectacular payoffs even when they win. Far fewer people pay much attention to the firms, however, that make the reins and bits required for horses to win.

For investors, studying component manufacturers and owners of spectrum can bring greater rewards than investing in Apple, AT&T, Verizon or Vodaphone. I stumbled across a small firm in upstate New York that made relays for cell phone towers. Relays are a small portion of cell phone tower cost and minuscule in the entire cellular phone industry, but this company manufactured the best relays available in the low-cost environment of an obscure, rural town.

I met some of the sales people in the company and discovered the firm had good values—the kind Collins and Porous talk about in Built to Last. The company invested in technology, but also invested heavily in personnel training. After examining its public reports, I could tell its financial management was conservative, with little debt and aggressive expense control. The company was unknown to Wall Street stock gurus, the best kind of stock to own. Cell phone sales soared and so did my investment in this tiny, entrepreneurial firm, much more than if I had invested in the communication giants or even Apple.

There's one more thing you might want to consider as an entrepreneur or investor. When you hang up your spurs and head south where you can wear shorts all winter, you'll be glad you invested in reins instead of horses. The reason is the "valuation" your company will be given by potential acquirers.

In an exit strategy, entrepreneurs are typically valued as a multiple of EBITDA (Earnings before Interest, Taxes, Depreciation and Amortization). If your firm is an ordinary, well-managed firm, you'll probably receive a multiple about 3-7 times EBITDA, perhaps a little higher with rapid growth. Your valuation will also be influenced by debt and type of assets in your firm. If your exit strategy involves an IPO (Initial Public Offering), you'll probably receive about 10-15 times Earnings Per Share (EPS), after the investment bankers and their accountants get through adjusting for personal perks that may be hidden in your expenses, excess owner compensation and their costs. You'll get a higher Price/Earnings ratio (P/E) if you have good prospects for future growth.

But, here's the wild card, a factor that could command far more than a normal valuation for your firm. If you market an essential component needed by the big horses in your industry, you may be treated as a "strategic acquisition" by firms with a lot of cash or high-value stock they are willing to pay for your firm. They are probably not buying your company to add to their own revenues or profits because your firm would be a minor contribution to those numbers. If you make or market a key component, software or service critically important to the acquiring firm and not readily available elsewhere, all bets are off in using comparable ratios or traditional rules. That's why eBay paid $1.5 billion when it acquired PayPal and Google paid $12.5 billion for Motorola Mobility and its 14,600 granted patents and 6,700 pending patent applications to strengthen Google's earlier acquisition of Android (and its founder, Andy Rubin) for "an undisclosed sum." A pretty large sum, I am guessing!

The bottom line is this. If you are an entrepreneur or investor in entrepreneurs, search for key components, circuit boards, software, specialized services or other products critically important to the big horses not readily available from other suppliers. And be sure to ask more than the $50,000 the inventors of DOS received from Bill Gates! The big money is in "reins and bits," not horses.

Pushing People to Perfection

Jobs was not enough of a technician to invent break-through products himself. He didn't even know how to write computer code, a continual subject for derision of Jobs by Bill Gates. Studying Jobs' path to success reveals this important secret: If you can't produce technology yourself, know how to push other people to perform that task to perfection.

The methods Jobs used to push people are not likely to be cited as a paragon of virtue in human relations textbooks. In the unofficial "official biography," Steve Jobs (Simon & Shuster, 2011), author Walter Issacson describes Jobs as "charming, loathsome, lovable, obsessive, and maddening." Employees feared him at the same time they loved him with the kind of passion that causes soldiers to die in battle for their general, not unlike what troops did for General George Patton in World War II. Former employees of Apple report incidents of rudeness, intolerance, injustice and intemperance. Despite the litany of horror stories about Jobs, some of those same employees admit Jobs "got them to do things they never thought possible." Jobs gave employees seemingly impossible tasks to accomplish, but he inspired them with the belief, "You can do this." And somehow, they did.

What should aspiring entrepreneurs learn from the personality and leadership style of Jobs? I never met Steve Jobs, unlike most of the other entrepreneurs in our conversations. With only a few exceptions, I know personally many of the people described in this book or have friends who worked for them and told me about their strengths and weaknesses. With Jobs, I have to rely on what I've read. So, I don't know, would he have been less successful without his intimidating, vexing leadership style, or would his achievements and their longevity have been even greater if he had the heart of a servant leader? I will leave the answer for you to ponder.

A Knight of Special Privilege

From the inception of Apple when Jobs met Wozniak, inventor of the Mac, until his death Jobs relied on other people to invent products solving customer problems so well, customers were willing to switch to Apple. One of those persons was Jonathan "Jony" Ive, Apple's chief designer, awarded knighthood in the United Kingdom as a Knight Commander of the British Empire.

Ive had a special relationship with Jobs and a lot of privileges within Apple, giving him rare instant access to Jobs and making him practically untouchable to anyone else. In addition to meals with Jobs and immediate communication anytime of the day or night, Ive has a private design studio on the ground floor of Apple's campus shielded by tinted windows and a heavy, locked door. Not even high-level Apple employees are allowed into Ive's office.

When it comes to design, Ive is not only the first word, but the last. Maybe that's the genius of Jobs—recognizing the genius in others, and taking extraordinary measures to insure they continue contributing to Apple's design dominance. It's an important lesson to learn for all entrepreneurs with the need to recruit and keep the best talent in their organization. I don't believe it is necessary to go as far as Jobs did in his eccentric treatment of people, but when you find employees with talent essential to the success of your firm, make sure they know how much you appreciate and value their continued contributions.

In our conversation about Steve Jobs, I've chosen not to spend time on the company or products Jobs produced. You can read and probably already have read voluminous and detailed descriptions in books, magazines and newspapers about the person and the company he created. His accomplishments in product development are probably in your hands before, after and perhaps while you are reading this book. Instead, I focus on lessons learned to build better businesses. I'll finish this conversation with a valuable theory explaining how Jobs built the most valuable corporation in the world.

He didn't invent this process either, because it is a combination of ideas from scholars and practitioners, but Apple exemplifies the concept I hope you understand making your firm a lasting success. It is central to the design and introduction of new products by any firm, whether start-up entrepreneur or mature corporate giant.

Design Strategy

If you want long-term profits, don't start with an innovative product; start with design strategy. It is a secret entrepreneurs are just beginning to learn, accounting for the difference between barely surviving in the introduction of new products and market-dominating, knock-your-socks-off success. Jobs didn't invent design strategy any more than he did the Mac or iPhone, but perfected its implementation, worthy of emulation by entrepreneurs desiring to grow small firms into large fortunes.

Jobs didn't study design, but designers study Jobs. For Jobs, mastery of design strategy appears innate rather than erudite, based partly on his love-hate relationship with Microsoft. Jobs expressed his disdain saying, "The only problem with Microsoft is they just have no taste."

Design strategy is much more than aesthetics. It is a discipline determining what to make and do, why do it and how to innovate considering all elements of the market environment and organizational realities, both immediately and over the long term. The process focuses on the interplay between design and business strategy, a systematic approach integrating holistic-thinking, research methods, and strategic planning. Social or psychological research methods are sometimes used to ground the results and reduce risks. It's a relatively new concept useful in all organizations, including non-profits, exhibited in such activities as Pelatonia a highly-successful cycling event to fund cancer research, sponsored by the Wexner Medical Center.

Design strategy integrates introduction with projected acceptance of new products over time. Apple is the master example of this approach, laying out the strategy for the iPod and iTunes ecosystem slowly over time, rather than launching all its products rapidly.

There are many other examples. Toyota designed the hybrid Prius to resemble the conservative Echo instead of making the Prius look high-tech and adventuresome. Evolution in the design of products is usually more accepted by customers than revolution, but it is necessary to know where you want the brand and product to end as well as when and how you want to evolve it. Design strategy helps avoid abrupt change, usually a fatal flaw in product policies and branding strategies, as JCPenney discovered when it changed rapidly to "Apple style" stores, alienating traditional customers faster than it attracted a new customer base.

Too Much Change in design is as dangerous as Too Much Capital! Trying to do things too fast is the reason an IT firm in Chicago with innovative ideas for new software and infrastructure soon became bankrupt. The well-funded start-up fund, backed by drooling VCs, blew through $718 million in 18 months with nothing left to show for the effort except the skeleton of an unfinished building still standing on the west side of the Loop in Chicago, and a myriad of brilliant, but now unemployed workers. Technology does not create fortunes, nor does ample investment capital. Customers do, based on the realities of consumer decision-making we talked about in Conversation 9.

Design strategy integrates business strategy with economic realities of manufacturing, distribution and brand strategy based on how buyers consume products. These elements are shown below, but are not linear as the diagram implies. Each element of the strategy affects and is affected by other elements. Design strategy is at the center, revised by production and marketing realities. Marketing includes all the "Four Ps"-- Product, Place (distribution), Price, and Promotion. The entire process is embedded in overall corporate or business strategy. Brand strategy communicates what the business or product does. Design strategy is continuously updated, modified by customer expectations and experiences.

Business Strategy > Brand Strategy > Design Strategy > Marketing Strategy > Production Strategy > Implement Plan

Plan these key elements if you want to be as successful as Steve Jobs. When he started, Steve Jobs changed an industry by pioneering Graphical User Interface (GUI).   By the time Jobs' life ended, he was again changing the nature of the business of computers and communications devices with Natural User Interface (NUI) with such design features as "Siri." When he commenced the development of a new product, he demonstrated a clear picture of where he wanted to end and how each product in the Apple portfolio would embed into the overall Apple Design Strategy. He was an "overnight wonder," but it took him thirty years to become one.

The genius of Jobs and the success of Apple are due not just to elegance and simplicity of design strategy. The genius of Jobs is expressed also in the integration of economic reality, manufacturing technology, and system compatibility solving problems for potential customers.

For example, the success of I-suite products is based partly upon the breadth and usefulness of "apps" quickly available for iPhones and other Apple products. How can Apple afford to offer 500,000 (more by the time you read this) different apps? The answer is simple. Apple designed an economic system—including ease of payments--to incentivize thousands of people ranging from students in their dorm rooms and college classes to design engineers in corporate laboratories to write a myriad of apps for every possible situation from flashlights and games to weather information, sports and personal performance monitoring. Apple shifted app development and other functions to their most efficient level in the demand chain.

Manufacturing strategy is also shifted to its most efficient level in the supply chain. To keep iPhones economically feasible for mass acceptance, Apple manufactures products in places such as China, achieving low costs, but also precision production and assembly. Apple has relatively few production employees of its own, but one of its contractors in China has one million very efficient employees.

When something does go wrong, Apple has its own resources close to the consumer and readily accessible. They are in hundreds of Apple stores, usually the coolest retailer in the mall, usually replacing rather than repairing a faulty device. When my relatively new iPhone went on the blink, I drove to a nearby mall, handing it to a well-trained Apple employee. He examined it a few moments, and asked me if I had everything backed up on my laptop. Fortunately, I did. He handed me a new phone, showed me how to download everything, and I walked out of the store delighted, at no charge. I had gone from loving my iPhone, to hating it, to loving it again, all within a couple hours. That's the kind of immediacy and customer-delight that Michael Dell and Jeff Bezos can't deliver. It's part of the strategy engineered by the Apple team designing a system that plans all elements from knowing how the minds of consumers work to delivering retail, manufacturing, logistics and economics as an integrated system focused on meeting customer needs and solving their problems.

Apple's master design strategy insures whether driving a car, "docking" your iPhone to play music or plotting a stock market chart on your iPad, everything works together perfectly, at least most of the time. When something doesn't work, a trip to the nearest Apple store gives access to "genius" help fixing the problem expertly, usually for free. How can you argue with a design strategy such as that? Especially, when accomplished with lofty, rapidly-growing profits.

There is not time in our conversations to describe intricate details of implementing design strategy in your firm; but I recommend you study how this process is changing product development and introduction. If it's a new topic to you, you may want to search some of the papers published by academics on the topic and web sites of organizations such as Ideo offering services in this area.

Focus on a Few

Design Strategy focuses a firm's resources on a few winners

rather than a lot of losers. When Steve Jobs returned to Apple after it acquired Next, he quickly put Apple's product offerings on a diet, choosing product depth over breadth. The result was more innovation with a smaller number of products, a result worth considering in any firm. There's more money to be made with quality than quantity.

Shortly after returning to Apple, Jobs called a meeting and asked employees what was wrong with Apple. No one was able to answer correctly, so he provided the answer: "It's the products. The products suck!"

He immediately began simplifying Apple's product strategy. Apple released one iPhone model each year, with a few variations. In contrast, competitors flood the market in what might be called "throw a lot on the wall and see what sticks." When Apple had three basic iPhones (3GS, 4, and 4S), LG had 27 different models (with Android and Microsoft Phone handsets), Motorola Mobility had 15, while Samsung and HTC had 53 and 50, respectively. Among those top four competitors, that's 145 different models compared to Apple's 3. Yet Apple had a market share of 44.9%. It's more profitable to sell a few really good products well than offering lots of products, hoping some will find market acceptance.

With a focused Design Strategy, Research and Design (R&D) costs go down as a percent of sales. Look at the chart below and compare the percentage spent by Apple on R&D with competitors. Productivity is as an important in developing products as manufacturing them.

Company	R&D (% of Revenue)	R&D ($)
Apple	1.6%	$758 million
Google	12.2%	$1.3 billion
Microsoft	11.3%	$2.4 billion
Motorola	11.1%	$384 million

Source: SEC filings, 2012, compiled by Motley Food analyst Evan Niu.

"I'm from the Government, and I'm here to help you."

When TMC is sponsored by government organizations, demise is usually more predictable and rapid than garage entrepreneurs built from private capital. A highly-visible example of how capital provided by government often ends in failure is Solyndra LLC, a solar panel producer that played a starring role in President Obama's green-jobs initiative. The U.S. Energy Department provided a $535 million loan and incentives for private investors to invest another billion to get the firm going fast. Too fast, it turned out.

Someone forgot to check the design strategy of Solyndra's product which used long and thin tubes covered in chemicals to absorb the sun's rays. That seemed like a good idea compared to existing manufacturers using conventional flat panels relying on an expensive material called polysilicon.

People designing products at Solyndra or Energy Department officials supplying half a billion in capital miscalculated in at least two ways. First, manufacturing of the new product was complicated, expensive and unreliable, not a favorable competitive position for a new entrant to the market. The more serious mistake was failing to understand what happens to costs and prices of innovations over time.

Competition forces firms to slide down the "experience curve," a well-researched process in which new products introduced at high prices decline in cost (and usually price) in predictable patterns over time. That's what happened with polysilicon, giving Chinese and other manufacturers a huge cost advantage over Solyndra. The result was bankruptcy for Solyndra, criminal charges against some if its executives, a major embarrassment for President Obama and a credible challenge to the idea government officials know enough about entrepreneurship to provide capital for start-ups.

Just because a technology is innovative doesn't mean the product will be better, cheaper or accepted by customers. If you or the technicians you employ projecting future input costs don't understand and correctly forecast the impact of the experience curve, your strategy is likely to be wrong. Very wrong, at Solyndra. If Design Strategy had been employed by Solyndra, these problems could have been eliminated and half a billion dollars diverted to some better purpose with lasting jobs, financial success, and massive savings to tax payers funding the project.

Government officials may correctly understand that entrepreneurs are key to creating new jobs for the nation, states or other jurisdictions. When they try to jump-start that process by deciding which entrepreneurs should be given tax dollars to fund new ventures, their decisions are often incorrect because of inexperience in entrepreneurial businesses (or perhaps lobbyist influence). The market place understands the entrepreneurial process better than bureaucrats.

Entrepreneurs may jump at the opportunity to obtain capital the market is reluctant to supply. That's understandable, I suppose, but when someone says, "I'm from the government; I'm here to help you," my advice is caution—and be prepared to say, "No, thank you."

Good Jobs? Or Bad Jobs?

Assessing the legacy of Jobs is not for ordinary observers like me. I'll leave that issue for you and perhaps Divine Judgment. Jobs was his own person, that's for sure, and there is much to be learned from what he achieved, as I hope you've concluded from this conversation.

Steve Jobs once commented, "Your time is limited, so don't waste it living someone else's life." But we can learn from his.

I hope you found food for thought in our conversation about Steve Jobs. If not, maybe you will find tastier fare in our next conversation.

13

Conversation THIRTEEN

Food For Thought

Perhaps our last conversation gave you food for thought about your business, especially Design Strategy, but if you concluded Design Strategy applies only to technology firms such as Apple, think again. Design Strategy is important to all types of entrepreneurs, even firms as traditional as grocery stores and restaurants.

Before we discuss what you learn from entrepreneurial restaurants, let me demonstrate how to build customer loyalty through design strategy revealed in a family-owned grocery store that keeps evolving, year after year.

Giant Eagle: From Apples to Oranges

Can a mass-market grocery store compete against niche players such as Whole Foods? Giant Eagle's answer is Market District, mammoth stores ranging from Hispanic produce and gelato to a place to park kids while parents sip wine by the glass. If you like food-on-the-go, you'll find a food court featuring any hot or cold item your family might like, with enough ambiance to enjoy it in the store, sometimes with live music.

Consumers in cities served by Wegmans ("best chain in the country, maybe the world"), Stew Leonard, Ukrops, Buehler's or other exceptional regional chains find similar attractions, but nothing exceeding Market District's array of products and services, including free Wi-Fi, churrasco-style foods, a kosher deli, Rosti bar, candy shop, Panini station, cheese cave and other options not offered in standard stores, including an onsite nutritionist in the pharmacy department in 127,000 square feet tailored to needs of ethnic and income segments, offering health care, banking and a wide array of floral, catering, and bakery services.

I've studied loyalty programs for two decades, but few are as well-designed or widely imitated as Giant Eagle's "Advantage Card," integrating Get Go gas with Giant Eagle grocery stores. Giant Eagle's Fuelperks® program allows customers to earn 10 cents off each gallon of gas (more in select markets and promotions or when buying gift cards) with fifty dollars of grocery purchases, moderating price-comparison shopping, a sensible objective with competitors as formidable as Aldi and Walmart. The loyalty card offers discounts and special offers, permitting customers to track savings on receipts, mobile apps and a website as well-designed as any I've seen this side of Amazon. Design Strategy is the strategic advantage for a firm selling everything from apples and oranges to gasoline, an Eagle soaring above predators such as Walmart, Aldi, Kroger and Whole Foods.

Would you like to know the margins, profits and other financials related to Giant Eagle? Sorry, like Wegman's, Meijer and other family-owned firms, that's private, but whether you are selling high-tech Apples or oranges in a bricks-and-mortar retailer, Design Strategy integrates planning needed by any enterprise wanting to grow small firms into a family fortune. Even with products as conventional as groceries and gasoline, I enjoy seeing an Eagle soar.

A Lethal Disease

The focus of our discussion about food for thought, however, is restaurants, but I must warn you. The desire to own a restaurant is a contagious disease, often lethal, plaguing even successful entrepreneurs in one field, wanting to branch into another. The disease is spread by patrons eager to tell friends, "I own part of that restaurant."

Wanting to "own a restaurant" can be profitable, but often is not. "Restaurantitis" is my term for the ailment, and I write from my own experiences as a shareholder of Wendy's, Cheryl's, and Max & Erma's. I am, I confess to you, a recovering restaurant entrepreneur. I survived, and you can too by mastering principles of prosperity for successful food entrepreneurs. If you are planning to open a restaurant, all you need do is be better than the 616,000 U.S. restaurants already in existence.

Restaurants: Profits and Pitfalls

To begin a discussion on how to start, operate or invest in a restaurant you should know two important facts.

First, the bad news. Most restaurants fail in three to four years. Many never make it past the first year. If you make it past the first year, you likely will work long hours and pay yourself little salary the first year, and perhaps many more years. The only way you will see much of your family is putting them to work in the restaurant, as Francesco Scali did in Conversation 2.

Second, the good news. It is possible to make money in the restaurant business with patience, reasonable expectations and willingness to work very, very hard and very long hours, thoroughly testing and modifying your concept in the laboratory of consumer response. That's the recipe for success as a restaurant entrepreneur. To be frank, that is the recipe for all successful entrepreneurs.

Secrets of Successful Restaurants

"I love to cook," is a frequent statement by people starting restaurants, as you remember from our conversation about the boyhood desire of Dave Thomas, starting Wendy's. Another kid who loved to cook was Steve Ellis, in the mountains of Colorado. With little capital, he converted an ice-cream shop near the University of Denver, focusing on details so passionately his friends called him a "control freak." Mastering details is essential for any entrepreneur, and vital in profitable restaurants.

Another secret of success is *limiting the menu to core products.* Too many restaurants place too many items on the menu, confusing consumers, driving up costs, and failing to have "signature" items causing customers to return again and again. When you start a restaurant, open with only a very few menu items---what you do best. Then perfect their taste, presentation and service. There's time to expand the menu and space later with profits from patrons instead of capital from investors. With eleven items on the original McDonald's menu, Ray Kroc provided fast service and maximum velocity in a confined (and therefore less costly) space, obliterating existing competitors.

Steve Ellis achieved menu precision with tortillas prepared by people who know good tortillas when they taste them. The restaurant doesn't serve coffee or desserts. That would detract from its core offering, reliably-good food in a carefully-controlled, cost-efficient environment. Ellis is also hypersensitive to perfecting visual and tactile surroundings. Everything is designed, measured and regulated from the temperature in a room to the (lack of) cushiness in a chair, a recipe for fast growth in over 1,150 stores and more than $2 billion in revenues. Sticking to basics is also the key to success at his chief rival for fast growth, Five Guys Burgers and Fries.

In case you didn't recognize the name of Steve Ellis, you probably realize by now that he started Chipotle. The "secret" recipe in his system is controlling everything to perfection, including costs. An additional advantage is the ethnicity of his most available and least expensive workforce adds an aura of authenticity to the image of Chipotle's as a Mexican restaurant.

Your chances of profitability and family fortune are enhanced by a design strategy integrating menu with an operational system delivering it. Chipotle is a blueprint for design efficiency. So was McDonald's original menu. At Max & Erma's, we had a rule that no new item could be added to the menu unless one of the least-bought items was removed. *Failure to "keep it simple" is a death sentence for restaurant entrepreneurs.*

You see these same principles in a recent start-up called Piada, reflecting entrepreneurial skills of the Doody brothers, who grew up working in their mother's upscale restaurant, Lindey's, a Columbus favorite for decades. Building on their restaurant knowledge, the Doody brothers founded Bravo in 1992, building it into a chain of 56 restaurants before selling a majority of the equity. Rick Doody remained Chairman of the Board of Bravo-Brio (BBRG) which went public in 2010.

After the sale, Chris Doody wanted more time with his wife and sons. He traveled throughout Italy, where he discovered the "PIADA" or "PIADINA" and formed THE PIADA GROUP, a concept with Chipotle-type simplicity, but based on Italian street food, and lots of growth potential. The recipe for success in restaurants is pretty basic, with ingredients worth understanding by entrepreneurs in any business.

Low capital, low labor cost, lower food costs (typically true for Italian and Mexican themes), and maximum opportunity for customers to input their own preferences quickly, focused on specific "signature" items. For investors, it's a delicious recipe for success. If you bought the IPO stock of Chipotle (CMG) in 2006, by the beginning of 2012 you saw your investment appreciate almost 500% as the company grew earnings per share (EPS) from $1.52 to $6.42 on over $2 billion of sales.

Few (if any) fortunes are created in the high-end segment of the restaurant business. People operating complex restaurants well may make a comfortable living as owner-chef-host, but they shouldn't expect to turn their efforts into a fortune. There's little profit because of intensive service, high capital costs, and scarcity of labor willing to work long, strenuous hours at low wages in the "white table cloth" segment of the restaurant business. Yet, plenty of investment dollars are readily available from people wanting to own a piece of an image, and perhaps the assurance of a preferred table. *Sell to the class, and you live in the mass.* Sell to the mass (or invest in firms that do), e.g. Chipotle, McDonald's or White Castle, and you have a much better chance of living in whichever class you choose.

The Birth of Fast Food

**Here are a few questions.
Do you know the answers?**

Which restaurant chain invented fast food?

What was the first chain to sell a billion hamburgers?

Which fast food chain has a menu certified by a university-based chemist as one in which a normal, healthy child could eat nothing but its sandwiches and fully develop his or her physical and mental facilities?

What national fast food chain has the broadest package of employee benefits and the longest longevity and loyalty of its employees?

What national restaurant chain refuses to franchise any of its units, retaining complete ownership and control of its units?

What national restaurant chain is open 24/7 every day of the year except Christmas?

What national restaurant chain has been entirely owned by its founding family for almost a century?

The correct answer to each question is the same. Some find the answer surprising when they learn it is White Castle.

The first White Castle was opened in Wichita, Kansas in 1921 on $700 of borrowed capital. The money was paid back in 90 days because of the philosophy of the man who built White Castle, "Billy" Ingram, who believed "he who owes no money cannot go broke." Even today, the firm has almost no long-term capital debt. Many say White Castle invented "limited-menu, fast-food service" and developed and perfected methods that have become standard in the industry.

Long before branding and "design strategy" became part of the entrepreneurial lexicon, the name was selected because "White" signifies purity and cleanliness and "Castle" represents strength, permanence and stability, originally inspired by a famous old water tower in Chicago. The style has been modified from time to time over the years, but the castellated walls and central tower still appear on White Castle stores. The guiding rule of operating since the earliest days has been infinite attention to the smallest detail.

From the beginning, White Castle designed and built its own buildings and most of its fixtures. In 1928, one of White Castle's associates invented a modular all-metal building and obtained a patent on it, the first successful use of porcelain enamel as an architectural material. Initially, White Castle used outside suppliers to manufacture the steel buildings, but this function shifted to the company when it acquired land and buildings in Columbus, Ohio, and established Porcelain Steel Buildings Company to manufacture its own buildings and fixtures, moving headquarters in 1934 from Wichita to Columbus.

In the early days, White Castle operators wore a cloth cap that unfortunately came in two sizes, too large or too small. Ingram sought a better solution and developed a sanitary, disposable, adjustable cap of paper and obtained a patent on it. It took four years to develop a machine to make the caps, but during those years, the company developed a process that could make a year's supply of White Castle caps in just two weeks. It should not be surprising that the experience and expertise White Castle developed in manufacturing its own products provided opportunities to sell them to other organizations, another ingredient in growing small firms into large fortunes.

If the United States is ever invaded by a foreign army, I plan on heading for the nearest White Castle. Its all-steel construction is the nearest place I know to being a fortress, a feature serving the company well as a stalwart of safety in sometimes-troubled neighborhoods. White Castle is safer from armed robbers than most banking offices!

White Castle's method of cooking is also unique. While others debate the merits of broiling, frying, or grilling, White Castle uses steaming. Its square hamburger patty uses the entire cooking surface, avoiding hot spots and wasted energy inherent with round patties on a rectangular grill. White Castle also uses a unique combination of dehydrated onions and water and hamburger patties with holes enabling it to cook the entire sandwich and warm the bun without turning over the patty. Its unique process produces an easier-to-eat, moist sandwich, especially appealing to children and people with less than perfect teeth. The high moisture content of the finished, fully-cooked sandwich is compatible with both modern freezing techniques and microwave reconstitution, important when the company later extended to home meal replacement in supermarkets.

Are you beginning to understand why most entrepreneurs in the restaurant business fail or have only limited success, while ones dedicated to continual improvement, details and functional shiftability build fortunes for their families? The chopped beef used in the White Castle hamburger sandwich is all-beef from selected cuts of American-grown beef, in specific proportions, shaped and compressed into squares with five evenly spaced holes on White Castle patented equipment to cook quickly and uniformly.

Children have always liked White Castle hamburgers. So, in 1930, the company retained the head of the physiological chemistry department at a major university to carry out studies of the food value of the sandwich. As a result, the food scientist signed a report that a normal, healthy child could eat nothing but White Castle sandwiches and water and fully develop all physical and mental faculties if two things were done: (1) add a small percentage of calcium to the flour used in White Castle buns to aid development of bone structure, and (2) maintain the proportions of meat and bun to give a balance of proteins, carbohydrates and fats. That's why the buns are built the way they are today. Today, of course, nutritionists recommend lots of fruits and vegetables and other nutrients, but White Castle was ahead of its time in attention to food nutrition issues.

You Win With People

Billy Ingram, founder of White Castle, said, "We have no right to expect loyalty except from those to whom we are loyal." Consequently, White Castle impresses on supervisors that a person can be strong without being brutal, can be firm without being mean, can exercise authority without being arrogant, can instruct, teach and guide without being unkind. Many of the company's executives started behind the counter. Promotion to supervisory and management positions is routinely internal. The family tradition continues with CEO Lisa Ingram, great-granddaughter of founder Billy Ingram.

Years before lawmakers thought of old-age benefits and retirement security, White Castle was practicing the principle as a natural part of the spirit of working together. In 1924, the firm installed a cash bonus plan for employees based on sales, shared by all employees on the basis of length of service, regardless of position or salary. That was unique in 1924 and still, today, among many companies. In 1927, the firm instituted a plan of company-paid group life insurance and sick benefits. In 1943, a pension trust was set up and hospitalization and major medical insurance provided. In 1949, a profit-sharing fund was started in addition to other benefits, allowing young employees who stay with firm throughout the career to establish large sums available for their retirement. Some entrepreneurs have such plans today because they are required. The Ingram family established these benefits because they believed it was the right thing to do. As a result, the company has what observers believe the longest longevity and greatest loyalty of any work force in the restaurant industry.

I hope you also conclude from our discussion of White Castle, the importance of innovations achieving chain-wide standardized methods. What Henry Ford did for car manufacturing, Ingram did for hamburgers. White Castle influenced, and some would say created, the hamburger industry as profoundly as Steve Jobs did the smart phone industry.

Entrepreneurs should, in my opinion, share with their community some of the gains from entrepreneurial success, and usually they do. White Castle pioneered that idea with the Ingram-White Castle Foundation, based on principles of treating people fairly, investing in the future of others, and sharing success with the community. Through the years, the Foundation has awarded millions of dollars in grants to support programs serving disadvantaged students and helping them achieve academic success, as well as scholarship support for employees and their dependents.

White Castle also pioneered its share of marketing innovations. One of those was the movie *Harold and Kumar Go to White Castle*, costing the company almost nothing except supplying a lot of hamburgers for the cast. It tells the story of a strange night for Harold and his roommate, Kumar, when they respond to their cravings and set out from New York, going across New Jersey to get White Castle hamburgers. I knew the company had a public relations *coup* when I saw Harold and Kumar-White Castle shirts sold by vendors on the streets of New York City. I still have the T-shirt I purchased in NYC!

Every year on Valentine's Day, White Castle offers to reserve a candlelit table for two, complete with a server and free desert. So far, I've never found anyone to accompany me for Valentine's dinner at White Castle, so I don't really know how well that works. Maybe someday, I'll get a date for a "hot and steamy" night at White Castle!

Starbucks: Take Care of Your Employees and They Will Take Care of You.

Taking good care of employees is also a key strategy of another spectacular star of the food industry, Starbucks. Formed by Howard Schulz in Seattle in 1971, the company operates 6,705 company-operated stores and 4,082 licensed stores in the United States; and 2,326 company-operated stores and 3,890 licensed stores spanning the globe.

If you haven't read *How Starbucks Saved My Life: A Son of Privilege Learns to Live Like Everyone Else,* by Michael Gates, I recommend it. The book yields insights into Starbucks and the principle for success in any industry: *Take care of your employees and they will take care of you.*

Bi-Polar Pricing

At the opposite end of price polarity from White Castle's original five-cent hamburgers is a relatively new food chain called Jeni's Splendid Ice Creams. I craved ice cream one day and spotted my favorite flavor in Giant Eagle's store brand, selling for $2.49 a pint. While reaching for it, I noticed next to it were pints of Jeni's Splendid Ice Creams, in flavors that caught my attention. When I saw the price, I fumbled for my glasses to be sure I was seeing the amount correctly-- $9.99 per pint. And judging from the quantities displayed, she must be selling a lot of them. I could only imagine what a full gallon would cost, and decided I needed to know more about the market segmentation strategy of an entrepreneur persuading consumers they needed these premium-priced pints.

When I met Jeni Britton Bauer, I knew in a moment she represents a different paradigm for food entrepreneurs. She is passionate about ice cream, explaining on her website her love affair with the delectable delight, *"We create ice creams we fall madly in love with, that we want to bathe in, that make us see million-year-old stars. We devour it out of Mason jars, coffee mugs—whatever we can get our hands on. Handmade American ice cream = Bliss with a big B. Every single thing we put in our ice cream is legit. Generic chemist-built ice cream bases and powdered astronaut-friendly gelato mixes? No, ma'am. We build every recipe from the ground up with luscious, Snowville milk and cream from cows that eat grass. With that exquisite base, we explore pure flavor in whatever direction moves us at any moment, every day, all year."*

When Jeni Britton Bauer and her team say they explore pure flavor in whatever direction moves them, she means places a galaxy away from normal ice cream. You can read her signature flavors (and order them for $12 a pint!) on Jeni's web site, and here are some you find: Bangkok Peanut, Brambleberry Crisp, Brown Butter Almond Brittle, Cherry Lambic Sorbet, Goat Cheese with Cognac Figs, Pistachio & Honey, Queen City Cayenne, The Buckeye State, The Milkiest Chocolate in the World, Ugandan Vanilla Bean, Whiskey & Pecans, and Wildberry Lavender. She saves the really adventuresome flavors for special times of the year.

Jeni Britton Bauer is not your average garage entrepreneur, or maybe she is, because she started with little capital and a big dream. It wasn't a garage that served as the maternity ward of her business; it was a funky, quirky place populated by a lot of start-up entrepreneurs called the North Market. When Vice-President Joe Biden visited Columbus in 2012, he specifically planned his trip to Jeni's Splendid Ice Creams to meet the entrepreneur creating new jobs in her emerging empire of ice cream stores.

Jeni and her husband, Charly Bauer, who works in the business, are fierce supporters of heritage farms and dairies, preparing their handcrafted flavors from grass-fed dairy products, simply flavored with the freshest local ingredients and responsibly-raised exotics. Her inspiration is her grandmother's garden and art studio, her own backyard and ingredients found in pastry kitchens around the world. While attending art school, Jeni worked for a French bakery, an experience inspiring her first recipes for ice cream. Drawing on that experience, Jeni developed her own techniques to make American ice cream less sweet and more flavorful.

She opened her first venture, Scream ("I scream, you scream, we all scream for ice cream" --- you get it, don't you?), and spent three and a half years studying ice cream, flavors and business. Jeni ended up closing the store to work on improving her recipes and write a better business plan. In 2002, she and husband Charly launched Jeni's Splendid Ice Creams; Charly's brother Tom joined as a partner a year later and a family friend, John Lowe, became CEO in 2009. Today, in addition to the original location, Jeni has additional locations in upscale, artsy areas of Columbus, several Columbus suburbs, Cleveland and Nashville, Tennessee . When I talked with her, she told me of planned expansion to more cities.

I once lectured at Ben & Jerry's Ice Cream and met Ben Cohen, who along with Jerry Greenfield co-founded the ice cream company bearing their names before they sold to Unilever. I heard Ben talk with passion about supporting local dairies and environmental issues, along with admiration of the Grateful Dead, the inspiration of a special flavor dedicated to Jerry Garcia. When I met Jeni Britton Bauer, I had the eerie feeling I was detecting a reincarnation of the passion and ingenuity I saw in the origin of Ben & Jerry's. Maybe someday she will sell to a giant conglomerate for a fortune as Mr. Cohen and Mr. Greenfield did, but for the present, Jeni is just a typical entrepreneur who, along with her husband, is having fun and making a living producing curious, but very tasty ice cream.

"The riches are in the niches," you've heard me say several times, and Jeni is personification of that principle. "An overnight wonder," some call her, to which I quickly add, "and it only took sixteen years to become one." After years of hard work and experimentation, she has won a lot of awards including Entrepreneur of the Year and national media attention. I suspect so far, however, the *riches* for Jeni are more in the taste of her ice cream than her bank account. But, that's the normal path for most entrepreneurs.

In-N-Out

No discussion of recipes for success in the restaurant industry is complete without analyzing the near cult-like devotion to a restaurant mastering the process of converting customers into fans. Celebrity chefs are among the many singing praises to this famed California burger chain, including Julia Child and Thomas Keller. Julia Child admitted to knowing every location of the restaurant between Santa Barbara and San Francisco, and she had the burgers delivered to her during a hospital stay. Keller celebrated with In-N-Out burgers at the anniversary party of his own restaurant, The French Laundry. In-N-Out was one of the few restaurant chains given a positive mention in the book *Fast Food Nation*, commending the chain for using natural, fresh ingredients, cleanliness and great treatment of employees.

You get more bang for the buck with good publicity than media advertising. That's a marketing principle I learned years ago, especially important to entrepreneurs with limited capital. In-N-Out uses a few billboards, a little radio , and some TV, along with bumper stickers willingly worn by customer-fans, but celebrities and free endorsements in mass media provide its most important creation of fans who recruit more customers. When Heisman Trophy winner Troy Smith raved about the In-N-Out cheeseburgers during a press conference before a BCS National Championship Game, a senior executive said, "It does not get much better than that for us. We're kind of a small company, and we do not have any celebrity endorsers. But I think we just got the best one we could have." Unpaid celebrity endorsements are more effective marketing tools than expensive advertising programs!

If you don't know much about In-N-Out, you're not from California or one of the western states where Harry and Esther Snyder started it in 1948. Today, its 268 stores are owned by their grandchild, Lynsi Torres. Its key ingredients, worthy of emulation by entrepreneurs in any industry, include:

1. Efficient logistics. No location is more than one day's drive from a regional distribution center; as the chain expands, it opens an additional distribution center to insure low costs, lean inventories, and fresh products.

2. Employee-centered personnel policies. Unlike other fast-food chains, In-N-Out pays significantly more than minimum wage.

3. Simple, "cookie-cutter" templates producing highly-efficient, nearly identical stores (with a few exceptions, such as Fisherman's Wharf) designed for available space and traffic.

4. Locally-acceptable image as a family-owned traditional business in communities often opposing corporate-owned, national chains such as McDonald's.

5. Exceptionally high ratings in customer-satisfaction surveys.

6. Efficient, limited menu.

There's one other element in the strategy of In-N-Out attracting some customers without offending others who might not agree with Christian beliefs held by the Snyder family. In-N-Out prints discreet references to Bible verses on their paper containers, consisting of the book, chapter and verse number, but not the actual text of the passage, in small print on an inconspicuous area of the item. Verses include John 3:16 (on beverage cups) and Nahum 1:7 on the double-double wrapper (about strength, in case you are not familiar with that verse, appropriate for a double-double wrapper). The firm provides key chains with a reference to I Corinthians 13:13, a familiar verse, saying "And now faith, hope, and love abide, these three; and the greatest of these is love."

That seems appropriate for In-N-Out, because there's probably no restaurant chain in the nation that gets more "love" from its customer-fans, than In-N-Out.

Bible reference on the bottom of an In-N-Out drink cup

Bible reference on wrapper of an In-N-Out Double-Double

Centrifugal City Growth

The principle of centrifugal growth applies to cities as well as companies. By that, I mean *cities tend to facilitate new entrepreneurs in areas pioneered by existing, successful entrepreneurs.* That's why software and computer firms are clustered in Silicon Valley, anchored by Stanford University and Austin, Texas, anchored by UT and Dell. In Seattle, it's Microsoft and the University of Washington, along with an abundance of coffee. When entrepreneurs excel, their employees start more firms in the same or related industries.

It's not surprising Columbus, Ohio, headquarters for square hamburgers, is also home to many restaurant chains. In addition to White Castle, Wendy's, Max & Erma's, City Barbeque, Cheryl's, Jeni's, Bravo-Brio, Donatos and Piada, chronicled in our conversations, there are more. Bob Evans brings food from "down on the farm" to cities all over the nation, started by a man with a coffee shop and market on his farm.

Cameron Mitchell is another entrepreneur who built a portfolio of restaurant concepts, ranging from Cap City Diner to "M," along with an extensive catering business. His formula for success includes a high level of service and attention to detail from the finest associates available. "The way we treat our associates is a secret ingredient in our recipe for success," Cameron states.

His entrepreneurial successes formerly included Mitchell's Steakhouse and Mitchell's Fish Market brands. He sold both to Ruth's Chris in February 2008. You may recall that was just *prior* to a recession causing a collapse in value of many restaurants. I include Mitchell's in our conversation for an important reason when investing in restaurants. Restaurants ride a roller coaster of popularity and consumer acceptance, making it *more important to know when to sell restaurants and restaurant shares than when to start or buy them.* Kenny Rogers gave good advice not only for restaurant owners, but for all entrepreneurs when he sang, "You got to know when to hold 'em, know when to fold 'em."

Cameron Mitchell started his restaurant career at Max & Erma's, a firm built on recruiting, training and retaining personnel giving such high levels of service and signature food items that customers couldn't wait to come back again and again. Max & Erma's is now owned by American Blue Ribbon Holdings LLC in Denver, but when it was headquartered in Columbus, the owners said *the most important asset on the balance sheet is one not on the balance sheet: The personnel training manual.*

If after this conversation about restaurants, you are still addicted to the idea of owning one, let me suggest a website that could be helpful. It focuses on restaurant startup and growth with a lot of resources including downloadable personnel manuals. Check out www.restaurantowner. com. If you have limited capital, want a high probability of success and profits, you might also consider a specialty coffee shop. You will find the recipe for profitability in 7 Steps to Success by Greg Ubert, consultant, wholesaler and specialty roaster for independent coffee houses and grocers. The approach to planning a new business is worthy reading by any new entrepreneur, even for products other than coffee. Details at www.crimsoncup.com.

Success Depends on How You Slice It

Another prototype for success is Jim Grote, who founded Donatos Pizzeria as a sophomore in college, eventually saving his money to buy the pizza store where he worked for $1300. His purpose was simple: "To make the best pizza and to treat others the way I would like to be treated."

Grote built trust with customers, a sense of goodwill in the neighborhood, and the respect of everyone who knows Jim. The firm grew consistently and profitably into a chain of nearly 200 restaurants in more than 170 neighborhoods in several states. In 1999, Jim cashed out, selling to McDonald's, reportedly for $125 million. Jim remained as guardian of product quality, but rapid expansion didn't pan out well in the eyes of McDonald's investors. The burger giant sold the business back to the family (at a far lower sum than it paid), proving, I guess, that it is possible to eat your pizza and have it too. Grote's daughter, Jane, is Chairperson of the thriving-again family-owned corporation, recently celebrating its 50th anniversary.

Grote is an exemplar of garage entrepreneurs, not only for founding a pizza chain from nearly nothing, but experimenting in his garage to develop a better slicing machine for the 99 pepperoni slices on every Donatos pizza. The result was the Grote Company, world's leading manufacturer of precision slicing and application equipment for the food processing industry. It started in his garage, but now makes and markets high quality equipment for everything from bulk slicing and portion control to slice-and-apply sandwich automation, focused on improving food processing operations. Some might consider machinery manufacturing mundane but any way you slice it, Jim is passionate about engineering solutions for the most demanding slicing and processing applications.

I like the company's slogan, "Innovation makes us a cut above." One restaurant grew to many, and pizza stores spawned slicing machinery applications. That's the pattern of centrifugal growth and financial success, turning tiny firms into family fortunes.

Centrifugal Cities

Centrifugal growth is also a way to keep cities dynamic with growing employment and tax base. That happened in Seattle by Schultz and Starbucks, as well as Gates and computers. Louisville has been a maternity ward for restaurants since Colonel Sanders started KFC with a handshake agreement stipulating payment of a nickel to Sanders for each chicken sold.

Columbus, often referred to as "Test Market USA," experienced similar clusters in retailing, logistics, consumer banking, health care and information systems. A few years ago, an economic development group asked me to moderate focus groups to determine why so many successful entrepreneurs begin and thrive in Columbus. After gathering CEOs together, I asked, "Why do entrepreneurs do so well in Columbus?"

"Because Columbus has so many experts on every subject who can answer any question from engineering, technology and logistics to retailing, restaurants and law," was the response from one of the group's members, mentioning Battelle Research Institute, The Ohio State University, Chemical Abstracts, OCLC and other institutions. They provided expertise for L Brands (formerly Limited), Wendy's, Cardinal Health, CompuServe (pioneer of on-line retailing, email and the first on-line newspaper), CheckFree (Electronic Funds Transfer) and Bank One (pioneer of innovations such as drive-in banking, the bank card, and America's first ATM) and other entrepreneurs.

"But there would be people in major cities such as New York and Los Angeles, who also have that level of expertise," I followed-up, as moderator of the group.

"The difference is," one of the entrepreneurs responded, "In Columbus, the people who know the answers are willing to tell them to you."

I hope the city in which you live has lots of people knowing answers to questions you face as an entrepreneur---and are willing to tell you. Shared knowledge stimulates entrepreneurial growth.

14

Conversation FOURTEEN

Cash is King

When speaking about Garage Entrepreneurs, I often ask the question, "Why do most entrepreneurs fail?" "Not enough capital," someone in the audience often responds. Then I explain the opposite is more accurate, clarifying why TMC creates the lethal luxury of not conforming to what customers are willing to buy.

"Poor cash management," is another answer sometimes given why entrepreneurs fail. When I hear that response, the person is usually an experienced, wise manager.

Poor cash management is a serious problem among entrepreneurs, often in non-profit organizations also. Obtaining cash to start a business and what to do with cash in successful businesses are critically-important issues. That's why I chose "cash" as a singular topic for this conversation, hoping the message will "soak-in" that a likely-to-survive firm is one in which the owner/manager recognizes Cash is King.

Cash Flow is King

Profits in a business are like blood in people. Both are essential for survival, but transfusions and life-support systems can sometimes keep both people and firms alive a while, demonstrated by Amazon going years without profits.

Cash, however, is like oxygen. Neither people nor firms survive long without the "oxygen" of cash. That's why cash flow is a critical measure of health in a business. Astute analysts examine *cash flow* more closely than Earnings per Share (EPS). Hint: If you are concerned about your investments, you should do the same.

Be miserly with cash. Resist spending. Cut costs. Don't yield to witless comments, "you have to spend money to make money." Banks or creditors don't foreclose on buildings or equipment when you have a hoard of cash to meet obligations, accumulated through judicious spending. Debt is devilish; cash is angelic.

Collect Fast. Pay Slow

The basic principle is simple. Collect receivables as quickly as possible and pay bills as slowly as possible without damaging relationships with customers or suppliers, a principle easier to proclaim than to execute. It is a fine line learned through experience and insight into the psychological make-up of both customers and suppliers. Cash management involves as much skill and judgment as being a race car driver, and almost as dangerous if you do it wrong. Too aggressive with customers or too considerate to suppliers can wreck your business.

Cash Balances

The advantage of tracking *cash flow* from operations is a clear picture of what is happening. "Sales" means different things to sales people, accountants and auditors, especially at the end of the month when bonuses are determined, or at the end of the quarter when an outside auditor checks revenues, inventories and shipments. Cash is unequivocal. It is in either a bank account or a lock box, permitting an "apples-to-apples" comparison between months, quarters, companies and management.

Most firms operate on the *accrual* accounting system, designed to explain differences between months or divisions in recording revenues, inventories, costs and the other essential activities of a firm. But cash is a fact; companies have either collected it or not, and either spent it or not.

Generally, *changes* in "free cash flow" measure how a firm is doing from year to year. In an accrual accounting system, it is possible to "manage the numbers" to smooth out earnings and growth from year to year, but cash is mostly an "oranges to oranges" measurement. Even with cash, however, there can be a few "lemons" squeezed into reported earnings.

If payments for sales and expenses were completely predictable, there would no need to keep cash on hand. But, of course, they aren't. So, entrepreneurs must stash some cash to pay expenses due before payments from sales are received. Knowing there's plenty of cash in the bank, raised from the sources of capital discussed below, makes it easier to sleep at night, but too much cash from TMC causes complacency in understanding what customers will buy at a profitable price.

Black Swan Events

Even for well-established entrepreneurs with years of profitable operation, a different risk exists. It's called a "Black Swan" event, something so cataclysmic that it can wipe out a firm without enough cash to survive the event.

The reason it's called a Black Swan Event is because most swans are white, a metaphor for a firm's normal environment. People hypothesized the possibility of black swans, but they weren't documented to exist until the eighteenth century. Today, when unexpected events occur causing major impact on firms, they are called Black Swan Events. You probably won't be able to predict when they happen, but if they do, you need cash available to deal with them.

The black swan problem was popularized by Nassim Taleb in *The Black Swan* (Random House, 2007) describing "outliers," events so extreme they play much larger roles than regular occurrences. He designates the Internet, the computer, and September 11 events as examples. Entrepreneurs need contingency plans and sufficient cash to survive situations where:

1. The event is a surprise (to the observer).

2. The event has a major impact.

3. After it happens, with hindsight, entrepreneurs realize it *could* have been expected.

Planning for Black Swan events is a reason to keep access to cash beyond what is needed for normal operations. In his book, Taleb states a Black Swan event depends on the observer. For example, what may be a Black Swan surprise for a turkey is not a Black Swan surprise to its butcher. You need enough cash to avoid being a turkey.

Ford Motor did that in 2006, but GM and Chrysler didn't. Ford mortgaged all its assets—factories, equipment, office property, intellectual property (including its patents and famous blue oval trademarks) and its stakes in subsidiaries--to raise $23.4 billion in cash. Many observers criticized raising so much cash through a secured credit line, but when the Great Recession of 2008 sailed in like a black swan on the normally placid lake of consumer car sales, Ford had sufficient cash to survive. GM and Chrysler didn't, ending in bankruptcies wiping out the equity of shareholders. Those who owned old GM stock got absolutely nothing.

Entrepreneurs can't predict when Black Swan events will happen or their exact nature, but they can plan what they will do to survive them, including having access to sufficient cash. The best time to borrow cash, or secure a credit line, is when you don't need it.

Sources of Cash

Throughout this book, you've heard me talk (preach?) about the evils of Too Much Capital (TMC). Obviously, however, you need some cash to start and bootstrap a business. I hope I've convinced you to ask for as little as possible from outside investors so you can keep most of the business for yourself. Some start-ups require more cash than the modest amounts needed in the garages of Packard-Hewlett, Michael Dell, Jeff Bezos, Steve Jobs, and other garage entrepreneurs, but starting a business "lean" entails minimum cash.

What's the best source of cash to start or grow a business?

1. Cash from Customers

The best source of cash to start and grow your business into a fortune is from customers. The formula is simple; you collect for the products you sell before you have to pay your suppliers. That's what Hendrik Meijer did with his start-up grocery store in Michigan, using merchandise from wholesalers betting on Meijer's experience as a barber, placing inventory in Meijer's low-cost space and permitting payment after selling to consumers. Les Wexner did something similar with his first few stores at the Limited.

I first learned the principle of starting and growing a business with customers' cash from Dr. Alvin Star, a founder of Shoppers World, Chicago's first major discounter. He told me how they bought merchandise and sold it fast, collecting cash before bills were due in the normal trade cycle. After building a chain of a dozen or so stores, the founders sold it for a ton of cash to a large organization with lots of tons of cash, freeing Star to go back to school and get a Ph.D. at Northwestern. I asked Al why he sold the stores for millions instead of waiting for billions.

"I realized a winter blizzard could delay sales enough days to cause a cash crunch putting us out of business. We sold the stores to a buyer with enough cash to survive a Chicago snow storm." I now realize that Al spotted a possible black swan in the midst of lot of white snow. BTW, I am pretty sure Al didn't need a student loan to pay for his Ph.D.

2. Cash from Personal Funds, Family and Friends

Most entrepreneurs start their business with personal funds and credit cards, or small investments by family and friends. That's the essence of garage entrepreneurship, illustrated by firms such as City Barbeque, Jeni's Splendid Ice Cream, Johnson Products (remember the "vacation" loan?), Walmart and thousands of others. As you turn the pages or flip the screen of this book, perhaps you are, or will be, one of those in the future.

Michael Dell illustrates how to start and grow a business with minimal cash, mostly gained from profits selling to customers. In the fall semester of his freshman year in college, Dell got active in the computer business, putting together and selling upgrade kits for personal-computer buyers. Michael explains in a lecture to college students, recorded by the Associated Press:

"Business was kind of booming, and I was doing quite well, and my parents heard about all of this, and they got pretty upset. They said, 'We sent you off to college, and you are supposed to be studying.' The dorm room sort of looked like a computer lab. There were soldering irons and all this stuff all over the place."

"They got really upset with me around Thanksgiving break in 1983. And they sort of made me promise to focus on my studies and not do the whole computer thing while I was supposed to be in school. And I actually tried to do that, and it worked for eight or nine days. I wasn't very successful as a student, as far as that goes. Then it was like: OK, this (computer business) actually isn't a hobby that I want to do while I am going to school. This is what I really want to do."

A customer who was a lawyer incorporated Dell's business in return for a hard-drive upgrade for his PC. Dell then discovered that state law required companies to have $1,000 to become incorporated. So he sold a few more computers to raise cash. The business was called PCs Limited, but the lawyer filed the papers as Dell Computer Corp. doing business as PCs Limited because PCs Limited was too generic to be suitable for a corporate name.

"My motivation was that I saw an incredible opportunity, and I just had to do it. When I was 19 years old, the risk-reward was overwhelmingly in favor of taking the risk. It was a $1,000 investment, and if it didn't work, I would go right back to school. And away you go." And he did go—very fast and well.

Dell thought he was "taking the risk," but, in reality, he was minimizing risk building the firm with his own cash and profits from customers. Starting with your own cash or credit cards makes sense if you have the patience to build the firm over time. When entrepreneurs seek investors rather than their own cash or small investments from friends and families, they give up much of their business to outsiders, making it difficult to build a fortune in the future. Sometimes it's necessary to seek outside investors, but only if you think you won't have a future without them.

An investment or loan from family or friends has many advantages. If you hit it big, it's good to have your family and friends as partners, sharing the wealth from your entrepreneurial skills and spirit. If you lose it all, they are less likely to do bad things to you, at least in most families. But there are caveats to consider when obtaining money from family or friends, as one tragic case I will describe.

I first met Lee in my undergraduate class. He was enthusiastic about his idea for an Italian-themed restaurant and asked if I would look at his business plan, which I did. I also referred him to a friend who owned a chain of Italian restaurants, who offered constructive comments on ingredients and restaurant equipment. I suggested the young entrepreneur attend auctions of restaurants going out of business or visit dealers specializing in used restaurant equipment to start his restaurant at minimum cost, and look for "second use" space, available at low rent.

After graduating from college, Lee opened the restaurant with plans to open several more. I ate at his first one, and the food was good. It was in a new (expensive) mall and he had new equipment. His retired parents were in the restaurant during its grand opening, obviously pleased and proud of their son. They believed in him so much, they refinanced their home with a large mortgage providing cash to open his restaurant first-class. Although they lived quite a few miles from the new restaurant, his mother even helped some during the grand opening.

During the recession of 2008, the sales of most restaurants tumbled. So did Lee's, so much that he went out of business. He couldn't repay his parents, and they lost their home. The lesson to be learned from this story is simple. Keep costs very low when you open a new business. You might consider refinancing your own home to obtain cash if you don't have a family to worry about where they will live, something one-third of all small business owners do, according to the National Federation of Independent Businesses. But, my advice is not to allow your retired parents to mortgage their home to put cash in your business.

Lee learned a lot. When I sent this section of the manuscript for him to review, this was his response:

"What I gained from the whole experience far outweighs the losses. I gained my family. We are so close now. It was a wake-up call. We all saw what was important. Not money, things, or houses but each other. If the restaurant hadn't failed, I know I wouldn't have the incredibly supportive and close family I have now. We all moved to another state and live within a few blocks of each other. I see my parents several times a week and I live with my brother and sister. It's amazing and I never thought I could have all of this. The bankruptcy was a huge blessing in disguise."

Lee and his brother are now working on a new start-up in a computer business. I am betting that it and Lee (and his family) will be huge successes in the future, because of lessons they learned from the past.

3. Cash from Your Credit Cards

It's expensive, especially if you don't pay on time, but a lot of entrepreneurs start their business on personal credit cards.

The president of MCI spoke to my class at Ohio State and explained the audacity of starting a new telephone company with no money, competing against the world's largest communications firm, AT&T. The breakup of AT&T began in 1974 when the Justice Department sued AT&T under provisions of the Sherman Anti-trust Act, the same law which led to the breakup of Standard Oil in 1911. The case was settled in 1982, by Judge Harold H. Greene, forcing the former monopoly to divest itself of local operations, splitting them into seven independent Regional Bell Operating Companies (RBOCs), called "Baby Bells."

The "Greening" of America left open the door to more competitors than the baby Bells. William G. McGowan, instrumental in the legal fight against AT&T, kicked down that door and walked in as the feisty founder (along with John D. "Jack" Goeken) of MCI Communications Corp. The son of a railroad engineer, McGowan worked his way through Kings College (and later graduated from Harvard Business School) used every dime of his own money, driving his own car, maxing out his and others' credit cards to pay for gas. It was another example of "little David" confronting Goliath, eventually creating the second largest telecommunications firm and providing millions of Americans more choices in telephone services at lower prices. Much of the early "capital" of the new competitors, was sweat equity and "living on the edge" with credit cards.

I love it when "little David's" of the business battleground slay giants, stone by stone. All that starts well does not always end up well, of course, because MCI was eventually purchased by WorldCom, ending up in what was at that time the largest bankruptcy in U.S. history. Eventually, it was purchased by Verizon. The case illustrates both the potential of starting a firm with minimal cash, and the dangers of not controlling cash carefully or reporting profits accurately.

4. Cash from Angel Investors

If your business needs significant cash to start or grow beyond inception, you may need the help of angels. The term "angel" originally comes from financing of theatrical productions by wealthy individuals who provided money to open shows, hoping to achieve big profits but usually content to get good seats and association with actors, directors and other stars of Broadway. Today, the term "angel investor" has moved off Broadway to include financing by wealthy individuals of new or growing entrepreneurial firms.

According to the US Small Business Administration, the number of individuals in the US who make angel investments is between 300,000 and 600,000. Most are successful entrepreneurs who made a lot of money in their own business, wanting to grow their winnings investing in other high-potential firms. The amount they invest can range anywhere from a few thousand, to a few million.

Many angel investors are retired entrepreneurs or executives, and may be willing to help you in ways other than cash, including management advice and contacts. Angel investors may seem like they're from heaven, but be prepared for them to fly away with a chunk of your company in return, at least 10 percent and perhaps as much as 50 percent.

To attract angel investors, you must also be able to offer an "exit" in the form of repurchase of their stock at a premium, a buyout from a larger firm, or an initial public offering (IPO). Some may desire, and you may want them, to be on your board of directors or advisory board.

Where do you find angels? Around universities that have Entrepreneurial Studies programs is a good place to start. Some cities and state development departments sponsor Business Incubators offering entrepreneurs reasonable rents, access to shared services, exposure to professional assistance and an atmosphere of entrepreneurial energy. You can also find formal or informal groups that share information and deals and invest independently or join together to fund a company. Once you locate and relate well to one member, they are likely to lead you to others.

Here are some actions you can take to find angel investors:

1. Call your chamber of commerce or state development office and ask if it hosts groups of angels or venture capital groups that will listen to your business plan, give advice, and maybe invest in your firm.

2. Ask accounting and law firms in your area if they have an entrepreneurial practice that will assist you. Many do, trying to sniff out potential good clients in the future.

3. Check out the local business newspaper; they often sponsor forums and seminars bringing entrepreneurs together with investors.

4. Study the proxy statements of public firms in your area or online finance sites to locate names of directors or retired executives who have cashed out big in other companies. They may be looking for good new companies in which to invest from their successes in the past.

5. Get to know bankers well, especially those active in making loans to smaller, growing businesses. Banks rarely invest in firms without a track-record of profitable operations, but they know people who do.

5. Cash from Private Equity Firms

Entrepreneurs sometimes acquire cash from Private Equity (PE) firms, limited partnerships managed by a general partner (GP), with capital from high net-worth individuals or cash-rich institutional investors, such as pension plans, universities, insurance companies, foundations, and endowments. PE firms want high returns, ownership of 51 to 80 percent or more of your business, a clear exit strategy and may or may not retain you and your management team, depending on how valuable they consider you to the business.

I know entrepreneurs who obtained cash infusions from PE firms at critically-important times, but PE firms are more likely to be involved in exiting a business or saving distressed firms than growing new ones. We won't spend more time discussing them, except to acknowledge they may become valuable to you when you want to take substantial amounts of cash out of your business, either to start another business or put shorts on and head south.

6. Cash from Venture Capitalists

When the thought arises about where to find cash for your business, your first idea may be Venture Capitalists (VCs). In my opinion, it should be your last idea, at least early in forming your firm, but VCs fulfill an important function, despite some people calling them "Vulture Capitalists."

VCs, angels, and PE firms are all "private" equity, since their funding comes from private sources instead of public offerings. VCs invest in companies too small to raise capital in the public markets nor matured to the point they are able to secure a bank loan or debt offering. Because they assume substantial risk by investing in emerging entrepreneurs, VCs request a lot of control over company decisions, as well as a significant portion of your shares. They usually expect to sell their shares to a larger company or IPO.

As an entrepreneur, you may consider the amount of control VCs demand a disadvantage, but the opposite is likely to true. Their constant involvement in management, branding, product development and other areas may keep you from making bad decisions. Beside cash, VCs often help make major sales to corporate customers and negotiate favorable terms from suppliers. Their network of contacts is often the greatest advantage VCs provide your firm. In addition to the cash, of course!

VCs hang around incubators and universities streaming out graduates with skills. They look for innovative technology, rapid growth, a well-developed business model, and an impressive management team. It's been estimated VCs invest in only one of about four hundred opportunities they review. Of the nearly 2 million businesses created every year in the U.S., only 600–800 get venture capital funding.

The people who operate VCs are entrepreneurs themselves. One of the most successful is Michael Moritz, Managing Director and Partner of Silicon Valley VC super star, Sequoia Capital. After immigrating to the United States, Moritz made his mark as a journalist writing a cover story for *Time* magazine about Steve Jobs, wrote a book about him (*The Little Kingdom: the Private Story of Apple Computer,* Overlook Press,

1984) and observed Jobs closely until his death. I had the opportunity to interview Moritz, asking him about VCs and Jobs. Moritz told me Jobs operated in a "single mode" --- Apple, and later in life, his family.

Moritz emphasized VCs contribute much more than cash. They create successful entrepreneurs by obtaining customers, attracting outstanding people to work for you and giving marketing assistance. Moritz should know because his investments, in addition to Apple, include Google, Yahoo! PayPal, Cisco, YouTube and others. (They also include Webvan; some VC investments do better than others). His investment in Google helped him achieve the number one listing in *Forbes'* "Midas List" of the top dealmakers in the technology industry multiple years. Moritz came to America with nothing, but did well enough that he and his wife recently donated $50 million to the college where he graduated.

You may have wondered why I haven't mentioned banks as a source of cash to start your business. The reason is simple; banks rarely loan money to start a business. There's too much risk to satisfy banks' conservative policies. They might loan enough money to buy a truck, and after you have a few years of profitable financial statements, they may loan you money to buy machinery, seasonal inventory or assets backing a loan, but banks don't loan money for start-up or speculative investments, at least not knowingly.

When I was a young teacher, I moved into our first home and bought new carpeting, leaving me with no cash. One of the men in the Sunday School class I attended was branch manager of a bank whose marketing strategies I believed better than competitors. At church one Sunday, he invited me to open an account at his branch.

"I don't have any money to deposit because I just bought new carpeting for my home," I told him. "And if I had any money, I would rather buy your bank's stock than deposit cash in your savings account."

"Banking rules don't allow us to make loans to buy stock," he replied, "but how did you pay for the carpeting?"

"Cash, from savings," I answered.

"Come by my branch, and let's talk," he said.

I did, and after a few questions, he loaned me the several thousand dollars I paid for the carpet, with the carpet as collateral. I deposited the proceeds from the loan, bought the bank's stock and sold it a few years later for several times what I paid for it. I tell this story, hoping you find it helpful in knowing how to obtain cash to start your business.

What to do When You Have Too Much Cash

"You can't be too rich or too thin." You've probably heard people say that, usually accompanied by a chuckle from listeners. Most of us would like more money and less weight. When people who aren't accustomed to a lot of cash win the lottery or inherit large estates, they often end up in bankruptcy or death from alcohol, drugs and other abuses, soon after receiving too much cash.

Companies can also have too much cash. The most notable example was Montgomery Ward, after World War II. Its management believed another Great Depression was inevitable and hoarded cash to be ready for it, while Sears and Penney spent their cash building new stores in mushrooming malls sprouting up in suburbs sprawling across America. It was too late to retaliate when Montgomery Ward realized its mistake and became little more than a note in business history books.

Executives of successful firms sometimes stare at balance sheets with hoards of cash or cash equivalents. What should be done with all that cash? Making the right choice depends on your long-term strategy for the value and future of the firm. It is the key to growing your small firm into millions or billions for your family and investors. Here are a few choices.

1. Give the cash back to customers

Sam Walton had a unique financial philosophy. When Walmart's expenses decreased and profits increased, Sam believed in giving the extra cash back to customers as "Every Day Low Prices" (EDLP). That's unfair, competitors complain, because it attracts customers to Walmart, allowing Walmart to grow even larger and more formidable, a strategy so daunting that Walmart is now larger than most of its competitors combined. Instead of paying cash to shareholders as dividends (it does pay some dividends, but not large ones) or excessive salaries to executives and employees, Walton believed in giving cash back to customers in the form of lower prices. It's a financial strategy that worked out well enough to make Waltons the richest family in the world.

2. Pay dividends

There are two reasons people invest in a firm, appreciation in the value of its stock and dividends. When cash is used to fund rapid growth, most investors, especially younger ones, typically prefer appreciation of share price more than dividends, and U.S. tax policies encourage firms not to pay dividends. Owning shares of highly-appreciating firms is a key to soaring IRA portfolios, but when growth opportunities moderate and shareholders near retirement, investor preferences shift toward dividends. Shares of firms consistently increasing dividends typically double value every five to seven years. When growth opportunities decline, dividends may be a good way to grow value.

3. Buy strategic firms

Remember the "reins and bits" firms we discussed in Conversation 12? Cash on the balance sheet might be just the ticket for acquisition of those companies.

The focal person of our discussion in Conversation 12 was dazzling in the job of accumulating cash instead of paying dividends. When Steve Jobs died, he left $150 billion in assets on Apple's balance sheet. If "growth" was the objective of Apple, it had enough assets to buy Netflix or perhaps even Sony or Disney, but that wasn't the design of Apple's strategy. Here are some of Apple's acquisitions over the years and their estimated prices, compiled by financial analyst Evan Niu.

Year	Company	Estimated Price	Intended Use/Purpose
1996	NeXT Computer	$404 million	Steve Jobs, Mac OS X
2005	FingerWorks	Unknown	Multitouch
2008	P.A. Semi	$278 million	A4, A5 processors
2009	Placebase	Unknown	Maps app
2009	Lala	$17 million	iCloud, iTunes Match
2010	Quattro Wireless	$275 million	iAd
2010	Intrinsity	$121 million	A4, A5 processors
2010	Siri	$200 million	Siri
2010	Poly9	Unknown	Maps app
2011	C3 Technologies	$267 million	Maps app
2011	Anobit	$500 million	Flash memory

You get the picture, don't you? With rifle-like precision, Apple made strategic acquisitions that contributed to its overall Design Strategy. Steve Jobs focused on small acquisitions of companies with solid technology that allowed Apple to build an offering from the ground up, not huge purchases of competitors or companies difficult to integrate into Apple's culture. The most strategic acquisition of all was when Apple bought NeXT Computer, getting Jobs himself in the package.

Note also the absence of the word "billion" anywhere in these acquisitions. It is easy to get into a bidding war when elephants fight, something that Apple under Jobs' leadership avoided with a discipline easy to lose without a clear, strategic purpose of spending cash to buy other firms.

I've observed that when competitors merge, or large companies such as Hewlett-Packard buy firms with problem cultures such as Palm, the result is often reduced value for shareholders of both companies. Studies by finance academics reach the same conclusion. Cash is king when used strategically, but shotgun weddings turn kings into paupers.

Have I convinced you Cash is King? I hope so. Managing cash well involves obtaining it grudgingly, spending it miserly to build a sustainable business and knowing what to do with cash when you accumulate a lot of it.

As important as cash is in building small firms into large ones, there's something more important, as you'll see in our next conversation.

15

Conversation FIFTEEN

"You Win With People"

Woody Hayes, one of the most successful coaches in collegiate football history, explained his victories in *You Win With People* (Typographic, 1973), winning football games with principles you can apply to the game of entrepreneurship. If you play the game of entrepreneur alone, you lose as surely as a quarterback exposed and vulnerable without strong offensive linemen. You really do win with people.

Developing reliable team members takes time. Most people starting a business, especially with limited experience managing people, need to learn who they can depend on and who they cannot, and not only when to trust, but its limits. That takes time and patience.

Everyone knows a QB is usually the highest-paid player on NFL teams. Perhaps less well-known is the left offensive tackle, at least for right-handed quarterbacks, is often the second highest-paid player.

It is a lesson worth learning in building a team for your firm. If you find a really good player who "protects your blind side," pay him or her well---maybe as well as yourself. Along the way to success, you need a "left tackle" on your entrepreneurial team, a person "who's got your back." You saw that in our conversation about Steve Jobs. He might never have started Apple without "the other Steve" (Wozniak) nor taken Apple to its zenith without design guru Jony Ive. They had Jobs' back, and he needed protection of his back!

If you don't have such a person on your team, take your time in finding one. Too often, hiring decisions are made quickly and firing decisions are made slowly. The opposite is better. Don't hire people until you've had a few casual dinners and perhaps a pick-up game on the basketball court or football field. Google is considered one of the best places on the planet to work, but it averages four or five interviews and intensive background information before asking anyone to join its team.

It's difficult to recruit or retain great talent, and sometimes entrepreneurs are reluctant to delegate key activities to them, but in the long-run you'll make more money if you learn when and how to delegate. Building a team of winners allows you to retire someday, perhaps as a billionaire.

Entrepreneurs Are Coaches

Great entrepreneurs are great coaches, but "coach" is a difficult role to learn. The reason is good entrepreneurs usually start doing everything themselves, making it difficult to "let go" of details. But players win games, not coaches. At the same time they learn to delegate, entrepreneurs must never lose empathy for every part of the business nor fail to understand details making a firm's products better than competitors. That's important even though Steve Jobs "couldn't write code" any better than Woody Hayes could pass a football. Entrepreneurs often believe, "I can't find anyone to do what I do as well as me." But you must, and some of them will do it better than you.

I talked with a man who started a new airline. He was an impressive entrepreneur with an engaging personality, and raised millions of dollars from investors. He was an accomplished salesman to civic-minded leaders supporting the airline, soliciting both capital and passengers.

With all that money, he was able to start the airline with a major marketing campaign and an expansive fleet flying to several cities.

In our conversation, I described a flight in which we took off, "with a heading of 270."

He looked me at me quizzically as if I were speaking a foreign language. I continued the story, again referring to a "heading of 270."

"I don't know what you are talking about," he said.

"Were you ever a pilot?" I asked, knowing that a pilot or anyone who has spent much time in the cockpit of a plane knows a heading of 270 refers to 270 degrees on a compass, or due west.

"No," he replied.

"Did you spend much time riding in the cockpit of your airline's planes," I asked.

"Never went inside the cockpit," he said. "That's the pilots' job, not mine. I was the President."

I knew why his airline crashed into bankruptcy, soon after it took off, taking all employees with it.

In contrast, the nation's third largest cargo airline was started in 1974 by Gerald Mercer, who began flying a single-engine plane from a distant town in Michigan to Pontiac (near Detroit) to deliver cancelled checks overnight. Using his earnings as a pilot, he bought the plane and hired another pilot part-time. Gradually, he patched together a fleet of aging planes delivering checks overnight throughout the nation, competing with the U.S. Federal Reserve System and its shiny fleet of new jets. It's difficult to compete successfully with the U.S. Government, but he did.

Mercer had a fleet of Cessna Caravans, Cessna 210s, Piper Navajos and Beech Barons and gradually, Lear 35s, providing reliable service at low cost. His real advantage, however, was superior knowledge of flying and a passion for flight safety. Pilots trusted and respected Mercer because he was one of them; he knew the loneliness of flying through the night in all types of weather, under the peril of precise schedules. He understood flying skill and plane maintenance as well as any of the airline's intrepid night pilots.

What happens when a founder such as Mercer retires? The answer was Joe Biggerstaff, successor as CEO. He was not a pilot, but when he assumed leadership, he spent much of his time with people who were. He learned to speak their language and knew the "right stuff" about safety requirements, flight conditions, and capabilities of a diverse fleet of planes. When contract negotiations came around, he had the trust of pilots, obtaining salary levels and work rules that allowed the airline to compete head-to-head against airline giants and the Federal Government.

I had the opportunity to hang around the company's hangars and fly in the jump seat on some of those overnight flights, talking personally with pilots, hearing their flight communications as "Star Check One," the identifying code used for its planes. Never have I observed a work force so completely dedicated to a corporate mission. Signs on the wall said it simply, "We fly fast. We fly safe."

To continue growing, the company needed capital. It went public in 1998 as AirNet Systems, and was purchased in 2008 by Bayside Capital. AirNet didn't create billionaires, but it did create millionaires and thousands of good-paying jobs for pilots, ground personnel and office workers.

With the passing of the Check 21 Act, and increased electronic banking, AirNet faced what could have been its own Black Swan event. It recognized that possibility, and shifted its focus to other time-critical documents and packages, especially in the scientific and medical field. Today, AirNet Mission Critical (AMC) delivers substantially later pick-ups for overnight package shipments, early AM delivery, shorter pick-up-to-delivery cycles, high security, and persistent chain of custody of the most sensitive, valuable, and urgent shipments. It "sells time" to niche markets, providing door-to-door and door-to-airport service in 33 countries around the globe and is now the third largest cargo airline in the U.S. It all started with one plane flying through the night by a reluctant entrepreneur who knew how to fly planes fast and safe, and built a team that could do the same. When you are "little David" battling corporate giants, including the federal government, the "stone to sling" is *exceptional people.*

Servant Leadership

"You Win With People" is the theme of this conversation, but the most important person making that happen is *YOU.* You must be the leader even if you don't like the spotlight, don't like public speaking, and don't like responsibility. President Harry Truman, possibly America's most courageous president since Lincoln, said it well with a sign on his desk, "The buck stops here."

What is a leader? Dwight Eisenhower, another decisive U.S. president, said, "Leadership is the art of getting other people to do what you want to do." Leadership is mostly about followship. When asked what it takes to be a "leader," my answer is simple, "followers."

Over many years as a college professor, I observed student groups working on projects, usually five or six bright individuals. Some had high grades, some had engaging personalities, some were sharply dressed and attractive, but as I watched the groups function through the term, I observed that one individual usually emerged as the person whose opinions what the group should do were met by nods of agreement, notes for follow-up and murmurs of "That's right; let's do it."

The emergent leaders were often not students with the best grades, best clothes, or best personality, but in a setting where everyone had the same status or position and the same need for getting work done effectively, one person became the leader. It was almost always the person that worked the hardest to achieve excellence in the final project, putting team performance above his or her own needs. The teams that received an A on their team project were ones with a servant leader.

I followed some of them over the years and observed those same individuals, often not the ones with the highest cumulative grade point, later became successful entrepreneurs or CEOs, CFOs and CMOs of successful corporations. *The test of leadership is whether or not people follow your ideas.*

If they do, you're a leader.

If you've read about sheepherding, you know the best shepherds don't lead sheep. They stay at the side or toward the back, letting sheep dogs lead the way and attack predators along the journey. Effective entrepreneurs adopt the same strategy. Leaders don't always need to be "out front," but are often alongside the sheep, encouraging them, keeping them from straying from the right path, deciding when it's time for rest or be fed. *Servant leaders lead from the side of their flock.*

If you have time to read only one book on great leaders, in my opinion it should be Jim Collins, *Good to Great: Why Some Companies Make the Leap & And Others Don't.* It's sold millions of copies and translated into 35 languages. It's a "must read" for every entrepreneur, along with *Built to Last*, his earlier best-seller co-written with Jerry Porous. One of the functions of a leader is motivation. Although skeptics sometimes criticize the value of motivation, classic motivator Zig Ziglar observes, "People often say that motivation doesn't last. Well, neither does bathing – that's why we recommend it daily."

You probably will want also to read *Servant Leader* by Ken Blanchard or *Servant Leadership* by Larry Spears and Robert Greenleaf, if you have not already done so. Principles of how to be a servant leader, accomplishing extraordinary results in the city of Jerusalem, are also illustrated well in the memoir of construction entrepreneur Nehemiah, in the Bible. Or you could simply go to the source on servant leadership, studying the central character of the New Testament.

Does a "servant leadership" philosophy work in today's super-competitive world? I asked that to Bill Mullet, CEO of ProVia Doors, nestled in the rolling hills of Sugarcreek, Ohio, heart of the nation's largest Amish population. He started the company in a garage over 30 years ago, growing into a nationally known manufacturer of high quality entry door systems, energy efficient windows, super polymer vinyl siding and artfully-crafted, manufactured stone. On its website, the company explains one of its values as servant leadership ("lead by serving with humility") and how it moves forward, under a common purpose: *"To let our light shine before others, so that they may see our good works and give glory to our Father who is in heaven."* The firm's other eighteen values are described on its website, providing thoughtful ideas for any entrepreneur.

ProVia built a reputation for quality, old-world craftsmanship and personal care for customers, distributing products throughout most of the United States. It remains privately owned, investing continuously in its employees, facilities, customers and research & development, making products of outstanding quality with a team of nearly 500 people. Bill Mullet told me, "Servant leadership is built on love of our employees. It's the only type of leadership that works in the long run. All other types of leadership are resisted and create push back." He added, "Servant leadership is measured by achievement of our employees. It's more important to equip our employees to succeed than to succeed ourselves."

Should Employees Who Make Mistakes Be Fired?

The national leader I respect most in recent world history is Nelson Mandela. He was imprisoned for 27 years by South Africa's political leaders, including President P.W. Botha. When finally released, some expected a blood bath against the former leaders of Apartheid. Instead, Mandela appointed a "Truth and Reconciliation Commission." Its purpose was to tell the truth, but then to reconcile past grievances peacefully. Botha didn't apologize for the injustices Mandela endured. Nevertheless, Mandela said to Botha, "I forgive you." If you feel empathy for Mandela and agree with what he did, you have characteristics of a leader.

When an employee, partner or colleague disappoints you, how will you respond? Will you fire that person? Explode in anger? Berate the person with a "tongue-lashing?"

How you respond goes a long way in establishing your leadership. An employee who finds "truth and reconciliation" instead of humiliation and retribution can become one of your most loyal and competent employees. If you "taught him a lesson," should you "fire" that person, or would you prefer the lesson learned be applied the rest of the person's career in your organization instead of a competitor?

And remember, the Lone Ranger was not really alone. His faithful companion Tonto scouted the territory bringing essential information to his leader, and in the thick of the battle, Tonto had the Lone Ranger's back. Be sure you develop a Tonto in your organization.

Who's Number One?

Although this conversation is focused on winning teams, don't forget the most important people to serve—customers. A debate exists whether it is more important to place customers first, or employees. Southwestern Airlines has an enviable record of growth and earnings stability, started by one of America's most colorful entrepreneurs, Herb Kelleher. His philosophy places employees' interest first, and the results are impressive. Kelleher's colorful personality created a corporate culture in which Southwest employees became well-known for taking themselves lightly—often singing in-flight announcements to the tune of popular theme songs—but their jobs seriously. Southwest has never had an in-flight fatality and is consistently named among the Most Admired Corporations in America in *Fortune* magazine's annual poll.

Fortune once called Kelleher perhaps the best CEO in America. Unlike the failed airline I described earlier in this conversation, Kelleher spent almost as many hours in the planes, tarmacs and offices, as the pilots and flight attendants, ground crew and office workers. He embraced and hugged workers so warmly, he worried his employment lawyers.

Southwest differs a bit from companies proclaiming they put customers first. At Southwest, the policy is to put employees first---and let them determine how to serve customers best. It's a tricky argument about whether customers or employees should be Number One, but the policies of Southwest work well. By placing employee needs first, customers love Southwest and its shareholders love the results achieved by Kelleher as servant leader.

Here's one more question. How well should you pay yourself as the leader?

Remember our discussion of Jeff Bezos? His salary as CEO of Amazon is $81,840, the same as previous years. Paying himself less has paid off so well that the company spends more on his security than his salary. Look at leaders such as Warren Buffet, CEO of Berkshire-Hathaway, and you see the long-term value from serving others well instead of paying yourself a high salary. James Senegal, founder and former CEO at Costco focused on serving employees and customers first, paying comparatively high wages to Costco employees and a comparatively low salary to himself. The strategy of paying himself less than comparable CEOs earned a fortune in the growth of his stock. Study successful firms, and you discover an important principle. CEOs who earn less in salary earn more from the value of their company.

Employee Benefits

Your employee benefit program is one of the most challenging expenses faced by entrepreneurs. Without arduous control, benefits eat away at the profits of otherwise successful firms, but an effective benefit package is a salient attribute of success. In my experience, I have seen entrepreneurs make two fundamental mistakes:

1. Ignoring details of health and other benefits, often blinded by preferential health care and disproportionate personal perks for the owner.

2. Delegating the "benefit package" to the HR department, without closely monitoring details of costs and employee morale.

Don't make either of those mistakes. Either or both blunders lead to excessive costs and inability to build a winning team. As leader of the team, you need to "feel the pain" of team members, insuring they believe you care about their health and lifestyle.

One of the most effective devices to control costs and improve health is a Health Savings Account (HSA). An HSA puts employees in the driver's seat of their health costs, and in charge of their own health. If HSAs were adopted on a widespread basis, the health care costs of the United States would drop significantly. That's the theme of *Consumer Driven Health Care*, a book I wrote with Dr. Tom Williams and Alan Ayers, showing how to lower costs and improve health, encouraging consumers to be as concerned about buying health care as buying groceries, clothes or a car. Health and wellness among your firm's work force demands as much attention and effort as strength training and nutrition among collegiate and professional athletic teams.

What benefit package makes your firm a best place to work? Variations are infinite, but I suggest you read *Fortune* magazine each January describing programs at the Top 100 "best places to work." You'll read Google is famous for providing "free food," SAS provides exceptional working conditions and free education K-12 for its employees, and lots of other ideas from firms demonstrating it's possible to be highly profitable as well as a great place to work.

I visited the SAS campus in Carey, NC, and was blown away by the quality of a computer-laden school for children of employees, complete with swimming pool and superb athletic facilities. While working for SAS, I was granted access to wander around, observing employees (including its entrepreneurial founder and former professor) writing code. The one place I didn't have access was the day-care and elementary school. "Entry to our children's school is our most restricted access," I was told, "because families of our employees are our most important assets." When a company puts that kind of philosophy into its everyday policies, you can bet it helps create winning teams.

A Man of Steel

One of the most successful and colorful entrepreneurs I've ever met and worked for was John H. McConnell, founder of Worthington Industries, a billion dollar firm in the highly competitive steel industry. The son of a steelworker in Pugh town, West Virginia, he used the GI bill to attend Michigan State University, where he played football and studied business.

McConnell began working in the steel industry upon graduation and saw a need for custom steel processing. He used his 1952 Oldsmobile as collateral for a $600 loan to found Worthington Industries, buying and selling from the trunk of that car, another variation of "garage entrepreneur." The firm grew into a $3 billion global organization, widely recognized for its employee-based philosophy as one of the Best Companies to Work for in America.

McConnell practiced MBWA (Management by Walking Around), often walking factory floors of Worthington, talking with employees, many he knew by name. His views on open door policies and two-way communication were the basis for the company's success, in stark contrast to some manufacturing firms where office and factory workers seldom meet. He used to drive a golf cart around the factory on hot days with cold beverages, personally distributing them to workers and expressing his appreciation for their efforts.

"Doing the right thing" was at the center of everything in McConnell's life. Through this philosophy, he became recognized as one of the region's most generous citizens, lovingly referred to as "Mr. Mac." The firm started innovative wellness programs and donated large sums to establish the McConnell Heart Hospital, providing treatment and prevention services for heart-related illnesses. From a $600 loan on his old car to making the list of America's billionaires was a long journey, marked most, I believe, by his life as a servant leader.

If the business newspaper or magazine in your city sponsors a "best place to work" issue, study it carefully to find ideas that work in your city or region. If you are forming an advisory board for your firm, an executive from one of those firms might be an ideal candidate. If there is a banquet honoring those firms, attend with key members of your team for ideas and inspiration.

Passionate People

Chris Irion is an entrepreneur passionate about technology, the environment, and charitable giving. He co-founded e-Cycle to address problems of mobile recycling and corporate responsibility. Basically, the firm acquires phones and recycles them instead of watching them dumped in land-fills. Based on a personal concern about cancer, Chris started the firm when he figured out how to raise $60,000 for the American Cancer Society by returning $2 each for 30,000 abandoned phones the organization received as donations.

Naïve investors might look at the soaring sales of IPhones, Droids and other mobile suppliers, concluding the bigger payoff is investing in those firms. Others observe every time those devices are discarded, it's an opportunity for e-Cycle. When phone contracts expire, usually after two years, a lot of them are stashed somewhere with owners wondering what to do with them. Closets, drawers and corporate storage rooms are Chris' biggest competitors!

What happens when a firm sees such a major problem and solves it? The firm grows annually 100% or more, with recent current year sales more than all of its earlier years combined. The e-Cycle solution reduces dumping potentially-hazardous materials in landfills and increases security of corporate data.

"We listen to customers, and do what they want," Chris comments, but he also knows great people build great companies. How do you fill the firm with great people? Chris personally interviews all new recruits, asking, "What is your passion?"

My advice for entrepreneurs is to build your firm on people passionate about something. It might be sports, family, technology, disease or the environment, but people with passion for something can develop a passion for an organization with effective solutions to strongly-felt needs. You win with people, especially passionate people.

Respond. Don't React

Most anyone can be an entrepreneur, but only a few make it to the finish line of financial success. High performance by great athletes, great leaders, and great entrepreneurs is about pushing boundaries in sometimes seemingly impossible situations. There is a Chinese saying, "The temptation to quit will be greatest just before you are about to succeed."

If you are an entrepreneur, I can almost guarantee that just when you believe you are on the way to success, disasters will happen. You may believe the new product is ready for market, ready for shipment, and ready to generate revenue. Usually at the last moment, something happens to delay or prevent one or all of those from happening. It may be a delay in a government permit or regulatory requirement. A key supplier may contact you and say, "I can't fill your order now." A truck breaks down or a rail or dock strike hits just as you are ready to ship. Sometimes it's a bank refusing to extend a line of credit or a key customer saying "no" to what you thought was a sure sale allowing you to pay pressing bills. Just when you think you've climbed to the top of the mountain, you fall over a cliff.

How do you handle such setbacks?

Many people, perhaps most, react. They explode in anger at anyone unlucky enough to be near them. They become confused and fail to seek new solutions. They throw in the towel. Some become depressed, a sure route to more and deeper problems, with a likely outcome of failure.

Psychologists warn parents against disciplining children when angry, or reacting instead of responding to misbehavior. The better approach is calculated response, carefully considering causes of the behavior and how best to correct their consequences. That's also good advice for entrepreneurs.

If your personality is one that *reacts* to difficulties in anger or by instantly choosing another action, you may be headed for defeat. Don't react to unexpected outcomes; respond. Let your response to a difficult situation be measured, carefully considering alternatives recognizing that most won't work, but persevering in the belief that a solution does exist if you approach it with enough creativity and diligence. Einstein said, "It's not that I'm so smart, it's just that I stay with problems longer. I think and think for months and years. Ninety-nine times, the conclusion is false. The hundredth time I am right." *Successful entrepreneurs view setbacks as installment payments toward victory.*

Perhaps you're seen or read the story of Bonnie St. John. If not, I recommend reading her book *Live Your Joy* or visiting her website at www.bonniestjohn.com. I was fortunate to hear her speak, and instantly recognized her life illustrates the pattern of success for garage entrepreneurs.

Bonnie St. John knows what it is like to be down, to struggle financially, to have big emotional challenges, and to grow spiritually in order to overcome them. She also knows what it is like to be on top of the world; Bonnie was the first African-American to win Olympic medals in ski racing, winning silver and two bronze medals in the 1984 Paralympics in Innsbruck, Austria. She also won scholarships and graduated with honors from Harvard University and a Rhodes

Scholarship to Oxford. She worked for IBM until she was appointed to the White House National Economic Council. She was featured on *The Today Show, Montel Williams, CNN, Good Morning America,* as well as *People magazine, The New York Times, Essence* and many others.

There are a few other facts about Bonnie that you should know when you face seemingly impossible challenges as an entrepreneur. She grew up in an impoverished neighborhood, was abandoned at birth by her father and faced the challenge of her leg amputated at age five.

In her motivational seminars, Bonnie quotes research revealing why some athletes win and others don't. Playing better is a matter of recovering better. Tennis players who win most are five times faster getting their heart rate back to a normal response rate between points. The speed and quality of recovery allows winners to reframe and recover instead of react. Resilience wins matches, and emotional and physical resilience is required to recover and respond, instead of reacting.

In one of her most challenging downhill ski events at the Olympics, Bonnie was almost down the slope, about to win gold. But she fell. Bruised, broken and in great pain, she knew the medal she cherished wouldn't happen if she didn't get up and cross the finish line. With extreme determination, she forced herself to get up and won the Bronze medal.

Crossing the finish line as an entrepreneur is much the same as for Bonnie St. John. High performance is about pushing boundaries beyond what the human body and psyche can endure. Those who win medals of monetary gain get up, no matter how painful it sometimes seems, and push boundaries beyond what most human beings are capable. "If a one-legged, African-American girl from San Diego with no money and no snow can go to the Olympics as a ski racer..." garage entrepreneurs should remind themselves, "surely I can follow my dream and find the joy in my life."

Remember, if you plan on making it as an entrepreneur, *respond; don't react.* Instead of worrying about past problems, learn to think creatively about possible solutions. Worry is like a rocking chair. It occupies your time, but doesn't get you anywhere.

Woody's Three Principles
Woody Hayes had three guiding principles:

1. Paying Forward

2. Hard work

3. Education

All three principles are fundamental for entrepreneurs.

Paying Forward

"Paying Forward," refers to building a better future by giving back to the community part of the results from your past success. That's something I hope you observed in our conversations about many of the entrepreneurs in this book. It is exemplified in the lives of Bill and Melinda Gates (the most generous couple on the planet), Les Wexner, Dave Thomas, the Ingram family at White Castle, John McConnell and many others. Not so much, however, in the life of Steve Jobs.

Paying forward, or improving the community where you live, is usually the mission of non-profit organizations. Some do it better than others. I recently met a leader at Redeemer Presbyterian church in New York City, coming away understanding that even non-profits need to "pay forward."

Redeemer is an historic church, led by highly-respected pastor and best-selling author, Dr. Tim Keller. There are lots of growing "mega-churches," as there are congregations of other faiths, but what impresses me about Redeemer is its mission not to build a great church, but "To build a great city for all people." Instead of building a bigger church, it focuses on planting other churches, in cities all over of the world, many in different denominations than its own. Instead of focusing on the needs of upper-class parishioners and their contributions, Redeemer provides resources to organizations serving poor and marginalized people with a special emphasis on young people near its Broadway location in Manhattan.

Does "paying forward" really pay as well as soliciting people to contribute to a church? The numbers representing effectiveness of its ministries are astounding, and I won't bore with you them here. If you are interested, read about them on www.redeemer.com or "Google" the impressive accomplishments of Redeemer Church and Tim Keller, the coach of its winning team. The one statistic that impressed me most, however, is the average age of Redeemer's congregation: 27. "Paying forward" for the future is an effective strategy for having a future.

Hard Work

Education is a word with many meanings. Some people believe education means attending the right university or college—one inculcating a culture as well as knowledge and a network of future contacts. Entrepreneurs also know that other leaders, such as Dave Thomas, graduated from "the school of hard knocks."

Successful firms recruit graduates with a strong work ethic and excellent values. One indicator is whether or not graduates work during college to pay expenses. A CEO of a highly-successful firm told me, "I love it when the CEO of my competitor is a rich kid whose parents paid for his education. If my competitor is headed by a poor kid who made it at an elite school, I know I am probably in a fight for my life. There's no more effective competitor than a firm with a CEO who knows how to fight like a junk yard dog. When that happens, I know I have to be extra-smart or he'll kick my ass, but if my competitor is owned by someone who grew up rich, I can relax a little."

When I was at Ohio State, I frequently went to lunch with recruiters on campus, and asked which graduates turned out most successful. The Executive Vice-President of a bank explained she looked for graduates who could maintain an entrepreneurial mind-set even in a large organization.

"I look for jugglers," she said.

"What do you mean by jugglers?" I asked.

"People who can keep a lot of balls in the air at one time," she explained. "I look for someone who worked in college or was outstanding in competitive sports, was an effective leader in at least one organization or cause, and maintained good grades---B or better." If they excel on only one dimension, they are not likely to have much of an entrepreneurial mind-set or be effective as leaders," she expounded.

Then she added, "I won't hire someone who never held a job, even if they have a 4.0 cumulative grade average." When you recruit team members for your firm, consider her advice. If you want your children to succeed you in your own firm, I recommend that you start them in a real job as early as possible. "A real job," an entrepreneur friend of mine told me, "is one in which at least one body part hurts at the end of the day."

Educated

As an entrepreneur, recognize the difference between team members who are well-trained and those who are well-educated.

Training transmits knowledge about *how* to do things well. The function of your corporate training program and most trade schools is to train people how to do jobs well, whether those jobs require factory or office skills, medical laboratory tasks or other competencies. Every firm needs well-trained employees.

Education goes beyond training, understanding not only *how* to do things well, but *why* they work well. Organizations need workers who know how to do things well, but they also need team leaders who understand *why* things work well, so they can change things before they stop working well. Even effective methods eventually stop working well. Successful firms recruit people who evolve and continuously improve things to meet and beat competition.

A winning team needs members who are both well-trained and well-educated. Great coaches teach a lot of Xs and Os in "skull sessions," but if Woody's team lost on Saturday, his players knew they would spend next week practicing the basics of blocking and tackling.

One of the great sales-trainers and motivators is Carl Stevens. He grew up in Tennessee and lived much of his life in Texas, which meant his speech was a little more colorful than Ivy League graduates. Carl cautioned, "You can't no more expect someone to do what they ain't been taught, that you can expect them to go back to where they ain't been."

Carl's country euphemism clarifies a basic truth every entrepreneur should ask when a team member makes a mistake. Was the mistake the fault of the employee? Or was the mistake the fault of the firm's training? It is a mistake by managers when they assume employees know how to do a task well, if they have not been trained well. When things go wrong, proper training about company policies is also a primary defense in legal liability suits.

Woody Hayes didn't quote the Bible much, but if he did, he would have liked this famous truth in the book of Proverbs: "Lazy people are soon poor, hard workers get rich." (Proverbs 10:4) Oh yes, one more thing. I wish Woody had understood the principle better of responding, rather than reacting. His career would have lasted longer.

16

Conversation SIXTEEN

Anyone Can Be a Millionaire

There is a simple strategy allowing anyone to be a millionaire, stated succinctly in two words: Start young.

You don't have be an "Einstein" to make a million if you start young. Einstein's favorite theory is the key, as I will explain in just a few pages. Martha Stewart sagely advises, "Start planning before you think you should."

Wexner Wisdom

Do you remember the lessons learned about Les Wexner and the Limited? And the three valuable marketing concepts from Conversation 5 his firm demonstrates?

At a recent shareholders meeting, Wexner responded to a question about investing in his firm. He said people buying $1000 of Limited stock when it went public in 1969 would now have $40,000,000 with splits and dividends. After the meeting ended, a spokeswoman quickly informed the media Mr. Wexner's calculation was not quite correct. The actual amount was $50,000,000.

You don't have to be an entrepreneur to make a fortune like that. You don't even have to have much money to become a millionaire, but it is a lot easier if you understand theories we've discussed in our conversations together.

I was fortunate to live only a few blocks from the first Limited location and noticed the store in its early years. The more I heard about it from customers shopping there, read about it the media and studied its market segmentation strategy, I became convinced Limited shares would be a winner. That's a pattern for identifying potential big payoffs investing in entrepreneurs.

I was a young teacher on a small salary with little cash left after raising my children and paying the mortgage, so I didn't have much to invest. The Limited looked good because Wexner was doing right things right. Most of his thousands of competitors in apparel retailing were operating the way they had for decades, not very efficiently. I didn't know Wexner and didn't meet him until years later, but I could see high-growth potential for his business. With difficulty, I scraped together a few hundred dollars to buy shares. Within a few years, my investment more than doubled. I could have sold the shares and been delighted with the gain, but I didn't. Three decades later when I needed money, I finally sold my Limited shares for almost $1,000,000.

My point is this. Most of this book has been about how to grow small firms into fortunes. Wexner has definitely done that, and he created tens of thousands of jobs for people working in stores, warehouses and headquarters. But—and this is the point--you don't have to start a firm to benefit from understanding why some entrepreneurs grow large and others don't. You don't have to be an entrepreneur to make millions, but you do need to understand entrepreneurial theory.

Knowing what makes entrepreneurs successful enables you to make almost as much as an investor as people who do the hard work of starting and growing firms. You can earn a fortune understanding theories that enrich entrepreneurs. You can do it even with small amounts of cash, based on knowledge, diligence and patience.

You Can Be an Einstein at Investing

Albert Einstein didn't invent relativity. He invented the *theory* of relativity, but people who understood the power of his theory invented the atomic bomb, nuclear energy and a host of other break-throughs. If you apply theories you read in this book, perhaps you'll be known as an Einstein. But, anyone can be an Einstein by investing with a secret that only a few apply.

If asked to name the most powerful theory in the world, you might expect Einstein to say, "The Theory of Relativity." He didn't, calling compound interest "the most powerful force in the universe, the eighth wonder of the world." He added, "He who understands it, earns it…he who doesn't pays it."

However you quote Einstein's words about compound interest, one thing is clear. When you adopt in your youth the theory of Compound Annual Growth (CAG), letting appreciation and dividends grow over time, you are almost certain to be a millionaire when you retire, even with small amounts of savings. When compounding your investments in *successful entrepreneurs* instead of mature corporations, you likely will become a multi-millionaire.

Let's look at an example of the power of CAG for ordinary investors. If you put $5,000 just one year in an IRA when you are 21 in mutual funds averaging the same return as the stock market the past century (10%), you will have over $700,000 when you reach 72 (more if compounded quarterly or monthly). If you can't manage $5,000, investing less, but for three or four years, you are still likely to be a millionaire. If you save $5,000 each year throughout your career, you probably will have over 8 million dollars and twice that amount if you wait another seven years.

Search "IRA calculator" on websites of financial firms and input your own numbers to calculate what is likely to happen by the time you retire. The power of CAG turns most everyone into a millionaire if they just start young, even with small investments.

You might object, saying people age 20 to 30 don't have an extra $2,000-5,000 to place in an IRA. That's true, of course, unless you consider they could probably cut out alcohol, buy frozen pizzas at Aldi prices instead of delivered pizzas, refrain from buying new school clothes every year (or buy at a thrift store), or a combination of these, and they will have enough for a substantial contribution to their IRA each youthful year.

Save or spend, that is the question. Those who decide to save in an IRA instead of spend on a variety of desired but unneeded (and sometimes harmful) purchases are able to retire with a million dollars---and perhaps many millions. Many people *save* the amount left over after they *spend*. The wisest investors *save first*, and spend what is left over. If you want a good book about how to decide how much to save (and other important issues in life), read Andy Stanley, *The Best Question Ever* (Multnomah Books, 2004).

Warren Buffet in a letter to shareholders described investing as "The decision to postpone current consumption in order to have ability to consume more in the future." You can decide to spend on little things now and be poor all your life, or postpone spending on little things, invest the savings, and have a million – or many millions—later. CAG is a brilliant tool for becoming a millionaire, making anyone an Einstein at investing.

Warren Buffett started his billion-dollar empire as a teenager, delivering newspapers. With a penchant for numbers and an eye on the bottom line, he started a business in high school, accumulating $10,000 by the time he graduated from college. If you consider it too late to accumulate much because you're 50 instead of 20, it's not too late to teach CAG to your children or grandchildren. Maybe they will take care of you in your old age.

The Great Fear

The great fear facing maturing investors is their assets will expire before they do. Longevity continually increases, so that living to a hundred or more is a reasonable expectation for many people. If you want to estimate how long you are likely to live, Google "longevity calculators" and answer a few questions about your health, lifestyle and relatives to estimate your expected life. One I like is on the Northwestern Mutual website at www.media.nmfn.com, but there are dozens of good ones. Whether you are 20, 50 or 70, a longevity calculator may motivate you to max out your IRA while you still can.

It is tempting when approaching retirement to convert a portfolio of growth equities to fixed-income investments such as CDs and bonds, a conservative strategy reducing risk from stock market declines. That strategy doesn't work well in an environment of low interest rates, inflationary price increases, and declining value of the dollar. Lengthened longevity requires both income and appreciation from investments. If you are a maturing investor, use the content of our conversations to select companies likely to pay dividends plus a few entrepreneurial ones likely to keep your portfolio increasing alongside your age.

What happens when your life *after* retirement is longer than your working life *prior* to retirement? You'll probably need your assets to keep working long after you leave the firm where you worked. And don't count much on Social Security or a company pension in the future. One solution, of course, is never to retire. I read the wisdom of one centurion who was asked his secret of living to 100. His reply was, "Don't smoke, don't drink, and never retire!"

Whether you retire, change occupations or just adjust the nature of your work, you probably will need to continue growing your income from investments. You'll probably also need equities that grow, but provide dividends to maintain your lifestyle. If you have most of your portfolio in a traditional IRA instead of a Roth, you will be required to withdraw a required minimum distribution (RMD) each year after turning 70 ½. Doing that usually requires a portfolio with lots of upside potential, and very little down side. You can see why understanding how small firms grow into large fortunes is critically important for retired readers.

Regardless whether you are just starting your IRA hoping for CAG to make you a millionaire or you are retired hoping your portfolio will last as long as you do, how do you find investments likely to grow rapidly?

The S-Curve of Entrepreneurial Growth

Few areas of behavioral economics are as predictable and consistent as the diffusion of innovations, validated by both scholarly research and practical experience. Literally thousands of studies about the diffusion of innovations demonstrate consistent patterns you can use in choosing entrepreneurs likely to grow rapidly.

Studies of innovation are anchored in the seminal book by Everett Rogers, *Diffusion of Innovations* (Free Press, 1962). A modern version of Rogers' theories became a best-seller by Malcolm Gladwell, *The Tipping Point* (Back Bay Books, 2002). I wrote the "Diffusion of Innovations" chapter through ten editions of *Consumer Behavior*, and it was an easy chapter to write because the theory never changed. Diffusion is the same whether explaining how influenza spreads, the popularity of children's books, or the adoption of personal computers and the Internet. Some of my students wrote doctoral dissertations on diffusion of innovation, studying products as diverse as the ATM, personal computers, interactive television, online shopping and Electronic Funds Transfer (EFT). They all concluded innovations fail or succeed by gaining adoption by consumers in the pattern originally identified by Everett Rogers, shown below.

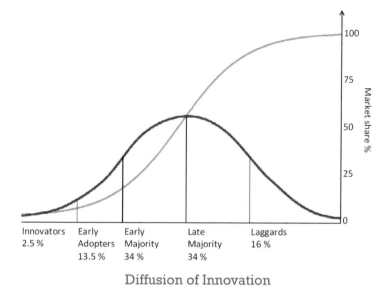

Diffusion of Innovation

You pretty well know whether or not a start-up firm will succeed by observing closely the 2.5% of people who determine the future of new products. A few will try anything, but when you see a rapid increase in innovators, it is a signal, called the inflection point. Most firms are not public during that time, but when you see the transition to early adopters, it's time to consider buying shares when they go public. Compare changes annually in "fastest growing" lists of business magazines and newspapers.

Don't be in a hurry to buy a company until adoption hits the inflection point. You might pay a few dollars more per share by waiting, but that's OK. You need time to assess the competence in distribution, production, channel relationships, customer satisfaction and the ultimate question, can the business be operated profitably? That's essential to keep from losing money on stocks, something you never want to do! Stocks at the top of the diffusion curve should make enough money to generate dividends and stock buybacks. Stock market declines are opportunities to buy good companies. Buy low and sell dear!

Cumulative adoption forms an "S" curve, represented below. If you recognized that Michael Dell revolutionized the computer supply chain transforming it to a demand chain, an investment of $10,000 rose to $5.7 million, but Dell and many tech companies also illustrate the importance of knowing *when to sell*, usually when rapid growth slows.

It is not essential to "get in from the beginning." Investing in Dell anytime in the first three or four years produced similar gains without the risk of buying stock in a company before it is clear whether or not it is a winner. Buying too early is just as risky as buying too late. "Early adopters" are key to sizzling returns.

How do you spot winners before other people and Wall Street do? By understanding theory. Universities were some of the first to see the advantage of customer-configured demand chains, causing me to notice Dell before Wall Street did, and I knew from my study of theory that education is associated with early adoption of technology products. Knowledge of functional shiftability and the innovation of Dell shifting inventory financing from computer manufacturers and retailers to consumers, convinced me the company's stock was worthy of investment. Wall Street analysts are often not aware of what happens in the Midwest until shares of firms like Dell and Walmart have made their greatest gains. When sales migrated to the late majority, growth slowed and share prices declined. Understanding diffusion of innovations is highly profitable in achieving dramatic growth in your portfolio and knowing when to switch to dividend stocks.

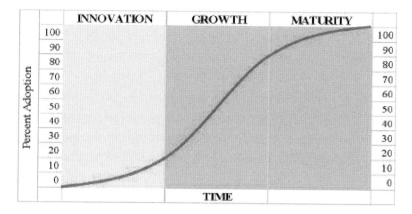

S-Curve of Entrepreneurial Growth

Where to Find Stocks for Your IRA

How do you get ideas about firms with stunning growth in value? By walking around and studying products you understand.

As a speaker and professor, I often toured corporate facilities. Since my largest consulting client was IBM, I usually asked to see the computer room, pleased when they were decorated mostly in blue. Most computer rooms were dominated by IBM and a few other major suppliers, but I began to see one piece of equipment in a corner of a different color with the logo "EMC." I asked techies why they bought one piece of equipment different than the dominant brand.

"In digital storage, EMC is just better than what I can get from the major computer manufacturers," they repeatedly said. When I returned home, I read about the company, inquired about the values of management and directors, and studied their financials---and bought EMC stock, well-before Wall Street analysts widely-touted the stock. It did well.

What was the fastest growing stock of the past twenty-five years?

IBM? Apple? Google? Sorry, if you guessed any of those, although they did well. It is a firm in Winona, Wisconsin, started with $30,000 to rent a basement and seven residential garages, equipped with a $25 used roll-top desk and kegs of bolts. When its founder, Bob Kierlin, now 73, started the company he bought 30,000 surplus toothpaste cartons to display the nuts, bolts and other fasteners the firm sells in its stores. "Had you visited our stores in that era," says Kierlin, "you would have thought we were selling toothpaste rather than fasteners. We did it on the cheap." TMC was not a problem in the formation and growth of this firm.

Its innovation was not new products, but a new level of service and logistics efficiency, similar to what Wexner did in apparel retailing. I first heard of the company when talking with industrial suppliers and construction companies who were customers. Scott Semerar, one of my former students who was a stock broker, researched its values and financials. Customers had one word to describe the company's service, "Best."

Have you guessed the name of the company? It's not quite as well-known as Coca-Cola, P&G or Google, although today it has 2,600 stores throughout the nation with over 11,000 technically-sophisticated and customer-responsive sales people.

The company is Fastenal, the biggest gainer of the past quarter century in the Russell 1000 index trading for at least 25 years, surging 38,565 percent, not including dividends, according to Bloomberg. Adjusting for splits, the stock has gone from 13¢ in 1987 to a recent price around $50.00. A nice addition to anyone's IRA.

Recently, while studying annual reports, something caught my attention—the location of a firm in a small Arkansas town. As I studied the firm's documents, I noticed it operated in a fragmented industry of inefficient, independently-owned retailers of used cars. The name of the company reminded me of its nearby neighbor in Bentonville and thanks to the Internet, it was possible to view presentations at the shareholders meeting and listen to conference calls by the firm's executives. The strategy was nearly identical to the one we discussed in Conversations 4 and 7. It exhibited the same philosophy of controlled decision-making, disciplined purchasing of the goods it sells, an emphasis on training of sales people, efficient technology, and centrifugal growth reminiscent of what we've discussed in conversations about Meijer, Max & Erma's, and Walmart.

The firm is Car-Mart, the nation's largest "buy-here/ pay-here" auto retailer, even though it operates only in a few states surrounding Arkansas. The average vehicle sells for under $10,000 and most of its Accounts Receivables are self-funded. Its diffusion curve is steadily increasing, its EPS growth is consistent and its branding fits its market target. Most importantly, not many people knew about the company, especially on Wall Street.

"Sell to the mass, and live in the class," I reminded myself, but the event that convinced me the stock might be right for my IRA was the conference call. Some of the other listeners were financial analysts, including one from Wall Street.

"How are you handling the volatility on Wall Street?" the analyst asked.

"Well, we don't pay much attention to Wall Street," the CEO responded, "We just try to take care of our customers and run our business well." That's when I decided to buy shares of CarMart.

When you and I have our retirement funds in a 401K, we are affected by Wall Street and the Dow Jones average whether we want to be or not because 401k funds are mostly mutual funds, run by giant Wall Street traders handling billions of dollars. The performance of a small, rapidly-diffusing firm in Arkansas doesn't usually catch Wall Street's attention. That's why an IRA, where individuals can find fast-growing entrepreneurs offers opportunity for large gains creating millions instead of miniscule increments in a 401k. The price of Car-Mart shares was $22-$24 when I bought them. I hope it is substantially more by the time you read these pages, helping my IRA outlast me.

The Process is the Same; Only the Speed Varies.

The process is the same for all entrepreneurs, whether they sell products, services or ideas. But the speed of diffusion varies, as the following graph displays. Some firms are like the curve labeled "Innovation I" with immediate and rapid ascendency. FaceBook and Pinterest are examples, with wide-spread diffusion within months. Typical entrepreneurs are represented in the curve for "Innovation II," typical of many technology stocks. Some, such as Walmart and Fastenal, are like "Innovation III," permitting cautious investors a few years to study and buy the stock. Observe customers closely to determine in which category an innovation fits.

Remember one additional principle. All innovations eventually slow in their growth, usually left with P/E ratios too high to be sustainable, causing big drops in the stock price. When you see growth begin to slow, it is time to consider selling the stock and looking for another. If the firm has a good plan for increasing profits and substituting dividends in place of rapid appreciation, you may still want to hold it as part of your portfolio, but the time to sell a stock is when you would no longer buy it.

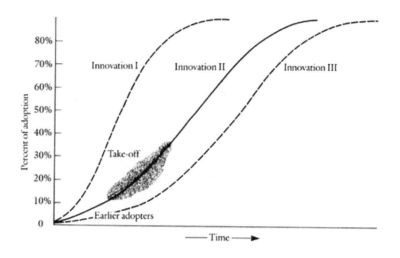

Determining How Fast Innovations Grow or Fail

The key to high returns is to wait until the new product has moved from innovators to early adopters . That is when spectacular increases in share price occur. Firms with rapid ascendency may not be profitable, but don't buy the stock unless you can clearly determine how and when profit is possible. No path to profitability is a reason to avoid innovative entrepreneurs. Humility helps know when to exit if something isn't as great as you thought it was.

The more gradual curve is less risky because slow growth gives you time for evaluation. When firms have the kind of growth represented by Innovation 1, they often fall as fast as they rise, making exit even riskier. I saw the rapid growth of Facebook, studied the rise in "dormant accounts," the public pronouncements of advertisers doubting effectiveness of Facebook advertising and the lack of experience of its CEO. When people asked me for advice on what to do when Facebook went public, I simply said, "Sell short."

People ask, "How do you know which innovations will succeed?" The answer is one of the most researched and best understood topics in marketing. The five factors determining success are:

1. **Relative Advantage**—The degree to which consumers perceive the innovation to offer substantially greater benefits than the product currently used.

2. **Compatibility**—The degree to which a new product is consistent with existing practices, values, needs, and past experiences of potential adopters.

3. **Complexity**—The degree to which an innovation is perceived as difficult to understand and use. The more complex, the more difficult is acceptance. How frustrating will it be to customers when evaluating or learning how to use an innovation? How much time will customers have to devote to learning how to use and care for the product? Apple designed the use of its products to be simple, and the results turned out rather well.

4. **Trialability**—New products are more likely to be accepted if experimenting or using the products is made easy. That's why P & G is the master of sampling; so is Jeni's Splendid Ice Cream.

5. **Observability**—The degree to which results from using a new product are visible to friends and neighbors. If customers can see others using a new product, that innovation is likely to diffuse faster than when the product is used privately.

Keys to Investing in Family and Friends

Most of the rules we've just discussed apply to investments in public corporations, but you may have opportunities to invest in private firms just getting started. They may pay off spectacularly, but I learned from experience, it is usually better to leave really risky investments to angel investors and venture capitalists. When investing with family members and friends, here are three rules.

1. Don't invest money with entrepreneurs if you are not prepared to lose it all, both financially and emotionally.

2. Don't invest in entrepreneurs who don't understand and apply most of the principles in this book.

3. When someone, even a family member or close friend, asks you to loan or invest money in his or her venture, ask why the new firm is better than anything currently on the market. If the entrepreneur can't explain how her or his firm solves important customer problems better than current solutions, go back and read rule #1.

I have invested in a substantial number of start-up firms, but always in amounts I could afford to lose, and emotionally prepared to do so. Most of those investments were in the range of $25,000 to $100,000, and some resulted in gains of several million dollars. Most didn't, ending up valueless. Some of the losses occurred when I was younger and didn't know the principles we've discussed in this book. Some were in the 1990s during the technology boom when I participated in the irrational exuberance of the era. My objective in writing this book is to help you learn from those experiences, so you can avoid mistakes I made in my youth. I wish I had read this book years before I wrote it!

I'll finish our conversations about how to grow small investments into large fortunes with a summary of making investments with the least chance of losing money and the best chance of large gains. I call the summary "the Future Millionaire's Oath."

Future Millionaire's Oath

1. I will not buy stock in a company if I cannot tell an average person what the company does and explain why its products and services are better than competitors.

2. I will not buy stock in a company until I have researched the values of the people who run the company and are on its Board of Directors.

3. I will not buy stock in a company until I have studied its math, analyzing its P/E ratio, Gross Margin (and trends), its debt-to-equity ratio, PEG ratio, dividend policy (including payout ratio), its balance sheet and P & L statement, and other key measures of the company's health.

4. I will examine those numbers compared to competitors and changing market conditions at least twice a year.

5. I will examine a chart showing the stock's movements over as many years as possible, looking for seasonal or market conditions affecting when to buy the stock.

6. I will look for bad news in the stock market or unusual events that cause a price dip in the share price of a company I want to own.

7. I will not buy a stock I don't plan keeping at least five years.

8. I will sell the stock when I would not buy it today.

You may consider living by this oath to require a lot of time and effort. "Good luck" in the stock market is highly correlated with homework and disciplined decisions. Becoming a millionaire or multi-millionaire is hard work!

But how will people prosper if they don't earn enough money to be in the prosperous middle class? If entrepreneurs don't have money to start a firm, where will they get it? If mature citizens have more life left than savings, how will they survive? The answer is explained by understanding who survived in the past, especially during the 1800s, on the American Frontier.

Frontier Consumers

In the American frontier, people who survived could shoot faster and better than other people, mostly shooting wildlife needed to feed the family, but occasionally to protect what their family owned. Survivors not only shot better; they cut trees faster and made better homes, cleared ground faster to grow larger crops, and generally were better at handling problems than people who didn't know how or weren't motivated to do the work required to survive and prosper on the frontier. There were no social safety nets, except neighbors.

Frederick Jackson Turner's essay, "The Significance of the Frontier in American History" is perhaps the most influential essay ever presented at the American Historical Association's annual conference. In the years after it was delivered, it became part of American History reflecting on the meaning of the "frontier" in American culture.

Turner's thesis explained why American people and American government were different from European counterparts. Turner saw the "land" frontier ending, and speculated as to what this meant for continued dynamism of American society. The frontier influenced the rise of American capitalism and Captains of Industry such as Rockefeller, Carnegie, Ford, Edison and a host of other rugged entrepreneurs who bootstrapped firms and pioneered new industries.

Has the motor for change ended? No, but there are new frontiers which involve different processes, such as the frontier of technical innovation. President Kennedy promoted his policies as the "New Frontier," making space the new frontier, sending astronauts to the moon. The "frontier" metaphor, meaning the mainspring of social process, continues today as an explanation for the rise of capitalism in the 20th century, explaining the success of Google, Amazon, Apple and a host of others. In the 21st century, a new type of "frontier consumer" is emerging, one that not only determines which families prosper and which ones don't, but shapes the customer environment determining which firms survive and which ones don't. If you want to own more goods and services than your credit-burdened neighbors, read any of the many books by Dave Ramsey, or his philosophy is on the web site www.daveramsey.com. I won't try to explain the details, because I could never do it as well as he does in his lectures and books. Ramsey's rules are simple: Live debt free, spend wisely and save to create financial freedom.

Entrepreneurs are saving America, a process described as "creative destruction" by Austrian economist (and chief rival of Keynes), Joseph Schumpeter in his book *Capitalism, Socialism and Democracy* (Harper Perennial Modern Classics, 2008). If you are an executive and don't feel threatened by this process, you definitely should also read *The Innovator's Dilemma* (HarperBusiness, 2011) or other excellent books by Clayton Christenson.

There are two ways to accumulate wealth. Earning a high income is one, but you can't go can't go long without noticing a lot of people with high incomes, spend so much of it they end up with little wealth. They buy a lot of things, but end up with few assets. People who acquire high incomes rapidly, such as sports and other celebrities, or people who win a lottery, often spend high income into personal bankruptcy. When people resist temptation to spend income, living frugally, they are practicing the second pathway to wealth, savings. They may invest their savings in their own business as aspiring entrepreneurs and or by investing in entrepreneurs.

Here's a secret you may not want to know: The easy days earning a living with abundant consumption are ended. Median household income has been stagnant or declining for a decade and demographic realities in Europe and the U.S. dictate further decline in the future. The new frontier for consumers is saving money and investing it, rather than spending it. If you earn high income and spend most, all, or more than you earn, you end up a pauper in poverty. If you earn a modest income, saving some through frugal spending, you end up wealthy --- if you invest it wisely. Investing wisely is the focus of this final conversation.

Having enough money to invest, even on low income, rests on the discipline *not* to spend all you earn. What you *have* (your economic net worth), is determined by what you *save* more than what you *earn*. That's why *frugality is the new frontier for American consumers.*

Frugality is the lifestyle of millionaires, according to Stanley and Danko who identified seven common denominators of real millionaires:

- They live well below their means.

- They pursue wealth very efficiently.

- They have little interest in social status.

- They received little or no financial help from their parents.

- Their adult children pay their own way.

- They identify profitable markets.

- They choose occupations wisely.

In my years as a professor, I encouraged students to do such things as buy a car (probably used), but after paying it off, continue making "car payments" to their own savings account for a few years before buying another car. When they do that, they build a savings account large enough to buy cars "free" the rest of their life, never having the burden of car payments, and eventually the ability to buy more and better cars than buying on credit.

Does this really work for young people? I receive hundreds of letters and emails from former students telling me about their savings from frugality and sometimes the size of their IRA accounts, but this one from a former student caught my attention:

"To: Professor Blackwell

Subject: Got a car for free thanks to you

Hi, Dr. Blackwell. This is not an advertisement even though the subject line reads like one. I am a former student of yours and I wish to give thanks for your commitment to the students of The Ohio State University. I graduated and moved on to life in the corporate world but wish to keep in contact with people from which I have been inspired by. Obviously, you would be one of those people.

I also wish to share some good news with you.

I remember an example you gave about how to get a car for free. I wanted to share with you that I accomplished the feat!! I had managed to start an CD account in high school that has earned a sizable amount. I put that money in another account that puts the dividends in my checking account so it will take care of the payments I need to make for my car loan. Along with my well-maintained trade-in, I managed to pay $0 for a used Dodge Stratus. I am sure I could have done more with the money but I could not postpone the purchase of a car. Anyway, I just wanted to let you know that the lessons you teach really make a difference in a quantitative as well as qualitative way.

Regards and Thanks for the free car!

"Omar"

There are many ways to live frugally, saving enough to invest toward becoming a future millionaire, but they require more time than we have in our current conversations. I could probably write a book on the many ways to save rather than spend. Maybe, someday, I will.

For people who want to live like a millionaire without being one, the rule is simple: Spend less; Save more.

I've heard people say that spending less is like eating sushi; people don't think they like it, but after trying it a few times, they love it. Spending less and saving more is like that. After you've done it a while, you wonder why everyone doesn't love it. More importantly, you learn what you have is not determined by what you earn as much as what you save. You are a "two marshmallow" person. That's the new frontier for American consumers. It's also how to obtain capital to bootstrap your business.

I hope you enjoyed our conversations in this book. If they help you create jobs, fix the economy and become a member of the prosperous middle class, send an email (rblackwe@columbus.rr.com) or letter letting me know I've accomplished my mission.

A LIFE OF EXCELLENCE

Simmons confronts the question that frustrates most every one of us: Why is there such a gap between the life I have aspired to and dreamed of, and the life I am actually living now? Simmons says, "My hope is to help you dramatically shrink that gap."

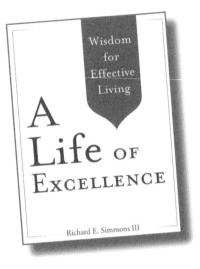

RELIABLE TRUTH

"This book offers powerful and compelling evidence why the Bible is valid and true."

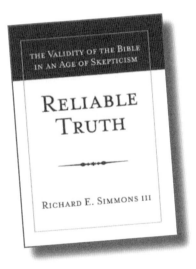

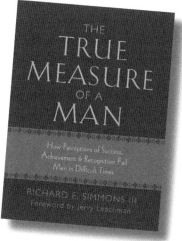